fertility and faith

fertility and faith

the ethics of human fertilization

Brendan McCarthy

Inter-Varsity Press

INTER-VARSITY PRESS
38 De Montfort Street, Leicester LE1 7GP, England

© Brendan McCarthy 1997

First published 1997

British Library Cataloguing in Publication Data
A catalogue record for this book is available from the British Library.

ISBN 0-85111-180-7

Set in Garamond No. 3

Typeset in Great Britain by Parker Typesetting Service, Leicester

Printed in Great Britain by Clays Ltd, Bungay, Suffolk

Inter-Varsity Press is the book-publishing division of the Universities and Colleges Christian Fellowship (formerly the Inter-Varsity Fellowship), a student movement linking Christian Unions in universities and colleges throughout the United Kingdom and the Republic of Ireland, and a member movement of the International Fellowship of Evangelical Students. For information about local and national activities write to UCCF, 38 De Montfort Street, Leicester LE1 7GP.

contents

Preface

The Warnock Report represents one of the most significant ethical landmarks in the social life of the United Kingdom in the twentieth century. The debate surrounding the Warnock Report culminated in the 1990 Human Fertilization and Embryology Act, which established the Human Fertilization and Embryology Authority. In many ways the debate continues today as this authority continues to make ethical decisions based on its Code of Practice, first published in 1991.

The salient features of the debate, highlighted in this book, are to be found in the Warnock Report, subsequent Government papers, various Christian submissions to the debate, and the 1990 Act. While it would be interesting to examine the Warnock debate from the perspective of humanist or feminist or medical contributors, the objective of this book is to concentrate on ethical and theological implications of the debate, viewed from a Christian perspective. I do not wish to imply that other viewpoints are unimportant, only that, apart from those expressed in the Warnock Report and the 1990 Act, they lie outside the scope of this study.

Even with this limited objective it is by no means a straightforward matter to decide what to include in this enquiry. A balance has to be struck between surveying the content of the debate, establishing ethical and theological principles pertinent to the debate, and analysing the various areas of the debate in order to define a Christian approach to the techniques and treatments dealt with in the Warnock Report. I have attempted to balance these interests while offering a particular Christian viewpoint.

Because of the pivotal position of the Warnock Report in the debate, the book begins with an examination of the agenda it established. Even though few contributors to the debate set out to establish a coherent theory of law and morality and the relationship between them, many did criticize the allegedly utilitarian basis of the Warnock Report. Consequently, I have included a brief examination of the relationship between law and morality, with particular reference to the Warnock Report. This is prefaced by a discussion on the nature of Christian ethics.

It is essential that ethical and theological principles relevant to the debate be established before the various areas in the debate can be analysed properly. In the debate, the greatest single concern reflected in most submissions, in the media and by Mary Warnock herself, was the status of the human embryo. This book reflects that concern, and consequently I devote much space to establishing a defensible position regarding the status of the human embryo. Also of widespread concern in the debate was the question of marriage and family life, especially the relationship between the unitive and procreative aspects of sexual union. This too is given close attention. Other topics, such as the wider implications of scientific intrusion into the processes of reproduction or the distinctive insights of feminist theology, are not dealt with here; interesting as these topics are, they were not to the fore in establishing current United Kingdom legislation.

Much of the actual debate surrounding the Warnock Report addressed various practices related to infertility treatment or research: artificial insemination by husband, donor insemination, egg and embryo donation, *in vitro* fertilization, surrogacy, embryo research, gamete and embryo storage and, at a later stage in the debate, abortion. In this study, I map out, in some detail, the positions adopted by the Warnock Committee, the reaction of the Government in subsequent papers, the law established by the 1990 Human Fertilization and Embryology Act, and the array of Christian submissions. Each area of the debate is then analysed, and detailed conclusions are reached and defended regarding Christian practice in the area under scrutiny.

In establishing ethical and theological principles it is, at times, difficult to decide how far back to first principles one ought to go. A notable weakness in many Christian submissions was that little or no attempt was made to defend the ethical principles which were being promoted; consequently it is reasonable to believe that some, at least, of these submissions were less effective than they otherwise might have been. In this book, within the confines of limited space, I have sought to establish principles rather than simply promote or defend them. My intention is to argue towards a position rather than from one.

The Warnock debate touched on a wide range of subjects. Inevitably, it has not been possible to cover all of these fully. Many subjects, such as the nature of the human soul or the interpretation of Scripture, are fascinating in their own right, and merit detailed and lengthy investigation. Here, however, they are introduced as parts of wider arguments, and consequently they are explored only to the extent that they are directly relevant to this study. Inevitably this leads to some frustration, but this cannot be avoided in a relatively short work.

Any study dealing with the subject-matter of the Warnock debate covers territory well travelled by others; the status of the embryo and the nature of marriage are areas of almost universal concern. This book attempts to provide a comprehensive approach to the subject, within the confines of available space. The debate and its underlying principles are explored from legal, medical, philosophical, ethical, theological and practical perspectives. One of the disappointing features of the debate which took place was that contributors tended to approach the subject from too narrow a perspective; this is also true of many books written since the publication of the Warnock Report. Equally, Christian opinion has often been presented by commentators as being unified and predictably conservative. A fuller investigation of Christian submission shows this to be entirely false. This study examines Christian submissions in some depth, and the pattern which emerges is varied and by no means uniformly conservative.

In evaluating the debate it is, of course, necessary to provide one's own opinions on the various techniques under scrutiny. I have attempted to establish principles which act as guides through the complex territory of fertilization and embryology. These principles lead to certain conclusions which do not coincide completely with the opinions expressed by any of the contributors to the debate or with any of the other authors referred to in the body of the text.

Where possible, arguments which have been clearly expressed by others are attributed to them and are often used as stepping-stones to reaching a conclusion regarding the principles underlying the debate. Where space has permitted, I have either quoted or summarized such arguments in the text, thus making it unnecessary to refer to the notes other than as references.

Finally, I wish to thank my wife and family for their support, patience and encouragement during the writing of this book.

Brendan McCarthy

1

The agenda set by Warnock

The starting-point

Two very reasonable and very different questions may be asked at the outset of this chapter. For those who have a professional or strong personal interest in human fertilization and embryology, the question springs to mind: why start with Warnock? For others who have an interest in the subject but are relative newcomers to it, a more pressing question is: who or what is Warnock? Both questions deserve an answer.

The whole area of human fertilization and embryology has become a moral and legal minefield. Scientific progress is rapid and ongoing. Attitudes and beliefs are held with a conviction that, at times, can be disturbing in their intensity. It is essential, therefore, that we take time to understand the issues properly. It is tempting to jump in at the deep end and start debating *in vitro* fertilization or surrogacy or some other intriguing topic. As with all temptations, however, the urge must be resisted. What is needed most of all is a careful, even painstaking, examination of all the techniques, treatments, principles and issues involved. This includes investigating the history which has brought us to where we are today.

In July 1982 the British Government appointed the Committee of Inquiry into Human Fertilization and Embryology under the chairmanship of Dame Mary (now Baroness) Warnock. Universally, this became known as the Warnock Committee. Exactly two years later this committee published its report.[1] In commissioning it the Government gave the committee the following terms of reference:

> To consider recent and potential developments in medicine and science related to human fertilisation and embryology; to consider what policies and safeguards should be applied, including consideration of the social, ethical and legal implications of these developments; and to make recommendations.[2]

In grappling with this brief the committee concentrated on two main areas of debate: infertility treatments (including surrogacy), and embryo research (including allied scientific techniques). Predictably, much of the report consisted of a summary of the existing medical and legal situation. Nevertheless, the committee members also exercised their minds in debating the ethical issues involved in these areas. As requested, they made a series of recommendations in each regard.

Before coming to their own conclusions, the committee members sought the views of interested groups and individuals. The response was encouraging, with 288 written or oral submissions forthcoming. One seventh of these came from churches or Christian-based organizations. Not surprisingly, it soon became clear to the Government that the Warnock Report had, itself, become the centre of the debate, and before legislation was eventually passed by Parliament, two further Government papers were published. In December 1986 a consultation document was published[3] and in November 1987 a framework for legislation was issued.[4]

By becoming the centre of the debate on human fertilization and embryology, the Warnock Report, in effect, set the agenda for others to follow. This was so not only in terms of the techniques and treatments to be covered by the debate. With only one notable exception, it was also true of the ethical standards which eventually found expression in legislation. The Warnock Report did more than provide a framework for subsequent discussion; it also determined the direction of the whole debate in regard to basic attitudes to infertility treatment and embryo research. We can trace these attitudes and ethical standards through subsequent Government papers and on into the 1990 Human Fertilization and Embryology Act. Today, in many circles, they go virtually unquestioned as the received wisdom guiding future developments.

To be fair to the Government, we must also acknowledge that, at every stage in the debate, opportunity was given for contrary opinions to be expressed. All votes in Parliament were free but, nevertheless, the findings of the Warnock Committee proved seminal.

The only major recommendations of the Warnock Committee which were not incorporated into the 1990 Act were those dealing with surrogacy. Even then, the discrepancy was only partial. Also, at a late stage in the debate the subject of abortion was introduced, even though this was outside the remit of the Warnock Committee. This intrusion into the debate did not, however, alter any of the recommendations of the committee. There is no evidence, either, to suggest that it changed the basic positions of any of the participants in the debate. We can be sure, then, that the correct starting-place for our investigation of human fertilization and embryology is to examine the agenda set by the Warnock Report. The Warnock debate was not concluded by the publishing of the committee's report; it still continues today.

The context

The Warnock Committee did not meet in a vacuum. Existing laws provided a basis for the committee's deliberations, and those laws carried with them the ethical principles on which they were founded. It would have been asking too much, perhaps, to have hoped that the Warnock Committee would have returned to first principles in examining crucial issues such as the status of the human embryo. Almost inevitably, the committee chose to build on existing laws and attitudes without any detailed questioning of their underlying principles. Similarly, while other countries were grappling with the thorny issue of legislation in this whole area, there is little evidence to suggest that the Warnock Committee was swayed by debates conducted in other jurisdictions.

In some of the areas of debate covered by Warnock, no Acts of Parliament existed to provide guidance, though other committees and commissions had previously reported their recommendations. We will look at these shortly. In one important area, however, the statute books did have something to offer: the status of the human fetus.

It was the abortion debate, rather than a debate on human fertilization and embryology, which gave rise to these laws. Nevertheless, they did contribute to the environment in which any serious discussion on bioethical issues could take place. These laws were unquestionably in the minds of the members of the Warnock Committee and those responsible for drafting legislation. To be accurate, the Warnock Committee was interested in the embryo rather than the later fetus, but already existing laws and attitudes regarding the fetus inevitably had an effect on the perceived status of the embryo.

The Offences Against the Person Act 1861

In picking our way through the labyrinth of case law and legislation, we must recognize that before Warnock the human embryo or fetus derived its legal protection indirectly through legislation which sought to protect either a woman's rights or the rights of an infant. The basic law in this regard which guided all subsequent development was the 1861 Offences Against the Person Act in England and Wales. This Act proscribed self-induced miscarriage, procuring the miscarriage of a woman by a third party, attempted procurement of miscarriage and supplying the means to do so.[5]

This far-reaching law made no distinction between therapeutic and criminal activity, and, consequently, it was argued, led to wide-scale back-street abortions. Importantly for our discussion, it was also used to support the opinion that the life of the fetus, at all stages of development, was of paramount significance. Technically, this law could be used to prosecute a doctor who performed an abortion in order to save the life of a woman whose illness was pregnancy-related.

One loophole was left in the law, however, which led to the introduction of a new Act. Under the 1861 Act it was not an offence to kill a child in the process of its birth. This alarming prospect was possible because to commit such a deed was neither to procure a miscarriage nor to take the life of an independent human being.[6] While we cannot guess how often this loophole was exploited, it did cause sufficient unease among the legislators of the day to pave the way for a new Act of Parliament.

The Infant Life (Preservation) Act 1929

This new Act made it a criminal offence for anyone to cause a child to die before it had independent existence. Crucially, the caveats were added that any such child must have been capable of being born alive and that the act which led to its death was both wilful and done with the intention of causing death.[7] For the purposes of the Act it was assumed that any fetus which had reached the twenty-eighth week in its mother's pregnancy was capable of being born alive.[8] A further fundamental departure from the 1861 Act was the introduction of a clause which allowed for the destruction of a fetus at any stage of development if this was deemed necessary in order to save the life of the mother.[9]

We need to be clear at this point on just how great a difference there is between the 1861 and the 1929 laws. Curiously, an Act which was designed to close a loophole in the law between abortion and infanticide resulted in enshrining in law two new principles which led to the exploitation of greater legal loopholes. The 1929 Act declared the twenty-eighth week of pregnancy to be the stage at which a fetus became viable and hence deserving of specific protection under the law. This left open to question and even legal challenge the status of the embryo and early fetus. The Act also introduced the now almost universally accepted concept that the life of the mother may be given priority over the life of the child. This opened up the way for a debate on whether the quality of life of the mother could be weighed against the continuance of life of the fetus. This Act, in effect, created a new environment for further ethical and legal discussion on the question of abortion and led in due course to the 1967 Abortion Act.

The Abortion Act 1967

As with so many important social changes, the progress from the 1929 Act to the 1967 Act was not made in a single step. First, an important precedent was established in case law before pressure built up to introduce a law specifically covering abortion.

The pivotal case was that of R. V. Bourne.[10] This case served to establish a firm link between the 1861 and 1929 Acts. In so doing it exposed inadequacies in both laws and paved the way for the 1967 Abortion Act.

Mr Bourne, an obstetrician, had performed an abortion on a fifteen-year-old girl who had been raped. He made no attempt to hide his actions and was subsequently charged under section 58 of the Offences Against the Person Act 1861. His barristers concentrated on the term 'unlawful use' found in this section. They argued that if there was an unlawful use of an instrument to procure a miscarriage (as the Act stated) then there must also be a lawful use. They further reasoned that the grounds for such lawful use were to be found in the 1929 Act which allowed for abortion on the grounds of endangerment to the mother's life. On this basis Mr Bourne was acquitted.

The most significant point in this case, for us, is the fact that at no time did Bourne believe that the pregnant girl was in danger of dying as a result of the pregnancy. He carried out the abortion because he believed that the health of the girl was at risk due to the psychological pressures placed upon her by the rape and pregnancy. The judge, in his summing up, stated that if the continuance of a pregnancy was likely to result in a woman becoming a physical or mental wreck, then a doctor who performed an abortion in that honest belief can be said to have acted in order to preserve the woman's life.[11]

The significance of this statement cannot be emphasized too strongly. It drew a clear distinction between preserving the life of the mother and preventing her death. This, in effect, said that the quality of life of a pregnant woman could, in certain circumstances, outweigh the continuance of life of her fetus. While this case was not binding on other courts dealing with alleged cases of abortion, it did have enormous impact on the legal profession and on public opinion.

In 1967 this principle was enshrined in law. The Abortion Act 1967 allowed for abortion if two medical practitioners agreed that the continuance of the pregnancy would involve risk to the life of the pregnant woman. It also allowed for abortion if the continuance of the pregnancy would be likely to cause mental or physical injury to her or to her existing children, greater than if the pregnancy were terminated. Abortion was also allowed if it was considered that the fetus would be born with a serious physical or mental handicap.[12] The Act, which has been hotly debated on many occasions by Parliament, provided the basic framework for all subsequent legal and ethical discussion on the matter.

Because of its brief, the Warnock Committee did not discuss abortion directly. There can be little doubt, though, that neither the Warnock Committee nor the Government had any desire to question the principles already established in law. Foremost of these were that the woman's mental and physical health and that of her existing children must be given primary consideration, and that the possibility of serious fetal handicap provided adequate grounds for abortion.

The 1861 Act still stood, however, and as such provided some continued protection for the fetus. Abortions carried out other than under the conditions of the 1967 Act were still illegal.

The Congenital Disabilities (Civil Liabilities) Act 1976

This Act has not hit the headlines or captured the public's imagination in the way that the Abortion Act has. It too is important, though, in our attempt to understand the background to the current situation regarding human fertilization and embryology. This Act allows for damages to be awarded to a child for injuries sustained while still in the womb as long as the child survives for at least forty-eight hours after birth. Because of this Act, some have concluded that it is an offence to cause injury to a fetus which later is born alive, but it is not an offence to cause death.[13]

This opinion is, however, disputed. It is also argued that it is a criminal offence to act in such a way as to cause a miscarriage in which the child will be born alive but will not be able to survive because of the manner in which the miscarriage was procured.[14] This situation, coupled with increasingly sophisticated neonatal care, has given rise to the question of a doctor's responsibility in sustaining the life of an aborted fetus which has proved to be viable, given adequate medical and nursing care. The net result of this was to raise the question of whether or not the status of the fetus should be enshrined in law as a topic in its own right.

The Feversham Committee

Abortion has always been a subject which has created controversy. Strongly held opinions, both for and against, are expected. Infertility treatment, however, has only recently become a matter for public concern and debate. Before Warnock, only one other Government-constituted committee had reported on infertility treatment. Even then its brief was restricted to human artificial insemination.

Despite the fact that the first recorded case of artificial insemination by husband (AIH) dated from 1790, when a Scottish doctor, John Hunter, was reputed to have artificially inseminated the wife of a London linen-draper,[15] public opinion was not aroused until the middle of this century. In January 1945 the British Medical Journal carried an article which was seen as rendering a favourable account of artificial insemination by donor (AID, now known as DI, donor insemination).[16] Public interest was stimulated to such a degree that the Archbishop of Canterbury set up a commission to enquire into the practice. This commission reported in 1948, and was critical of DI to the extent of recommending that it should be made a criminal offence, and that a woman receiving DI should be considered as having committed adultery.[17]

Continued concern led to the Government's establishing a committee under the chairmanship of the Earl of Feversham.[18] This committee addressed the following brief:

> To enquire into the existing practice of human artificial insemination and its legal consequences and to consider whether, taking account of the interests of individuals involved and of society as a whole, any change in the law is necessary or desirable.[19]

The Feversham Committee examined the subject carefully from medical and ethical perspectives, though its major concern was legal. Its tone was generally conservative in character, though it did depart from the recommendations of both the 1948 Archbishop of Canterbury's Commission and the submissions made to it by the Roman Catholic Church.[20] In particular, it did not consider DI to constitute an adulterous act or AIH to be in any way morally suspect. Moreover, it specifically recommended that DI should not be a criminal offence, indeed going so far as to argue that it should not be regulated by law.[21]

In all, the committee made one recommendation in regard to AIH and six other recommendations in regard to DI: successful AIH, resulting in the birth of a live child, should debar either partner from proceeding with a nullity case on the grounds of impotence;[22] DI without a husband's consent should be made a new ground for divorce;[23] sterility should not be a ground for a decree of nullity;[24] DI which results in the birth of a live child, and to which both husband and wife consented, should debar either partner from applying for a decree of nullity on the grounds of impotence;[25] a DI child should have the same automatic rights of inheritance or maintenance as an adopted child;[26] no change in the laws of legitimacy or birth registration should be made, thus DI children should continue to be technically illegitimate;[27] and a wife should not be allowed to take divorce proceedings against her husband on the ground that he donated semen for DI without her consent.[28] This was agreed despite the earlier recommendation which gave a husband the right to take divorce proceedings on the ground that his wife had received DI without his consent.

The Feversham Committee's work has been largely superseded by both subsequent medical practice and the Warnock Committee. Nevertheless, its recommendations are important for two reasons.

First, the committee developed the debate on human artificial insemination. Its recommendations broke new ground in that many of them rejected the more conservative approach of the churches and in particular the findings of the Archbishop of Canterbury's commission. Feversham clearly set a more liberal and essentially secular agenda for discussing artificial insemination. Of note, for example, are the statements that DI does not constitute adultery, and that successful DI should be seen as removing, in law, the existence of impotence.

Echoes of a more conservative age are still to be found, though, in the argument that while a woman may not receive DI without her husband's consent without facing possible divorce, a man may donate semen for a DI programme without any such fear. It is also worth noting that, as far as the Feversham Committee was concerned, only married women should be offered DI services.[29]

Secondly, the Feversham Report helped shape the approach of the Warnock Committee. Much the same ethical issues surfaced in the Warnock debate as in Feversham. Naturally, Warnock reflected Feversham in some of its recommendations. It is reasonable to believe that the more liberal attitudes expressed in the Feversham Report had a considerable influence on the Warnock Committee, while the more conservative recommendations were passed over. The expression of dissent appended to the Feversham Committee's report, suggesting the extension of legitimacy to DI children, also found favour with Warnock.[30]

The Feversham Committee reported in 1960 when moral attitudes were still quite conservative by the standards of two decades later. In the decade which followed the publication of the report, the 1967 Abortion Act was passed. Attitudes generally became more liberal and medical and scientific knowledge advanced to a stage not anticipated by the committee. By 1970 the issue of research using fetuses or fetal material was a real one. Once more the Government had to intervene to provide guidelines for medical and scientific practice. It convened the Peel Committee, which published its report in 1972.[31]

The Peel Committee

The Peel Report did not deal directly with embryo research, but with research on fetuses at a later stage of development. Nevertheless, there is sufficient common ground between the two topics for the Warnock Committee to recommend that legislation should be introduced which took a uniform stance on the whole area of such research.[32] Warnock argued, correctly, that the situation must not arise where research would be prohibited on four-week-old embryos but, by the possible exploitation of a legal loophole, could continue on a four-month-old fetus.

It is useful to get a flavour of the Peel Committee's findings. Peel identified fifty-three ways in which fetal research could be of value. The committee recommended that in the case of miscarriage, maternal permission had to be obtained in order for any research to be carried out. In the case of abortion, however, the mother should merely be asked if she has any directions to offer regarding the disposal of the fetus. In the absence of specific directions, research should be allowed to proceed.[33]

We noted earlier that the law gave some limited protection to the fetus if it is capable of being born alive or if it is injured *in utero* but lives after birth for at least forty-eight hours. The Peel Committee recommended that twenty weeks' gestation should be the point at which a fetus is deemed to be viable,[34] and that the first consideration of the medical profession should be the preservation of life.[35] While the committee did speak of the possibility of reckless injury to the fetus, it did not consider how such an offence could best be dealt with in law.

As far as the earlier fetus is concerned, the Peel Committee granted in principle that research under regulation should be allowed, but not beyond the stage when a fetus weighs more than 300g. Presumably this was to allow for a sufficient margin of error in determining the age of a twenty-week-old fetus, which may be expected to weigh between 400g and 500g.[36] In addition, the committee expressed concern regarding the possible sale of fetal parts for research, and the even more objectionable thought of abortions being performed for commercial reward.

Even this brief review of the Feversham and Peel Committees helps us to see the extent of the shift in public and professional opinion in the space of little over a decade. Scientific progress continued apace, so that by 1982 the Government stepped in once again and appointed the Warnock Committee to investigate the whole area of human fertilization and embryology.

Warnock inevitably inherited the legacy of the late 1960s and early 1970s. This legacy was not altogether consistent. On the one hand it said that the fetus should not be afforded the legal rights of a member of society, while on the other it expressed concern that the fetus should be given some statutory protection. This was one of the knots that Warnock had to attempt to untie.

The international context

At the same time as the Warnock Committee was investigating the many facets of human fertilization and embryology in the United Kingdom, other countries were also grappling with the same issues. There is little to suggest that the Warnock Committee, or anyone else for that matter, took their cue from any of the debates taking place outside the United Kingdom. Nevertheless, a brief summary of what other countries were doing at this time may help us to set the overall context more firmly in our own minds.

Within Europe a number of countries, including Belgium, Italy and the Netherlands, chose not to formulate any specific legislation in the area of human fertilization and embryology. At a federal level the same was true of Canada and the United States, though Kentucky, Illinois, Louisiana, New Mexico and Pennsylvania had laws that specifically mentioned *in vitro* fertilization. Each state took an independent approach to the subject.

Some countries were ahead of the United Kingdom in promoting legislation. Norway, Spain and Sweden all had laws covering IVF and embryo research, as had the states of Victoria and South Australia. When the 1990 Human Fertilization and Embryology Act was at the Bill stage in Parliament, France and Germany also had Bills in progress, while Denmark had just established a National Ethics Council to examine the subject.

The range of opinion regarding infertility treatments and embryo research was as wide as could be imagined. In Norway, for example, embryo research was prohibited, and a moratorium was declared in Denmark, while no legal restrictions at all were imposed in Belgium and Italy. Similarly, in Australia and Sweden only married couples or those living in a permanent relationship were allowed to enter IVF programmes, while in Spain all women, regardless of marital status, were eligible for treatment.

What this indicates is that the Warnock Committee could not have hoped to have gained much help or guidance by examining the law (or lack of it) in other countries. Throughout the 1980s most countries with the scientific and medical capabilities to provide IVF or engage in embryo research were struggling with the issues involved. The Warnock Committee in the United Kingdom reached its own conclusions, some of which were similar to the approaches taken by other countries. While similarities and differences are interesting to note, they do not assist us greatly in reaching an understanding of the agenda set in the United Kingdom by Warnock.

The Warnock Report

To the disappointment of many, the Warnock Committee did not seek to establish by detailed argument the moral grounds on which it made its recommendations. Equally crucially, it did not attempt to justify the particular link it made between morality and law. These were major omissions, since both these important concerns were clearly central to the committee's remit. Rather, following a terse statement regarding morality and law, to which we shall return later, the committee moved to an examination of the practices which it considered to be within its brief.

These practices and techniques may be listed under the headings of artificial insemination by husband (AIH), donor insemination (DI), egg and embryo donation, *in vitro* fertilization (IVF), surrogacy, embryo research, and use and storage of gametes and embryos. All of these topics remain areas of major concern today.

In addressing this agenda we need to map out clearly a reasoned and comprehensive approach. A weakness of many Christian contributions to the Warnock debate was that they failed to cover adequately the fundamental ethical issues on which the debate was based. Opinions were expressed concerning this or that technique without first establishing a defensible moral framework for the discussion. We have noted that this was also a failure of the Warnock Report, but this does not give us licence to make the same mistake. In the years that have followed the publication of the Warnock Report, few attempts have been made to formulate a comprehensive Christian approach to the whole area of human fertilization and embryology.

First of all, then, we must examine the moral basis on which a Christian contribution may be made. We must also explore the link between this moral base and its legitimate impact on legislation. This can then be contrasted with the moral base chosen by the Warnock Committee and the link it established with legislation.

Secondly, bearing in mind the detailed techniques and practices listed above, we must examine the relevant ethical and theological principles which should guide us in a Christian evaluation of the debate. Unless these principles are firmly established, it is impossible to examine properly the actual techniques dealt with by the Warnock Committee.

Thirdly, with the moral base established and guiding principles firmly set, we must then evaluate the debate which actually took place regarding the various techniques dealt with in the Warnock Report. This will be done by examining the Warnock Report and subsequent Government papers, the eventual legislation contained in the 1990 Human Fertilization and Embryology Act and the various contributions made to the debate by Christian churches and groups. The arguments which surfaced in this debate are, by and large, still the arguments which circulate today. Our evaluation of the debate must include clear, consistent, detailed statements of a Christian response to the techniques and practices under review. In particular, it must show in which areas Christians may argue on moral grounds alone and in which areas Christians may argue that legislative measures be taken to control or prohibit a technique or practice.

This is quite a demanding exercise. It is one which is absolutely necessary, however, if we are to take seriously the fundamentally important ethical considerations involved in the ongoing debate on human fertilization and embryology.

2

Warnock, morality and legislation

Christian morality

Our first step in analysing the moral position of the Warnock Committee
and the ethical basis of current United Kingdom legislation is to propose
a Christian basis for morality. At one level this may be established quite
quickly by asserting that the correct basis for Christian morality is the
will of God. To act in a morally correct manner is to act in accordance
with God's will. Certainly, it is difficult to see how a Christian could
argue that to obey God's will would be to act in an immoral manner or
that to disobey it would be to act in a moral manner. Nevertheless, there
are problems with this simple answer which must be explored, even
though it is the answer which many Christians would automatically give
to the question: how ought a Christian to act?

The problems may be dealt with by answering three further questions.
Is this approach defensible? Is it necessary? Is it intelligible? That is to
say, we must first examine challenges to what philosophers call a divine-
command theory of morality, which state that any such theory is either
meaningless or ethically unacceptable. (Is it defensible?) We must then
note alternative theories available to Christians, focusing particularly on
the relationship between reason and revelation. (Is it necessary?) Finally,
we need to look at the actual content of a divine-command theory with
particular reference to the place of the Bible. (Is it intelligible?)

This may all seem a rather complicated way of defending God's will as the basis of Christian morality, but it is precisely in failing to address this issue properly that many Christian arguments become unstuck.

Divine-command theory

The classical statement which purports to embarrass any proponent of a divine-command morality is found on the lips of Socrates when he asks Euthyphro, 'Is that which is holy loved by the gods because it is holy, or is it holy because it is loved by the gods?'[1] We can restate this to ask whether a deed is right or good because God wills it, or whether God wills it because it is right or good.

This philosophical conundrum presents us with a twofold problem. If we affirm the first part of the statement (a deed is right because God wills it), morality is said to be dependent upon the arbitrary choice of God. If God commanded it, therefore, torture of children would be a moral act; clearly an unacceptable conclusion. At the same time the statement 'God commands what is good' is said to be open to the charge of being a meaningless tautology since 'what is good' is defined as being God's command.

Equally, if the second part of the statement is affirmed (God wills something because it is good), it is claimed that a knowledge of God's will is not required for establishing morality. Indeed, if God himself is to be a moral agent, his will must conform to a morality which has an existence independent of him. Consequently, his omnipotence and sovereignty are called into question.

Brunner, Barth and Bonhoeffer

This challenge to an instinctive Christian belief that morality is based on God's will has long been recognized by philosophers and theologians. It is useful to note, then, that it has not embarrassed all theologians, causing them uniformly to abandon a divine-command morality.

The first half of the twentieth century saw two world wars, the advent of weapons of mass destruction, systematic genocide and many other evils. Under these conditions the whole concept of morality and the very existence of God were widely questioned. Precisely at this time, however, some of the century's greatest theological minds were defending divine-command morality.

Brunner, for example, argued that

. . . there is no such thing as an 'intrinsic Good'. The hypostatization of a human conception of the Good as the 'idea of the Good' is not only an abstraction in the logical sense; it is due to the fact that man has been severed from his Origin, to that original perversion of the meaning of existence which consists in the fact that man attributes to himself and his ideas an independent existence – that is, that man makes himself God.[2]

He continued, 'The Good is simply what God wills that we should do, not that which we would do on the basis of a principle of love.'[3]

Similarly, Barth wrote:

We cannot translate the truth and reality of the divine command into a necessary element of man's spiritual life, or the realization of human reason, or the realization of the good as achieved by man himself, or a value position anchored in the transcendent.[4]

He concluded, 'For me the good is to cleave to God. Every ethics which is at least half serious, aims consciously or unconsciously to say this.'[5]

Equally Bonhoeffer, who had more reason than many theologians to grapple with the reality of moral decision-making, argued, 'In ethical discourse what matters is not only that the contents of the assertion should be correct but also that there should be a concrete warrant, and authorization for this assertion.'[6] His argument led him to the conclusion that 'God's commandment is the only warrant for ethical discourse'.[7]

Impressive as these thinkers are, it is not enough to appeal to them in support of a divine-command morality. While their reflections may help to steady a few theological nerves, we must also indicate how such a morality is acceptable in principle. A number of approaches to the question have been taken by Christian thinkers.

Contemporary Christian thinkers

A. Phillips Griffiths, voicing the reaction of many Christians, likens the dilemma to a type of medieval puzzle which asks what we should say if God commands us to disobey him. He argues that 'it just won't happen'. Similarly, he notes, 'I am unable to conceive of any circumstances in which someone can be judged to have been commanded by God to do something wrong, evil or wicked.'[8]

This does not seek to solve Socrates' conundrum, but it does indicate that the dilemma may be apparent rather than real. After all, it is unthinkable that a Christian could argue that God and good are ever separable. This approach has the merit of cutting through the sophistry, but most philosophers will not let us off the hook that easily.

Tackling their concerns, Stewart Sutherland seeks to escape the charge that the statement 'God commands what is good' becomes a meaningless tautology if good is defined as 'what God commands'. He draws a distinction between the statements 'God always wills the good' and 'The God of Christian (or any other) theology always wills the good'. The former, he claims, is an analytic truth and would lead to a tautology, but the latter, he asserts, is a synthetic truth. In our moral decision-making it is the role of theology to give content to both the terms 'God' and 'good'.

This means that the Christian conviction that God wills only what is good must lead Christians to accept as commands of God only those things which they can defend as being good. Such a defence must be made on the basis of ethical standards which are open to investigation. The crucial point that Sutherland makes is that in Christian or any other theology we deal with our understanding of God and his will, not directly with God himself. We need checks and balances in our thinking to enable us to discover the good that is God's will. He concludes that this asserts 'a fundamental belief about the ultimate compatibility and indeed interdependence of moral and religious beliefs'.[9]

Moving further into the philosophical maze, Richard Swinburne argues that the dilemma may be resolved by recognizing that some actions are obligatory because God commands them and that others are commanded by God because they are obligatory in any case. The first group of actions he describes as being contingently obligatory because it is the whole network of circumstances which causes the action to be right and only God can know what is the correct action in such cases. The second set of actions he describes as being necessarily obligatory since he views necessary moral truths as being analytic. He argues that this does not limit God in any way, since 'By definition God is unconstrained . . . of logical necessity a being unconstrained and omniscient does not choose the bad.'[10]

This argument is not the easiest to grasp, but it is worth persevering with. What he is saying is that a being who is omniscient will always be able to recognize what is right. This is so whether many factors have to be taken into account or whether a necessary moral truth (one true by definition) is at stake. He further argues that an omnipotent being (one free from external constraints) will always choose to do what is right because there are no good reasons for acting otherwise. Consequently, 'God being omniscient and unconstrained of logical necessity chooses only the good.'[11] According to this thesis there is no conflict between seeing God's will as determining what is good and God necessarily approving of what is good.

Stephen Clark,[12] Robert Merrihew Adams,[13] Ronald Green[14] and others[15] stress that it is the character of the Christian God which assures us that he wills only what is good. This thought lies behind Sutherland's and Swinburne's arguments as well, but these writers are more explicit on this point.

Clark points out that God is not constrained to act in the same manner as he commands others to act. If Swinburne's contention is not accepted, God could command us to do good deeds and at the same time commit evil deeds himself. The fact that he does not do this (a fact known to us by his self-revelation) indicates that he is worthy of worship and trust. In other words we can believe that the dilemma is apparent rather than real, not because any god would always command the good but because the Christian God always commands the good. Furthermore, he has given us grounds for determining what the good is, so that we can safeguard against people claiming that God has commanded them to commit an evil deed.

This enables us to say that it is the character of the Christian God which renders the challenge to a divine-command morality ineffective. God, as Swinburne has argued, is unconstrained and omniscient and chooses only what is good, since to choose what is evil would be to enter into self-contradiction. Similarly, his self-revelation indicates that he chooses to act in a manner consistent with his commands to us. Consequently, we can have confidence that the Christian God does not act in an arbitrary fashion in determining morality since what is good is reflective of his character. This character is shown to be loving, gracious and praiseworthy in his acts of creation, providence and salvation.

The Christian God (as distinct from any theoretical god or gods) has also provided adequate means whereby we can judge the reasonableness of any interpretation of God's will. Goodness may stem from the character of God, but it is also reflected in God's revelation of himself in his creation. Thus 'God commands what is good' may, at one level, be a tautology, but it is not meaningless, since we have reasons in addition to a belief in God's command for asserting that something is good. Thus, 'God commands what is good' bears witness to the sort of God we believe in.

Much of this discussion may appear needlessly convoluted to many Christians. Believing that God's will is the basis of morality seems self-evident. Unfortunately, that is not how the majority of moral philosophers see it. In attempting to offer a Christian contribution to the ongoing debate on human fertilization and embryology, it is essential that Christians be able to defend the reasonableness of their moral basis. We may not expect everyone to adopt our viewpoint, but we do have an obligation to show that it is defensible. A Christian basis for morality cannot be dismissed out of hand if it demonstrates a proper awareness of the philosophical issues involved.

In defending the reasonableness of a divine-command morality, we have touched upon the contentious areas of revelation and reason and the relationship between them. Having shown that divine-command morality is defensible, we must now indicate why it is necessary.

Reason and revelation

An obvious way of dismissing divine-command morality is to argue, not that it is indefensible, but that it is unnecessary. After all, many will assert that it is possible to devise an adequate system of morality without reference to revelation. Even though divine-command morality may be defensible in theory, it is not needed in practice.

Among secular thinkers, the question of revelation does not arise, since the existence or relevance of God is denied. For such thinkers a purely human basis must be found for morality. While there is a variety of approaches to finding such a basis, the most influential contemporary method is utilitarianism. Among moral theologians, revelation is generally recognized, but its relationship with reason is disputed. Revelation and natural law are often seen as two alternative methods of discerning ethics, sometimes with one taking precedence and sometimes with the other. In determining a Christian morality we must face the challenge of utilitarianism and resolve the suggested tension between revelation and reason.

Utilitarianism

Contemporary exponents of utilitarianism have tended to move away from a calculation of pleasure and pain to a broader concern for 'best consequences'. This move makes good sense since, even if a consequentialist position is adopted, there are consequences other than pleasure or pain which must be taken into account. For example, a person injured in a terrorist bombing may suffer severe brain damage which renders impossible any enjoyment of normal life. Nevertheless, the injured person may actually be happier and experience more sensation of pleasure and fewer feelings of worry or pain than before the incident. If pleasure is made the only consequence of importance, then the terrorist attack has not been immoral.

Consequences, therefore, must include more than pleasure or pain, but even then utilitarianism encounters problems in presenting itself as an acceptable method of determining morality. There is the obvious difficulty of discerning the true consequences of any action. Equally, the fundamental tenet of utilitarianism, which states that each person's welfare is of equal importance, cannot be established on a utilitarian basis. Utilitarianism cannot provide an answer to the person who insists that his or her welfare is more important than that of someone else.

Furthermore, utilitarianism requires us to adopt the position of an impartial observer in determining our welfare and the welfare of others, but how can ordinary human beings attain this status? History and experience indicate that human beings have a strong tendency to adopt an inflated view of the importance of their own welfare and a correspondingly deflated view of the importance of the welfare of others. Since, in utilitarianism, we must make moral decisions on the basis of our own interpretation of any given situation, utilitarianism proves to be a very uncertain foundation for ethics.

Even if these objections were brushed aside, it is widely recognized that utilitarianism is inadequate when confronted with issues of justice, rights or promise.[16] It is not difficult to envisage situations where a utilitarian approach would lead to injustice or to a denial of rights or to broken promises. Utilitarianism would suggest that an innocent person could be executed in order to quell civil unrest. Minority groups within a society may be denied equality of treatment if the majority felt that society as a whole would benefit. A husband may break his marriage vows and have an affair if, by so doing, two out of the three people involved in the situation were happier as a result. Justice, rights and promise are important moral concepts; any ethical theory which does not take them adequately into account cannot commend itself to us.

Such problems have not, of course, escaped the attention of utilitarian thinkers. Consequently, utilitarianism has been refined by some from basic 'act-utilitarianism' (where each case is judged on its own merits), to 'rule-utilitarianism' (where rules are devised from what is considered to be the general balance of consequences of various actions). Thus punishing an innocent person is sometimes acceptable according to act-utilitarianism, but because such an action is believed generally to lead to bad consequences, rule-utilitarianism forbids it. Not all utilitarians are rule-utilitarians, however, and even for those who are, the problem remains of how to establish such rules.

Why be moral?

Utilitarianism, in so far as it highlights the need to take consequences into account in moral decision-making, does make a useful contribution to ethics, but in itself it does not provide an adequate basis for morality. Rule-utilitarianism will, in many cases, provide very useful guidelines for practical decision-making. It fails, however, to address the fundamental questions of why we should act in a moral fashion and why we should expect others to share our moral code.

Peter Singer, as a utilitarian, is reduced to saying that we act morally in order to give meaning to life, even though 'life as a whole has no meaning'.[17] This is a utilitarian argument in that it may be reasonably contended that the greater good of the greater number will be safeguarded by making life meaningful through moral activity. It fails, though, to give a reason for believing that a meaningless life ought to be given meaning, or that by so doing any good has been achieved.

Only if human life is inherently meaningful and of value can we be persuaded that helping people to live their lives in a meaningful way is to effect a moral good. If life is meaningless, no good is served in living an intentional deception; indeed, no good can exist.

This objection is fundamental in a critique of any secular morality. Whether we try to argue from a utilitarian perspective, or on the basis of intuition, or from a sociological doctrine of the coherence of society, we have to overcome the problem of the essential meaninglessness of life.

It is difficult to escape the belief that morality must be, in the final analysis, meaningless if human beings are to be understood as nothing more than the products of an impersonal universe. For humans to be of real value the universe must be the expression of a personal, moral agent: God. If this is not so, morality is merely a means of regulating human behaviour so that as many people as possible suffer as little as possible during their lives. While Christians may agree that this is a laudable thing, it is of no value if human beings are essentially valueless.

If we come from nothing and go to nothing and contribute nothing of eternal value, living our lives in an impersonal valueless universe, morality is also ultimately valueless. Any value given to it by society is illusory since it masks the fact that nothing really matters anyhow.

If I decide to kill as many newborn babies as I can, society may deem me to be a threat and consequently lock me up or even kill me, but if newborn babies have no ultimate value I have done wrong only in a relative way. This, of course, is not how most people see things. The fact that the importance of morality is generally accepted, though, is a sign that most people have not recognized the implications of secularism, rather than an indication that a truly valuable secular morality has been achieved.

Revelation

A divine-command theory of ethics is not rendered redundant by utilitarianism or other secular moral theories, but it is still open to challenge from a theological perspective. To what extent does morality depend upon revelation, and to what extent can it be discerned by reason based on the created order? For many Christians this is a much more pertinent question than any posed by advocates of utilitarianism.

The question facing moral theologians has been well put by J. M. Gustafson:

> Protestant theological ethics and Catholic moral theology
> currently share a serious quest, namely for a philosophical
> foundation for Christian ethical thought and Christian moral
> activity which takes the Christian tradition seriously, which
> provides a common ground with non-religious persons and
> communities and with other religions, and which has openness
> to historic changes and to personalistic values without
> becoming utterly relativistic.[18]

Unless a satisfactory position is reached regarding the relationship between revelation and reason, this quest will not progress far.

There are theologians, of course, who would contest the need for any common ground between Christian ethics and non-religious persons. Barth, for example, argues that theological ethics 'annexes' general ethics,[19] and he opposes any synthesis between the two, or any theory which views them as complementary approaches to moral decision-making.[20] Brunner, as we have seen, views the whole idea of an ethic independent of God's will as an act of human rebellion against the Creator.[21]

Not all Protestant theologians have been as hostile to natural or general ethics based on reason, but three common objections are made against what theologians call 'natural law'. It is argued that reliance upon reason fails to take sin seriously enough, that all attempts at reaching agreement on the content of natural law have failed, and that Roman Catholic interpretations of natural law reflect medieval social and cultural conditions.[22]

Roman Catholic theologians respond much more favourably to the role of reason in determining ethics and argue that natural law is scriptural, that it stems from God's creation of moral beings, and that Jesus, by becoming 'true humanity', has displayed the ethics of humanity as much as he has revealed the command of God.[23] This separation of revelation and reason into two rival sources for ethics is understandable, but mistaken.

Revelation v. reason

Placing revelation over against reason has often been an attempt to safeguard the sovereignty of God. Thus Luther and Calvin both defended the absolute freedom of God to determine morality, which can only be known with assurance through revelation.[24] The medieval Nominalists argued that morality so depended on God's will that if God revealed that he desired the death of an innocent person it would be meritorious to commit murder. God, it was argued, could even reveal that he desired human beings to hate him, hence making blasphemy commendable.[25] The absurdity of this position strikes at the heart of any radical separation of revelation and reason.

Emphasizing the role of reason over against revelation is also often done from laudable motives: to safeguard universal ethical standards or to provide a point of contact between theology and moral philosophy. Human reason, however, is manifestly too uncertain a foundation for moral decision-making. We have seen this to be the case in utilitarianism, but it is no less true in the case of Kantian ethics, where it is claimed that rational thought will always lead to correct ethical decision-making as long as one follows maxims which can be made into universal laws. As has been pointed out by critics of Kant, it is quite possible to devise irreconcilable but none the less rational ethical imperatives.[26] Reason, exalted over revelation, does not lead to clarity.

There is no good reason for supposing that reason and revelation are two mutually exclusive ways of apprehending God's will. Indeed, there is much to commend an approach which sees them as being complementary though unequal partners in assisting us in ethical enquiry.

Ronald Green argues persuasively that in both Judaism and early Christianity reason and revelation were complementary. Regarding Judaism, he notes that no-one raised 'the theoretical question of whether human moral reason and divine revelation can ultimately disagree: that they cannot is an implicit but defining tenet of the faith'.[27] He observes that in Christianity, 'faith is obedience to God in the conviction that the divine and human conscience cannot ultimately contradict one another'.[28]

Green argues strongly that even Aquinas, often seen as the leading proponent of natural law, viewed reason and revelation as being in harmony.[29] He sums up his position when he writes: 'Often lost in the fray (of reason *versus* revelation) was the naïve confidence of the early tradition, still evident in Aquinas, that human moral reason and revealed morality are one.'[30]

This harmony between reason and revelation must be seen as a real one, not merely an uneasy cohabitation. Unless reason and revelation are seen as being genuinely complementary, the danger still exists of their being viewed as alternative methods of discerning God's will. This point has been well made by Oliver O'Donovan:

> Creation and redemption each has its ontological and its
> epistemological aspect. There is the created order and there is
> natural knowledge; there is the new creation and there is
> revelation in Christ. This has encouraged a confusion of the
> ontological and the epistemological in much modern theology
> so that we are constantly presented with the unacceptably

> polarized choice between an ethic that is revealed and has no
> ontological grounding and an ethic that is based on
> creation and so is naturally known.[31]

Reason complementing revelation

If reason and revelation are genuinely complementary, how then are they related? Revelation of the divine command in morality presupposes that the recipients of such revelation are moral creatures. That is to say they must be able to recognize the divine command, and it must be recognized as a moral command. If this were not the case, God's self-disclosure would pass us by and we would be unable to assert that the command of God is 'good'. That we recognize God's command as being moral indicates that in creating us God has made us moral agents. This is, of course, no more than we should expect from God who is wise as well as powerful.

Nevertheless, we are creatures tainted by sin and its effects. Left to our own devices, we should expect to agree on many areas of morality but to differ on others, partly because of our inability to think clearly enough and partly because of our innate tendency to favour ourselves in situations of moral choice. Revelation is necessary to clarify our reasoning as well as to indicate clearly what the divine will is. Reason is also necessary both to safeguard against maverick interpretations of God's will and to apply revelation in detailed areas of ethical decision-making.

In a perfect world no conflict would ever arise between reason and revelation, but we do not live in a perfect world. Revelation must take precedence over reason on the occasions where reason is an uncertain guide, though we should expect reason to be able to endorse revelation in almost all cases. God's revelation of himself and his will does so much more than challenge and inform our reason, of course. It speaks to our whole being, calling us to respond personally to him. Here, however, we are concerned primarily with the relationship between revelation and reason.

Some Christian writers, such as N. H. G. Robinson, view revelation as correcting human reason,[32] and this is often how Christians engage in dialogue with society. A better way of viewing the relationship between reason and revelation is to say that revelation enables us to reason correctly. As Robinson admits, reason never creates the moral law; at most it discovers it.[33] Better again to insist that it endorses it.

This discussion on the relationship between revelation and reason leads us to an examination of the question of the intelligibility of a divine-command morality. If we accept that such a theory is defensible and that it is necessary, we have answered two of the three questions we set ourselves at the beginning of this chapter. We now need to address the third question, regarding the intelligibility of a divine-command theory of ethics. How can we know the content of the divine command? To answer this question we must examine, in particular, the role of the Scriptures in Christian ethics.

The Bible and ethics

Few Christians, if any, would argue that the Bible does not have a unique role to play in understanding morality. For those who adhere to a divine-command theory of ethics, that role is a central one.

Revelation necessitates that there be real content in what is revealed. Even if we argue that it is himself that God reveals rather than propositional truths about himself, we must still be able to talk about that revelation. We must be able to say that this rather than that has been revealed about God as a result of a revelation of God. Since, in any Christian evaluation of the Scriptures, the Bible is intimately associated with the transmission of God's self-revelation, it is important that we seek a clear idea of the role of the Bible in ethics.

Difficulties

Once again, we may be tempted to go for a simple, clear-cut statement of principle: the Bible is God's Word and must be obeyed. Without doubting that this is the case, we need to invest time and energy in understanding the issues that are involved in making such a statement. The difficulty facing Christians in this regard has been well put by J. M. Gustafson:

> If one holds to 'verbal inspiration', how does one resolve,
> theologically and ethically, discrepancies within the Bible? If
> one has a looser view of the authority of the Bible, how does one
> determine which theological and ethical principles will be the
> central ones for interpreting the Bible? If one uses biblical
> themes, like hope or liberation, to interpret the moral and

religious significance of current events, does one only come to
the threshold of ethical reflection, and, if so, how is an
appropriate course of action determined? If one uses moral
teachings of the New Testament, how are these nearly two-
thousand-year-old teachings applicable to the twentieth
century? How can one claim for teachings 'revelation' in a
Hellenistic Jewish culture a validity in a modern secular
culture? How can the beliefs and teachings developed by a then
insignificant and powerless minority community be applied in
a cosmopolitan world by Christians who are frequently
strongly identified with the culture of that world?[34]

R. G. Jones has summarized the problems facing Christians in their
use of the Bible in ethics as encompassing four main areas of difficulty:
the diversity of teaching within the Bible, the difference between
biblical cultures and our own, the difference between the ethical
problems facing biblical authors and the problems we face today, and the
questionable status of biblical injunctions even in biblical times.[35] We
cannot examine all of these issues in the depth they deserve; that would
require a separate book. What we can do, though, is to outline an
approach which is capable of addressing them.

Dead ends

A retreat into fundamentalism has proved tempting to many Christians
who seek to sweep away all doubt regarding moral action. Such a move is
unacceptable. Not only is it unsuccessful in achieving its aim, since
fundamentalists disagree on some moral issues, but it is based on an
incorrect view of the Scriptures.

As Allen Verhey has argued, there is a creative relationship running
throughout the Christian faith between the human and the divine. They
must not be 'confused, transmuted the one into the other, divided into
separate categories, or contrasted according to area or function'.[36] This
relationship is evident in God's revelation of himself and our
appreciation of that revelation.

Fundamentalism fails in that it identifies the words of Scripture with
the Word of God in such a way as to remove the human part of the
relationship. Little or no regard is given to the varying historical,
literary or cultural contexts in which the Scriptures were written. All

Scripture is interpreted in the same manner. Equally, in many cases, no regard is given to the varying contexts in which the Bible is to be applied today.

Similarly, the more extreme liberal views, which encourage us to accept biblical teaching only if it can be attested by reason based on historical, philosophical or sociological study, are also flawed. They remove the divine part of the creative relationship. The Bible is reduced to being just one religious book among many, albeit one which has a time-honoured position within the Christian tradition.

Verhey's 'Chalcedonian' approach, which insists on the importance of both the human and the divine in understanding God's revelation of himself to us, steers us towards a more thoughtful view of the role of the Bible in ethics.

The pivotal role of the Scriptures

Any Christian theory of ethics which is based on divine command must see the Scriptures as playing a pivotal role in the revelation of the divine command. Thus Brunner can say:

> The basis of the Divine Command is always the same, but its
> content varies with varying circumstances. The
> 'Commandments' of the Bible witness to the concrete Divine
> Command which has been proclaimed; they are thus
> authoritative expositions of the One Command.[37]

This does not require us to adopt a fundamentalist approach to the Scriptures, but it does indicate that the words of the Bible must be given a pre-eminent place in our thinking.

Similarly, Barth argues, 'The Bible not only instructs and guides us concerning the command of God, but also attests and mediates its revelation. It tells us, not only that God does demand and how, but also what He demands.'[38] He concludes:

> The witness of the Bible does not, therefore, refer to a
> temporary expression of the divine command which we have to
> divest of its temporary character if we are to deduce from it an
> eternal content valid for us. It refers to the divine command
> which has eternal and valid content for us precisely in its

temporary expression, and demands that we should hear and respect it in our very different time and situation.[39]

This does not mean that we can simply apply specific instances of biblical ethics to situations today without further thought. We must attempt to discover the divine command, witnessed to in the Scriptures, and apply it in our situation today. For example, the Old Testament acceptance of capital punishment does not mean that Christians today must accept this practice. It does mean that we must view murderers as having forfeited their right to life because of the enormity of their crime. We temper justice with mercy, and may argue that we ought not to take a murderer's life, but we do not lose sight of the essential principle.

In viewing the Scriptures as a vehicle for God's self-revelation, attesting and witnessing to God's acts in history, we must take seriously the tools of biblical criticism. This does not mean, however, that we have to accept the conclusions of exponents of the 'traditio-historical' school such as Von Rad and Bultmann. A better approach is to argue with Brevard Childs that the Scriptures must be seen as Scripture.[40] That is to say, while the mechanics of how the Scriptures came to be written are interesting and instructive, it is to the completed canon of Scripture that Christians turn when we want to discover the divine command.

This does, of course, mean that we have to believe that the God who revealed himself in history also took a providential interest in the transmission of that revelation. To believe otherwise is to suggest a very odd God indeed, who reveals himself to us but who is unconcerned with how that revelation is understood and passed on. This is not to say that we believe that every reflection of every author in the Bible is to be seen as indicative of God's will. Many of the Psalms, for example, contain sentiments which are the honest cry of a tortured soul. This honesty helps us in our relationship with God, but we do not have to agree with the sentiments expressed. We should be able to discern, however, in the canon of Scripture, the will of God for us. We too are drawn into the creative divine–human relationship in discovering the divine command today.

Bonhoeffer draws attention to this dynamic when he asserts: 'Respect for the holy character of the Scripture demands recognition of the fact that it is only by grace that a man is called upon to interpret and proclaim it and that it is also by grace that a man is permitted even to be a hearer of the interpretation and proclamation.'[41] In surveying the complex way in which we may arrive at an understanding of the divine will, he notes: 'It is only in conjunction, in combination and in opposition with one another that the divine mandates of the church, of marriage and the family, of culture and of government declare the commandment of God as it is revealed in Jesus Christ.'[42] Discovering the divine command and its application is not always easy, and it involves an understanding of contemporary society as well as of the Scriptures, but it is the goal of Christian ethics.

Interpreting the Scriptures

How then may we approach the Scriptures to find an ethical foundation for our actions? An investigation of Old Testament ethics underlines the essentially deontological basis of much of Israelite life.[43] This approach to morality, based on rule and duty, reminds us that we are not free simply to go our own way. We cannot rely on ourselves to discern right from wrong. The Scriptures, though, encourage us to move beyond a straightforward attempt to find laws which govern every situation. We are encouraged to look to the spirit rather than the letter of the law.

Those authors are surely right who draw our attention to the person and teaching of Jesus as our starting-point in Christian ethics. Thus O'Donovan argues: 'The foundation of Christian ethics [is to be found] in the incarnation. Since the Word became flesh and dwelt among us, transcendent divine authority has presented itself as worldly moral authority.'[44] Jesus Christ is the 'pattern to which we may conform ourselves, the bearer of a moral authority which belongs to the true order of human life in the world'.[45] Certainly it is inconceivable that any Christian could argue that a person may act in contradiction to the example or teaching of Jesus and claim to be acting morally.

Barth similarly focuses our attention on Jesus as the one who answers the 'ethical question' of 'what is the good in and over every so-called good of human action'[46] when he writes: 'The man Jesus, who fulfils the commandment of God, does not give the answer, but by God's grace He is the answer to the ethical question put by God's grace.'[47]

This is no more than we should expect if we believe in the reality of the incarnation. Equally, God's ultimate self-revelation in the person of Jesus must be the standard by which we judge all other witnesses to God's revelation in the Scriptures and in the church. The exemplary life of Jesus and his definitive teaching convey the divine command to us in its clearest form; anything at variance with this cannot command our allegiance.

The life and teaching of Jesus

The gospels present us with a picture of Jesus which indicates that he was a truly integrated personality. His character, teaching and actions were consistent with one another and with his understanding of the nature and character of God. This, in itself, sets Jesus apart from all others. It also suggests that he alone may become a definitive moral guide for us.

In his life and teaching, deontological (rule-based) motifs were present, but more significant was his insistence on getting behind the demands of 'the law' in order to perceive the character of God. The law reflects God's character and cannot be properly understood without reference to him. The 'letter of the law' is of very limited value without discerning the Spirit who engenders it. Jesus, in the Sermon on the Mount, constantly calls us to look beyond the words of the law to the meaning of the law. Consequently, he directs us to look beyond our actions. It is our moral character that is most important; our actions and motives stem from this.

When we look at the life and teaching of Jesus it is not difficult to discern what Christian character ought to be. Great moral virtues such as love, justice, sacrifice, honesty and piety leap out of the pages of the gospels. Deontological motifs (mostly references to the Old Testament law) help to define these virtues, but the greater preoccupation is with the forming of godly character.

In the gospels, in the rest of the New Testament and in the Old Testament we have a wealth of teaching on godly character. We can also refer to much supportive evidence of a deontological nature which gives us a clear indication of how we ought to act. The Ten Commandments, for example, state principles which help us to see how law and justice may be worked out in a number of practical situations. The specific ethical decisions made in particular biblical circumstances may not always provide a simple answer to the question of how we ought to act in similar circumstances today, but they do indicate the principles on which we may still act.

This emphasis on virtue in ethical decision-making has a long history,[48] but it is still relevant today as we seek a means of interpreting the Scriptures. As Ogletree has noted:

> What a Christian ethic must surely resist is the impulse to
> translate all moral understanding into consequentialist terms.
> We must be concerned about consequences, but our assessment
> of probable consequences and their associated values must at
> every point be constrained and ordered by perfectionist and
> deontological considerations.[49]

Such an approach is entirely in keeping with the life and teaching of
Jesus and the rest of the Scriptures understood in the light of the
incarnation.

All of this indicates that we can have confidence in using the
Scriptures in seeking solutions to today's ethical problems. We cannot
simply 'read off' answers from the Bible, but we can have confidence that
in the Scriptures we have a witness to God's revelation. When read in the
light of the incarnation, they lead us to follow certain cardinal virtues
which have been given concrete expression in deonotological teaching in
both the Old and New Testaments. The Bible will not speak directly to
every situation we may face, but its principles, and above all its witness to
the character of God, will guide us in moral decision-making.

Christian ethics

We have engaged in a thorough, if brief, examination of Christian
morality. We have resisted, at times, the temptation to go for a quick or
easy answer. Our investigation has been assisted by referring to others
who have trodden this path before us. Painstakingly, we have looked at
philosophical, theological and biblical difficulties before coming to a
conclusion. What then is a Christian approach to ethics?

Christianity is a revealed religion and every part of it is dependent
upon God and his revelation. The divine command is the basis of
Christian ethics. We also recognize that, because of God's character and
because he is the Creator, his command comes to us in a way that we can
appreciate. In most cases reason will confirm the divine command even if,
unaided, it could not discover it. Such a reliance upon revelation and the
divine command is essential if we are to avoid a plethora of competing
ethical theories none of which has a convincing foundation.

In discerning the divine command, we turn first to the Scriptures and
especially to their witness to the incarnation. In the light of the
incarnation we discern ethical virtues, chief among which are love and

justice, which reflect the character of God and which we ought to seek to attain. In giving these virtues concrete expression, the Scriptures provide us with deontological motifs found in biblical commandments. These, combined, help us to find a way forward in a variety of circumstances, enabling us to argue for a Christian ethic in all fields of life.

This means that Christian decision-making can be difficult and painstaking. There is no magical formula which we can apply to resolve all problems, but there is a peculiarly Christian approach which must be adhered to in the face of other, secular approaches.

Morality and law

Before we can begin to apply Christian morality to the issues involved in human fertilization and embryology, or before we can contrast a Christian approach to morality with the approach taken by the Warnock Committee, we must first examine another issue. The vexed question of the relationship between morality and law demands our attention.

The core question we need to answer is: should there be a separation, in principle, of law and morality? If this is answered affirmatively, then our discussion on a Christian basis for morality is useful only in seeking to persuade individuals to adopt such an approach as a matter of personal choice. If, however, morality and law may be to some extent linked, then there are grounds for arguing that in some areas Christian morality should be advanced as a basis for legislation as well as a basis for personal moral action. This issue is of fundamental importance for the topics covered in the Warnock debate, where both morality and legislation are central concerns.

We would be mistaken if we believed that this issue of the relationship between law and morality is one which concerns only those of a religious disposition. It is a live issue for those who deny that morality should be based on religious conviction, or who believe that religion should be kept out of legislation even if it does provide a basis for morality.

Because the Warnock Committee was established by the government of a liberal democracy, it had to formulate its proposals within a certain context: that of persuading Members of Parliament that a reasonable case had been made for legislation in the areas under review. Many of these areas touched on sensitive moral questions, so inevitably some relationship between law and morality would be seen to operate whether or not this issue had been specifically addressed. Parliament could hope to pass effective legislation only if it was assured that it commanded the support, or at least avoided the active opposition, of a majority of voters in society. Christian contributors to the debate had to make their submissions in the same light.

Consequently, even if we wished to argue that in all areas Christian morality should be enforced by law because it is the will of God, this approach would be entirely useless in the context of the Warnock debate. Liberal democracies simply do not react favourably to such absolute demands, so there is no practical point in making them. To do so is not to be a prophetic voice crying in the wilderness; it is to ignore the cultural and religious context in which Christians have to proclaim the Christian gospel. In fact, as we shall see, it is not the case that Christians should argue for an automatic correspondence between morality and law in every circumstance. Even if this were so, however, arguments advanced by Christians must be advanced with the proper political and cultural context in mind. This was too seldom the case during the Warnock debate.

Devlin v. Hart

In the latter half of the twentieth century, the central debate within the philosophy of law regarding the relationship between law and morality has been the debate between Lord Devlin, latterly Lord of Appeal in Ordinary, and H. L. A. Hart, latterly Emeritus Professor of Jurisprudence in the University of Oxford. This is so not only because of the debate between the two men themselves, but also because it has been taken up by so many others. We cannot make a meaningful contribution to the continuing debate on law and morality unless we first grasp the issues raised by Devlin and Hart.

While Devlin acknowledged that religion provided the historical background for the accepted morality of the United Kingdom, he and Hart were agreed that religion alone could not be used as a basis for legislation. Once freedom of conscience was granted in matters of belief, then morality based only on those beliefs should not be enforced.[50]

The debate, in effect, was between two liberal thinkers. Religious authority was deemed to be an unsuitable basis for legislation, though it may provide a basis for morality. If law and morality were to be linked at all, then a different basis for legislation had to be found. Both Devlin and

Hart argued in the context of the prevailing liberal thesis that the freedom of the individual was a primary moral consideration, even though they reacted differently to this proposition. Devlin took issue with the statement of the Wolfenden Report that it was not the function of the law to intervene in private morality,[51] while Hart showed himself to be more sympathetic to the position of the utilitarians who espoused a separation, in principle, between law and morality.[52]

Devlin posed three questions. Has society the right to pass judgment on morals? Has it the right to enforce morality by law? Should law be used in all cases?[53] In answering these question he argued that morality was an essential part of the fabric of a society and that if a shared or common morality were not firmly established in a society it would disintegrate.[54] Therefore a society had an interest in preserving its morality through legislation, since by so doing it was defending its own existence.[55] This does not mean that morality, and consequently legislation, may never change. Change, however, must be effected by a widely accepted shift in attitude in society itself before legislation should be altered.[56] Devlin was not arguing here for any particular morality, or that legislation should conform to correct morality; only that morality served a certain function within a society: to give it cohesion. This is a consequentialist argument, for it is the consequences of morality and legislation in keeping a society together that matter, not the content of that morality and legislation *per se*.[57]

Devlin argued that there should be no distinction between private and public morality, since no area of morality is incapable of affecting the cohesion of society. He preferred to argue that 'morality is a sphere in which there is a public interest and a private interest, often in conflict, and the problem is to reconcile the two'.[58] A balance has to be struck between the interests of society and the rights and interests of the individual. Thus he suggested there should be 'toleration of the maximum individual freedom that is consistent with the integrity of society'.[59]

How then are a society's morality and subsequent legislation to be determined? Devlin rejected both religion and philosophy as grounds for such determination, and argued that the opinions of society should be determined by the 'man in the street' or, more colourfully, 'the man on the Clapham omnibus'.[60] By this he meant not public opinion as reflected in a popular vote, but the opinion of the 'reasonable man', the person who epitomizes the most stable section within a society. This

45

person's opinion is to be articulated not on the basis of reason or religion but on the basis of 'common sense', on the basis of feelings of approval or disgust for particular activities.[61]

In answering the three questions he posed at the outset of his argument, Devlin proposed that society did have a right to judge morality. In its own self-interest, society has the right to enforce morality by law even though in practice morality should not be uniformly enforced. The content of a society's morality and the extent to which this is reflected in legislation are to be decided by the common sense of the average person in society. This is determined on the basis of feeling rather than on the basis of reason or religion, even though these may be factors in producing the feelings of the average person in question.

In his reaction to Devlin's thesis, Hart argued that, in principle, the core of the law and morality are not necessarily connected. He did accept that in interpreting certain parts of the periphery of the law, judgments have to be made regarding what the law should be. Hart argued that even this does not require a moral judgment, for he believed that social aims did not constitute morality.[62] Nevertheless, while espousing the utilitarian view that there is no necessary connection between law and morality, he did allow that in practice such a connection did exist. He believed that while an evil law, such as some of the laws in Nazi Germany, did not forfeit the character of law, it would be a bad law and so should not be obeyed.[63]

Consequently, he was prepared to argue that there should be a minimum connection between law and morality, since the survival of a species determined certain morals which should find expression in legislation.[64] The concept of justice he also recognized as a moral idea; one that is necessary for good law, though not necessary for law which is indifferent or bad.[65]

Hart took as his starting-point the contention of John Stuart Mill that the freedom of the individual should be curtailed only to prevent harm to others. He recognized that this was an insufficient basis for law, and extended it to include harm to the individual acting, and also harm to animals.[66] This introduction of paternalism is a marked departure from utilitarianism. Hart demonstrated his essentially utilitarian roots, however, when he argued that, while causing harm to others may be seen to include causing offence, nevertheless the principle of individual freedom outweighs this consideration.[67]

Hart differed most widely from Devlin, though, in arguing that the moral code of a society is not a seamless garment. Changing or contravening part of the shared morality of a society does not alter the rest of it, and does not have to lead to a lack of social cohesion.[68] Devlin, he believed, had stressed too much the interests of society over the rights of the individual. For Hart, Devlin's error was compounded by his insistence that morality was based on public sentiment rather than on reason. He observed that 'in the past intolerance, disgust and indignation led to witch-burning, racism, etc.'[69] and concluded: 'It is fatally easy to confuse the democratic principle that power should be in the hands of the majority with the utterly different claim that the majority with power in their hands need respect no limits.'[70]

Christianity and coercion

This debate, then, really centred on two issues: the rights of the individual over the needs of society, and the basis on which a society may determine its shared morality, some of which may find expression in legislation. Where does a Christian morality, based on the will of God as demonstrated supremely in the life and teaching of Jesus, fit into this debate?

It is clear that, in making us free moral agents, God has given us the capacity to choose whether or not to act in a morally correct manner. God does not coerce us into acting in accordance with his will, nor does he punish us in an immediate or direct form if we choose to disobey him. While we may suffer the consequences of our actions, and will be judged by God for any evil we have done, it is not correct to present these facts as coercion. The former is not generally recognized as punishment, and the latter is not considered by those who do not believe in God in the first place. We are not forced to believe in God, and we are not forced by God to accept his moral code.

This means that Christian morality is always one option among many which the individual may choose. It is always correct to advance Christian morality for the consideration of society, but society should not be coerced into adopting Christian morality for its own sake. Factors other than its religious basis and its inherent reasonableness must be evident before we can argue that it should be enshrined in legislation and so become coercive.

This means that Christian morality should be promoted both at the level of religious persuasion and also on the basis of its reasonableness.

Christians were right, therefore, to respond to the Warnock Report by advocating Christian morals, even though different groups advanced different understandings of Christian morality. What is also necessary, however, is an argument showing which of those morals should be reflected in legislation and which should not.

In this quest Christians today are as much prisoners of culture as are others in society. Previous generations of Christians may have believed that moral coercion was correct in all circumstances where it was felt this would be generally acceptable. Thus, laws prohibiting homosexual practices among consenting adults in private were thought to be as acceptable as laws prohibiting murder. Today, such an approach is unsustainable. Not only does it make morality a matter of coercion, which is itself repugnant, but it also separates Christianity and society at a fundamental level.

While Christian morality must be distinctively Christian and be prepared to argue its case before the rest of society, any attempt to coerce society into adopting Christian morality would be counter-productive as well as wrong. Reference to the Old Testament people of God is of no benefit in advancing a case for coercive morality, for there we are dealing with God's people who were covenanted to live in accordance with his will. Such a society no longer exists today; as far as legislation is concerned, there is no point in insisting that it should. Throughout history great harm has been done both to individuals and to the witness of the Christian gospel by Christians acting in a coercive manner. The burning of people at the stake in the name of the church or the name of Christ ought to act as a salutary warning of the dangers of Christian coercion.

A Christian approach to morality and law

What connection should there be then between morality and law? It is clear that, as Hart recognized, many laws are more a matter of social order than of morality. The preservation of historic buildings, for example, is a matter of social order in so far as a society deems itself to be more cultured, more sophisticated and aesthetically or spiritually richer if it preserves such buildings. This is a good thing, but it is straining the meaning of morality to make this an ethical issue.

Other laws, such as those governing taxes, may have a moral aspect in that it is right to pay what the government decrees. It is also a moral issue

48

that the government should determine fiscal policy fairly, but the purpose of taxes is to enable social order, not to promote morality. How taxes are spent may also involve moral decisions, but the concept of taxation has as its goal social order, not morality.

In cases where morality and social order overlap it is not always clear if law is there to uphold morality or social order or both. More often than not, both provide powerful arguments for legislation. For example, laws prohibiting murder clearly have both a moral and a social aspect. It is both wrong to kill innocent people, and injurious to social order. This may tempt us to say that morality should be enforced only when it is necessary for social order or when morality and social order coincide, but this would not do justice to the full range of activities which ought to be subject to legislation.

There are certain laws which should be enforced even when it is difficult to argue that social order as well as morality is at stake. Laws governing cruelty to animals or voluntary euthanasia, for example, have social order only as peripheral concerns. They are essentially moral in character and involve concepts of love and justice, dignity and rights, which are paramount. It may be argued that only a religious conviction can sustain such concepts, but that is not how most people see it. Stemming from a belief in human dignity and value, and an acceptance of human responsibility for other creatures and the environment, it is widely and correctly held that it is wrong for a society to allow its members to inflict injury upon one another or to treat animals cruelly or to ruin the environment. These mores are not always consistently applied, and at times they may conflict, but they provide an essentially moral basis for legal intervention in the freedom which a society allows its individuals.

It has therefore been suggested that the point of contact between Christian and secular morality is the conviction that persons matter.[71] This may be supplemented by the conviction that the rest of the natural order matters also. The basis for Christians accepting these moral principles is essentially a religious and, to an extent, a deontological one, though they may also be defended on a rational and consequentialist basis. Here common ground may be found between Christian morality and secular morality, and reason for coercion may be defended, for fundamental issues of love and justice are at stake, upon which Christians and others may agree.

Thus, a Christian approach to law and morality would be that the essential moral attitude behind those laws which incorporate morality should be a godly one, concerned with issues of love and justice. These principles, and not Devlin's feelings of disgust and repugnance, form the basis of morality, which does not have to be a shared morality in the sense of popular acceptance by the 'average man in the street'. Love and justice are not sufficient, however, to produce legislation. Lying, premarital sex and queue-jumping are all open to attack as denying true love and justice, but cannot be controlled by legislation, both for practical reasons of enforceability and also because morality then becomes coercive in all spheres of life.

Rather, if a deed is to be legislated against, it must not only be immoral; it must also threaten the essential order of society. In this respect Devlin was correct. Drunken driving, murder and theft are all examples of actions which are both immoral and threatening to society. In addition, those actions which harm or diminish the dignity of other human beings or which harm the rest of creation should also be subject to law. The acceptance by Hart of a degree of paternalism was also correct in so far as the young, the weak and the mentally handicapped should be protected by law against actions injurious to themselves. Unless social order is seriously undermined, though, it is unacceptable to argue that the law should protect healthy adults from inflicting harm on themselves, for example by deliberate suicide attempts, smoking, or drinking to excess.

The reasons we have advocated for combining law and morality are reasonable and defensible. Because of the inherent dangers of coercive morality, however, it has been wisely said that 'the onus ought to lie heavily upon those who would interfere in private behaviour even though a clear line cannot be drawn between public and private morality'.[72]

This is not a tidy solution to the question of law and morality, but tidiness is not our objective. This approach is a pragmatic one, but it is not merely pragmatic. It is based on the life and teaching of Jesus, the Scriptures and the created order. It also provides us with a meeting-point with the rest of society. In practice, in the context of the Warnock debate, it means that a specifically Christian morality may be advanced regarding all the issues covered in the debate, but that only some of them should be subject to legislation. To decide which moral issues should find expression in legislation it is necessary to show that not only morality but also society, the individual or the created order is at risk.

This risk must not be trivialized by suggesting that offence caused to some by AIH, for example, is sufficient grounds for introducing prohibitive legislation.

Before looking at further moral and theological principles which will help us to determine specific moral and legal attitudes to the practices covered in the Warnock debate, we must first compare and contrast the approach detailed above with that taken by the Warnock Committee, bearing in mind that its approach was pivotal in the whole debate.

Warnock and morality

The Warnock Committee, and Mary Warnock herself, have been the target of severe criticism from a number of sources. This has been so not only because individuals and groups have disagreed with the committee's conclusions but, more fundamentally, because they have disagreed with the report's approach to morality and the relationship between morality and law. Such critics are to be found not only in the ranks of churches and Christian organizations but also among those well versed in the academic study of jurisprudence and philosophy.

Critics of Warnock

Simon Lee has criticized the report for failing 'to clarify its attitudes to theories of morality and its approach to the relationship between law and morality'.[73] Furthermore, he suggests that a serious inconsistency exists in the committee's approach to the whole subject of morality. He has stated: 'On morality, the key recommendation [on embryo research] rests on a utilitarian approach even though the Report had already provided a damning indictment on utilitarianism.'[74] He follows this criticism with a further charge of inconsistency in the committee's thinking: 'At one point the Committee rejects the benefits of the research argument in deference to feelings, whereas its major recommendation would seem to imply the contrary.'[75]

The place of feelings in moral judgment has also been highlighted by John Harris, who argues that 'the crucial problem entirely ignored by Warnock is that not all feelings are moral feelings and not all outrage is moral outrage'.[76] Similarly, Michael Lockwood has noted with regard to the foreword to the report:

What is being urged here, is a conception of morality which
will allow us, indeed oblige us, as the strict utilitarian
conception does not, to take seriously the kind of intuitive or
emotive moral responses that the ordinary person actually
expresses.[77]

Such reliance on feelings has been most severely criticized by R. M.
Hare,[78] who also accuses the committee of failing to argue towards its
conclusions and failing to publish a well-conducted debate which he
believes would have been in the public interest.[79] He presses home his
attack:

The reason why the Committee was not able to help in giving
very solid reasons for these 'feelings' is that she [Mary
Warnock] is not a utilitarian, and all the reasons that in the end
will hold water are utilitarian ones.[80]

He concludes his appraisal with these strong words:

So we have in the Report some enquiry into consequences, but
it is not nearly far-reaching enough; and instead we have plenty
of appeals to intuitions, *i.e.* prejudices.[81]

The Warnock approach

In determining whether or not these criticisms are valid, we are fortunate
in that we have good primary source material which is open to analysis.
The foreword to the Warnock Report deals, albeit briefly, with the issues
of morality and law, and, in a personal introduction to the Report, *A
Question of Life*,[82] Mary Warnock has provided a fuller explanation of the
thinking behind the report. Michael Lockwood is right in arguing that
Mary Warnock's defence of the report in subsequent interviews and
articles demonstrates a close correlation between her own thinking and
that of her committee, and so some further comments made by Mary
Warnock are also illuminating.[83]

Using this source material, what picture emerges of the Warnock
Committee's approach to law and morality?

Turning to the foreword to the Report, we find a number of pertinent
comments. It is first stated that 'we had to direct our attention not only to

future practice and possible legislation, but to the principles on which such practices and such legislation would rest'.[84] The questions of morality and the link between morality and law are, therefore, acknowledged. The foreword continues: 'We have attempted to argue in favour of those positions which we have adopted, and to give due weight to the counter-arguments, where they exist.'[85] As we have seen, not all commentators believe that this goal has been achieved, but the intention of the committee is clear enough.

The committee's thinking is somewhat more difficult to follow when the foreword emphasizes that its views were based on argument rather than sentiment,[86] but then continues to expose inadequacies in a utilitarian approach,[87] and subsequently states:

> Moral questions, such as those with which we have been concerned, are, by definition, questions that involve not only a calculation of consequences, but also strong sentiments with regard to the nature of the proposed activities themselves.[88]

This is followed by the comment: 'We were therefore bound to take very seriously the feelings expressed in the evidence.'[89] A first reading would indicate, here, an ambiguity. On the one hand, argument and not sentiment is to be the basis for moral judgment, while on the other hand, consequentialist argument is inadequate, and sentiments and feelings are to be part of the process of moral decision-making. We need to look at subsequent statements to see if this difficulty can be resolved.

In *A Question of Life*, Mary Warnock outlined three approaches to moral decision: as 'a matter of feeling or sentiment', 'obedience to certain established rules', or utilitarianism understood as the assertion that 'an act is right if it benefits more people than it harms'.[90] In pointing out deficiencies in utilitarian and deontological approaches, she wrote concerning the work of her committee:

> We were bound to have recourse to moral sentiment, to try, that is, to sort out what our feelings were, and to justify them. For that a decision is based on sentiment by no means entails that arguments cannot be adduced to support it.[91]

She added with regard to the relationship between morality and law: 'The law is not, and cannot be, an expression of moral feeling.'[92]

Writing in the *Philosophical Quarterly*, during the course of her committee's deliberations, she observed:

> It is difficult to persuade members of committees that feelings or sentiments can have a central role to play in decision-making. Such people tend to believe that a moral judgment must be rational or else it must be based on religious dogma. Otherwise it will not count as a properly moral judgment. They find it shocking to accept that, as Hume put it, 'morality is more properly felt than judg'd of'. Yet I believe that it is to offend against the concept of morality itself to refuse to take moral feelings or sentiments into account in decision-making.[93]

Difficult it may be, but there is evidence to suggest that Mary Warnock was successful in her attempt to convince her committee of the important role of sentiment in moral decision-making.

Following the publication of the report, Mary Warnock further elaborated her views on the matter:

> If morality is to exist at all, either privately or publicly, there must be some things which regardless of consequence should not be done. Some barriers which should not be passed. What marks out these barriers is often a sense of outrage, if something is done; a feeling that to permit some practice would be indecent or part of the collapse of civilisation.[94]

Echoes, here, of Devlin's man on the Clapham omnibus.

Examples of Warnock's approach

The elements in moral decision-making already outlined were particularly evident in the Warnock Committee's deliberations on two complex and controversial areas in the debate: embryo research and surrogacy. Mary Warnock confirmed the importance of considered debate on the status of the embryo when she wrote:

> All the other issues we had to consider seemed relatively trivial compared with this one, concerned as it is with a matter which

> nobody could deny is of central moral significance,
> the value of human life.[95]

Her committee's treatment of this issue and the vexed question of surrogacy shows how the principles outlined above were applied in practice.

In explaining the committee's approach to embryo research, Mary Warnock has commented that this issue is 'a matter of public, and widely shared, sentiment'.[96] The approach adopted by the committee was further amplified:

> If, on broadly utilitarian grounds, the benefits from the use of
> embryos at this stage [*i.e.* before fourteen days' development]
> seemed very great, and if not only was there no harm in the
> sense of immediately felt pain to the embryo but also in
> addition there were no absolute outrage of general moral
> sentiment . . . then the majority argued that the embryo
> might be used for research.[97]

The conclusion was reached: 'The proposition was that, if the resulting benefits were manifest, an embryo at a particular and very early stage might be used.'[98] The report acknowledged that the appearance of the primitive streak, the point at which research must stop, is but 'one reference point'.[99] No detailed argument was advanced, however, why this particular stage of embryonic development was chosen as indicating an appropriate time to prohibit further research. While reference could have been made to certain objective criteria, we can only assume that sentiment played a large part reaching this decision.

For embryo research, then, the reasoning appears to have been that utilitarian arguments held sway as long as public sentiment was not outraged, but that a cut-off point of fourteen days was imposed because this was the time when the majority of the committee felt that further research would be inappropriate.

In dealing with surrogacy, the committee recognized that utilitarian arguments indicated that the practice would be beneficial to many, but also argued: 'That people should treat others as a means to their own ends, however desirable the consequences, must always be liable to moral objection.'[100] Stress was laid on the 'weight of public opinion'[101] which was against the practice. Consequently, the committee opposed the use of surrogacy as a means of treating infertility. Here, a similar approach was taken to that evident in the discussion on embryo research, but in this case public sentiment was believed to outweigh all utilitarian arguments.

The Warnock Committee's approach was, in the first instance, a utilitarian one. Likely consequences, both beneficial and harmful, were balanced in the decision-making process. Such a formula was, however, not allowed to determine the issue. The balance of harms and benefits had to pass the test of sentiment, that is, of moral feeling. If moral feeling were outraged, then, in spite of whatever benefits may result, a practice was considered to be unacceptable. The basis for such moral feeling was not explored; it may have stemmed from intuition or from religious conviction or from peer pressure within society. What was important is that such feeling exists and must play a pivotal role in moral decision-making.

With regard to the question of the relationship between morality and law, we have already seen that Mary Warnock has argued that law is not a mere reflection of moral feeling. The Warnock Report did not, however, make clear on what basis it recommended legislation other than to state that 'what is legally permissible may be thought of as the minimum requirement for a tolerable society'.[102] Mary Warnock acknowledged that her committee recognized that in some cases 'it was necessary to distinguish the issue of moral right or wrong, as we saw it, from a further, also moral question, whether it would be right to enforce a moral view, even if such a view were agreed'.[103] Precisely how the distinction was made in each case was not made explicit.

In the light of this analysis of the Warnock Committee's approach to morality and the relationship between morality and law, are the criticisms noted above valid? We will provide an answer to this question as we make our own critique of the approach taken by Warnock.

Evaluating Warnock

First, we need to recognize that the fundamental moral basis of the Warnock Report is flawed when viewed from a Christian perspective. The amalgam of utilitarianism, sentiment and stress on individual freedom is no substitute for a determination to do what is loving and just, acting on principles based on biblical criteria and reasoned argument. It would be entirely unreasonable for Christians to expect the Warnock

WARNOCK, MORALITY AND LEGISLATION

Committee to have acted from a Christian ethical basis, but it is important to note the divergence between the Warnock approach and a Christian one. This means that we are likely to disagree with many of the Warnock Committee's detailed proposals, because the ethical base from which we will argue is markedly different from that of the Warnock Committee.

The Warnock Committee had to produce workable recommendations which a liberal democracy would be likely to accept. In so doing, however, the moral basis for such recommendations should have been clearly outlined and defended, and other approaches noted and given due consideration. A report with such moral significance ought to have included such an enquiry and the committee ought to have seen this as part of its brief. Hare was right in viewing this as a major omission in the committee's thinking.

Our complaint with the report here is not that it did not adopt Christian principles (even though it is fundamentally flawed when viewed from a Christian perspective as a result), but that it adopted other principles without sufficient evidence that a full debate on the subject was ever conducted. Unfortunately, it is true that most Christian submissions to the Warnock Committee also failed in this regard. The seriousness of this omission can be seen in the fact that both the 1990 legislation and the current practice of the Human Fertilization and Embryology Authority indicate that the Warnock approach to morality may become, in some circles, a new orthodoxy.[104]

Secondly, the nature of the relationship between law and morality proposed by Warnock is also flawed. We have argued that morality should find expression in legislation in cases where social order is at risk, where individuals may be harmed and where the rest of the natural order may be seriously threatened or damaged. This is in marked contrast to the inconsistent approach of the Warnock Committee, which espoused the primacy of individual freedom in some circumstances and public sentiment in others.

The Warnock approach to legislation, applied to the detailed practices under consideration, indicates that a practice should not be proscribed if it is thought to benefit some people while at the same time not harming others. A definition of harm to others is not, however, adequately explored, and as a result the guiding principle is inconsistently applied.

For example, the status of the embryo is deemed to be such that harm to it is not considered to be 'harm to others', but no detailed defence of this view is offered. Harm to the structure of society by placing the institution of the family under threat is not adequately explored either. Public sentiment, however, is sufficient to proscribe certain activities such as later-embryo research and surrogacy. To argue, on the one hand, that individual freedom is to be granted where no harm to others is likely but, on the other hand, to allow public sentiment to interfere with this freedom is bound to lead to inconsistencies.

Surrogacy is a case in point. The Warnock argument against surrogacy is not that harm to the participants is likely (though the risk of exploitation is acknowledged), but that the practice is unacceptable to the public. This opinion depended partly on the committee members' own feelings and partly on the evidence submitted to it. This means, however, that public opinion may change and surrogacy may become acceptable in the future. Equally, embryo research may cause public outrage in the future and may consequently have to be proscribed. Thus, individual freedom is constantly under threat from public opinion, and all other arguments in favour of a practice will count for nothing if public opinion is outraged. Devlin's approach is really being accepted, though this is not acknowledged by the Warnock Committee.

The approach to the relationship between morality and law which we have outlined differs significantly from this view. We have argued that morality may be reflected in legislation only if it can be shown that individuals are at risk, that the fundamental order of society is threatened or that the rest of the natural order is seriously endangered. Public opinion can be a factor in deciding legislation only if it is so strong that to ignore it will create instability in society. This happens only in extreme circumstances; certainly not over surrogacy arrangements.

Thirdly, it is now clear what our approach ought to be in assessing the Warnock debate.

We must analyse first of all the status of the human embryo, from a Christian perspective. In particular we must discover the proper basis for determining the embryo's status. Was Warnock right in basing the embryo's status on a mixture of sentiment and functional ability, or are there other more defensible grounds for determining the embryo's status?

This is the central issue in the Warnock debate and will require a detailed investigation. This is so partly because Mary Warnock has acknowledged that the status of the embryo was of fundamental importance for her committee, and also because in Christian contributions to the debate this was very often the major concern. An evaluation of the debate must reflect this. It is also central for a more important reason: we have argued that morality should find expression in legislation if the interests of an individual are at stake or if nature is at risk of being destroyed or endangered. If the human embryo is to enjoy the same status as a human baby or adult, then it is clear that legislation regarding the embryo should uphold the rights of the embryo in the same way as any other human being. If the status of the embryo is more akin to that of an animal, as suggested by Warnock,[105] then legislation should protect it from pain and suffering and from being used in a way that would compromise its nature (such as cross-species fertilization); but it should not be accorded the same protection and rights as a member of society. If the human embryo is to be given the same status as an adult, then its protection must be a matter for legislation. If its status is inferior to that of an adult, then some may argue that protecting it from all research is still the correct moral position to adopt, but this must be a matter for individual moral choice, not a matter for coercive legislation.

Other topics are important too. Infertility treatments must be investigated to discover if there are issues there which require legislation. If it can be shown that social order is seriously put at risk by some activities which undermine the role of the family in society, or that nature is fundamentally compromised, or that others apart from those consenting to treatment are likely to be harmed, then legislation is appropriate. If not, infertility treatments may still be a matter of ethical concern, but Christians should not argue for coercive legislation.

Our task, therefore, is to examine the status of the embryo and then to examine issues of sexual ethics relevant to the debate on human fertilization and embryology. We must seek to discover moral principles in these areas, and also detail which areas are of moral concern only and which are also areas in which legislation should be employed. When this has been accomplished, we can then evaluate the debate which actually took place, examining the Warnock Report, the eventual legislation which emerged from the debate, and Christian contributions to the debate. We will examine each topic in the debate in this way, and then propose a practical Christian approach based on ethical and theological principles.

3

The status of the human embryo:
a biblical approach

Using the Bible

As we have already seen, an examination of biblical teaching on a given
subject will not exhaust Christian enquiry. There must, however, be a
beginning for Christian investigation. While it is essential to take into
account the findings of science as well as the insights of theology,
philosophy, history and contemporary experience, that beginning is to
be found in a survey of the Bible's teaching.

There are, of course, problems with this approach. As even the casual
reader of the Scriptures knows, the Bible does not always appear to speak
with a single voice on any given subject it covers. In many cases
differences of emphasis can be detected. In other cases the entire
approach appears to change with changing circumstances. We must,
therefore, expect to find a range of attitudes expressed regarding our
subject. It may be possible to synthesize these into a comprehensive
statement. Equally, it may be necessary to accept that, in some cases,
differing approaches to this issue were taken at different times.

An equally important difficulty is that the Scriptures do not always
deal directly with the subjects which we wish to investigate. We have to
acknowledge that the question of the human embryo's status was not one
which the biblical authors approached directly. It is, no doubt, the case

that many of them had a view on the subject within the confines of their medical knowledge of human development. The topic as such, however, is not treated directly in any of the books of the Bible.

This means that we are forced to base our understanding of the Bible's teaching on this issue on indirect evidence. By this we mean evidence which is found within the context of discussion of another topic. For example, the Scriptures sometimes speak of God's care and providence extending even to the time a person was still in the womb. They do so, however, not in order to indicate the status of the unborn but to underline the sovereignty of God. Similarly, a statement on God's choice of a person which stresses the eternal nature of God's will may also suggest that the person so chosen must have known God's personal love even while in the womb. Such statements are important in our enquiry, but the evidence they supply is indirect rather than direct.

Consequently, reasoning based not on direct scriptural evidence but on what may be seen as the implication of a particular biblical passage is unlikely to gain universal support. We must be careful that we do not draw the wrong conclusions from such passages, but such reasoning is not to be dismissed out of hand. While we may not hope to settle the issue of the status of the human embryo simply by conducting a biblical survey, this can, at least, provide a foundation for further study.

Biblical texts

In choosing texts which may help us to discover a biblical attitude to the human embryo's status we can divide the material into three main groups. These groups are not, of course, watertight compartments, but are useful in trying to gain an overall view of the biblical evidence. We can view, first of all, those passages which may apply personal language to the human embryo. Secondly, we can look at those texts which may indicate that God relates personally to the human embryo. Finally, we can examine those parts of the Scriptures which deal with the incarnation.

In addition to these three main groupings, we must also examine a single text which has often occupied centre stage in discussions on the embryo's status: Exodus 21:12, 22–25. This passage deals with the human embryo in the context of criminal law as applied by the primitive Israelite nation. As such it does not fit easily into any of our above categories. In any case, it deserves to be studied in its own right as a unique biblical text which brings the issue of the status of the human embryo into the realm of law and protection.

In looking for scriptural evidence on any subject, it is not always easy to ensure that all the relevant texts are covered. A word on the choice of biblical passages under scrutiny in this chapter is, therefore, necessary. The passages of Scripture which we will examine have been chosen because they have all been used by various Christian groups to support the argument that the human embryo is a human person. Some of them may appear more convincing than others. Indeed, some of them may be dismissed, after consideration, as having very little to offer to our investigation. Nevertheless, in an attempt to be as thorough as possible we will look at them all.

For reasons already stated, any evidence which we gain is likely to be of an indirect nature. It is unnecessary to give a detailed introduction to every text examined, indicating at length its historical, cultural and literary context. We need to accept, however, that in almost all cases the context is such that a statement on a particular subject is made which coincidentally appears to say something which is relevant to our study. Therefore, as we have already stated, great care must be taken in drawing conclusions from the texts to be studied.

One final word is needed before we begin to look at our texts. Inevitably, we will cover much the same ground in a number of passages. This means that a degree of repetition is unavoidable. This may not provide the raciest of reads, but it is essential if we are to be fair to the scriptures and exactingly honest in our enquiry. Once again, we must avoid the temptation to take shortcuts or to assume glibly that the true meaning of a text will simply jump out of the page at us. Our goal is to achieve the best understanding possible of all that the Scriptures have to say about the human embryo. By its nature this is a demanding task.

Texts applying personal language to the human embryo

> Let the day perish wherein I was born,
>   and the night which said,
>   'A man-child is conceived.'
>
> (Jb. 3:3)

This text was originally penned to indicate the bitterness of the response of Job to the many calamities which had befallen him. It was not intended to introduce a discussion on the status of the embryo, nor does the theme of Job's embryonic development play any further part in the debate which follows this verse. The debate continues with Eliphaz the Temanite on the question of the many miseries which beset the human race as a result of the natural human frailty of each of its members. It would, therefore, be misleading to suggest that the question of the human embryo's status was at all in the mind of the author when this was written.

The fact remains, however, that Job is presented as recognizing a continuity from the time of his conception to the time of his birth and on into childhood and adulthood. Job acknowledges that he was conceived and subsequently born, not that an impersonal entity was conceived which at some later stage gave rise to a child whom he identified with himself. While the text contains a reference to Job's conception almost as an aside rather than as a deliberate attempt to discuss the nature of conception, we cannot ignore completely its relevance for our study. This is particularly so since, unlike some other passages of Scripture which speak of the later fetus, this text brings us back to the time of conception and the early embryonic stages of development.

The main question here is whether or not this statement can be used fairly in our debate at all. Are we going too far in pressing poetical language into supplying evidence for an ethical discussion? Would it be equally wrong of us to ignore apparently personal language applied to conception simply because it is used in a passage of poetry dealing with one man's misery and misfortune? There is no obviously correct answer to this question. If we argue that the language is poetic and must not be used to infer an ethical standpoint, we may be guilty of ignoring a general viewpoint which enabled such a statement to be made in the first place. Equally, if we do argue that this text demonstrates that the author believed that the human embryo possessed a truly personal existence from the moment of conception, then we may be basing our argument on completely inappropriate grounds.

Unfortunately, commentators are of limited use to us in settling this issue. H. H. Rowley states: 'The language is vigorous and poetic. The ultra-logical mind should avoid poetry.'[1] A similar line of reasoning is employed by Marvin Pope. He states that the passage displays poetic parallelism and that 'one ought not to press the details too hard'.[2] A rather different view is taken, however, by Norman Habel. He argues that the reference to Job's conception is not merely poetic or coincidental but that 'his conception . . . became the vehicle for his entry into a life of bitterness'.[3] Many other commentators, of course, fail to raise the issue at all, but confine their remarks to the wider question of human suffering.

This sample of commentators' remarks does not enable us to decide definitively either for or against the admissibility of this text in our consideration of the issue of the status of the human embryo. This, however, does us a service. It demonstrates that while we cannot state without reservation that the author of Job viewed the human embryo as a personal being, we cannot state either that he was unfamiliar with the proposition. While none of the texts under scrutiny are to be seen as 'proof-texts', we can at least state that this particular text shows us that we must keep an open mind as to whether or not, at that particular stage of Old Testament development, the human embryo was seen as being a personal entity.

> Yet thou art he who took me from the womb;
>   thou didst keep me safe upon my mother's breasts.
> Upon thee was I cast from my birth,
>   and since my mother bore me thou hast been my God.
>
> (Ps. 22:9–10)

This text contains many of the characteristics of the text from Job noted above. It also is poetic in form and its context is that of a suffering individual grappling with the issue of God's love and protection in the face of personal affliction. Unlike the passage from Job, however, the attitude is one of reliance on God's power to alter suffering, rather than one of despair. Once again we are faced with the problem of trying to decide whether or not this text is relevant to our discussion. Equally, is it inappropriate to cite it as indicating a personal existence prior to birth, since reference to existence in the womb is introduced not in its own right but rather to indicate the depth of God's knowledge and care?

Our interpretation of this text is further complicated by difficulties regarding the translation of the first line. Both A. A. Anderson[4] and Mitchell Dahood[5] state that there are uncertainties over the meaning and etymology of the Hebrew term *gîḥa*, which is usually rendered 'took from' or 'brought forth' in English translations. Possibly as a result of this, the passage is often paraphrased by commentators as simply saying that God's care was with the psalmist from the moment of his birth, thus rejecting any reference to antenatal personal existence which was there to be 'brought forth' at birth. Anderson argues that the text means that God was the psalmist's 'protector of life from his very birth',[6] while Peter Craigie states that the psalmist is writing about 'his own experience from birth onwards'.[7]

In the light of these comments it would be unwise to argue that this passage indicates that the psalmist viewed his personal existence to have begun before birth. The text is too uncertain both in its poetic form and in its translation to support any detailed interpretation. In any case, the text could only be used to speak of the status of the fetus, not the human embryo, and so would be of very limited value in our enquiry.

> Behold, I was brought forth in iniquity,
> and in sin did my mother conceive me.
>
> (Ps. 51:5)

This text forms part of a psalm attributed either to King David or to a later author who meditated deeply on the details of David's life. It relates David's repentance following the arranged death of Uriah the Hittite subsequent to David's adultery with Bathsheba. The context is one of sorrow, self-abasement and honest confession of sinfulness. The text, once again, does not introduce the question of embryonic development in its own right, but refers to it in an attempt to underline the absolute acknowledgment by David of his sinful nature.

As such the text can be interpreted in two quite distinct ways. We can read the text to mean that David was conceived in sin, in the sense that he was conceived with a sinful nature already determined. From the earliest moment of his development he was 'in sin'. Alternatively, we can interpret the text to mean that David was conceived in sinful circumstances. In other words, David may be asserting that his entire family history was characterized by sin in that his mother had conceived him either when she was unmarried or as a result of an adulterous relationship. Similarly, we can argue that David was brought forth in iniquity in the sense that he already possessed a sinful nature even before he was born, or we can understand the text to mean that he was brought forth in the context of a sinful world environment. If we favour the traditional interpretation of inherited sinfulness, we will view this text as supporting the concept of personal, individual, human existence from conception onwards. If the alternative interpretation is followed, the text will be irrelevant to our discussion.

We must also acknowledge that if we do interpret the text to imply that personality may be attributed to the embryo from the moment of conception, we still have to take into account the fact that the text is poetic. In the context of the whole psalm it is not unreasonable to suggest that the author is engaging in hyperbole in order to voice his sense of profound sinfulness.

Most commentators prefer the interpretation which suggests that David's nature was affected by inherited sinfulness even before he was born. While it is possible to see this as a genetic flaw in the make-up of the human race, we cannot attribute sin to a purely biological process. If sin is said to be inherited in some congenital fashion, we are bound to ascribe some sort of personality to the human embryo and fetus. A genetic flaw in humanity's essential nature would truly be a tragedy, but it cannot be given the moral appellation of sin unless we argue, against the Christian belief in personal responsibility, that everything we do is genetically determined.

Mitchell Dahood simply states that 'all men have a congenital tendency toward evil'.[8] J. H. Eaton is surely nearer the mark, though, when he phrases the same interpretation of the text in a more personal fashion to say regarding all members of the human race: 'Wickedness characterises the very roots of their being.'[9]

A. A. Anderson goes further when he states that 'the psalmist confesses his total involvement in human sinfulness, from the very beginning of his existence'.[10] If these commentators are correct in seeing a reference to personal sin in this text, then it is difficult to escape the conclusion that some sort of personality must be attributed to the embryo.

We must be cautious, however, before we see this as a proof of early biblical testimony to the personhood of the embryo. Once more we must state that the text does not set out to discuss the issue of embryonic development, that the passage is poetic in its expression and that the text does allow a different interpretation, albeit one which is not widely followed. In consequence, it is best to view the text as suggesting belief in personal existence from conception onwards, but also acknowledging that the evidence falls short of proof that such was the case.

> The wicked go astray from the womb,
>   they err from their birth, speaking lies.
>
> (Ps. 58:3)

This text is of interest because it seems to suggest that sinfulness is a quality which can be experienced by an embryo or fetus developing in the womb. Rather like David's acknowledgment of his sinfulness from the time of his conception, this verse appears to indicate that moral imperfection is inherited. Certain people, at least, are inevitably going to behave in an evil manner once they are capable of making conscious decisions of a moral character.

We must note, however, that not only is this verse poetic in form, but also it is part of a psalm which is characterized by the violence of its imagery and the extreme frankness of its expressions. The righteous are enjoined to bathe in the blood of the wicked, God is called upon to break the teeth of the wicked in their mouths and evildoers are said to possess venom like the venom of a serpent. Such language and imagery suggest that the text under scrutiny should not be given a literal interpretation. Whatever we make of such an outburst of emotion and hatred, we are restrained from arguing that such a text can be used with any degree of certainty to support views of personal human development before birth.

It is, of course, true that the poetic imagery used in this psalm does not rule out the possibility that the author did believe that evildoers were already personally evil while still in the womb, but we cannot use this verse to argue that this was necessarily the case. The depth of the psalmist's feeling is not in question, nor is the obvious imagery he uses. The only doubt is whether or not such imagery should be understood literally in this instance. The context of the psalm would suggest not.

This is the interpretation of A. A. Anderson, who states that 'the expression is a poetic exaggeration'.[11] J. H. Eaton understands the psalmist to be using extreme language in order to underline his perception of the wicked as 'fundamentally evil'.[12] Mitchell Dahood paraphrases the text to read: 'They have been faithless to Yahweh because they were born loathsome children.'[13]

As we have already seen, such interpretations suggest that the psalmist did view his enemies as being evil from the time they were in their mothers' wombs. Nevertheless, because of the extreme nature of the imagery, we are correct to note the verse but are better advised not to employ it in our further discussion. In any case, even if the imagery were not as startling as it is, it would be difficult to use this text to support any theory of embryonic, as distinct from later fetal, development.

> For thou didst form my inward parts,
>> thou didst knit me together in my mother's womb.
> I praise thee, for thou art fearful and wonderful.
>> Wonderful are thy works!
> Thou knowest me right well;
>> my frame was not hidden from thee,
> when I was made in secret,
>> intricately wrought in the depth of the earth.
> Thy eyes beheld my unformed substance;
>> in thy book were written, every one of them,
> the days that were formed for me,
>> when as yet there was none of them.
>
> (Ps. 139:13–16)

This text forms part of a meditation on the mystery of the depth of God's knowledge of his creation. In particular, the psalmist rejoices in God's intimate knowledge of every part of his being and every aspect of his life. He argues that neither life nor death can hide him from God, and in that context pens the text above, demonstrating that even before his birth he was known by God.

A number of points need to be made regarding this text before we evaluate its significance for our discussion. First, as with other texts we have looked at, the focus of attention is not the life of the embryo or fetus but the infinite knowledge of God. While this text does have obvious implications for our study, we must be careful not to present it as a biblical passage written about the status of the human embryo. It is not; it is a psalm extolling the majesty and all-embracing knowledge of God which also, in the course of its argument, speaks of life before birth.

Secondly, we have to acknowledge that there is a difficulty over the psalmist's understanding of how human beings are formed. It is not altogether clear whether he is writing poetically and metaphorically when he states he was wrought in the depths of the earth, or whether he believed in some sort of personal existence prior to formation in the womb.

Thirdly, in spite of these problems and cautions, we must acknowledge that this psalm clearly suggests that the psalmist believed in

68

personal life before birth, and that God not only ordered such life but that that life was the object of his care and knowledge.

The important point to be noted here is not whether the psalmist presents us with a picture of antenatal development which appeals to our scientific understanding of the processes involved, but that he identifies himself personally with the embryo or fetus being formed in his mother's womb. He suggests that even in the womb he was the object of God's love. Thus, commentators' reticence to interpret the text unambiguously is not as important as it may, at first, appear.

A. A. Anderson writes: 'The reference may be to the formation of the embryo in the womb, or it is possible that the author is making use of certain mythological word-pictures which portrayed man as being created in the depths of the earth.'[14] Mitchell Dahood suggests that the latter is more likely to be correct: 'An impressive number of texts take for granted that men originated and pre-existed in the nether world.'[15] J. H. Eaton takes a more cautious approach: 'God's knowledge of him reached back to the mystery of his ultimate origin.'[16] Leslie Allen claims that the imagery used refers to embryonic development, stating that 'embryo is thus used in Talmudic Hebrew'.[17]

This serves to illustrate that we cannot base any scientific argument on this text, but it does allow us to say with some confidence that the passage furnishes us with evidence that at this period of Old Testament development, some, at least, viewed personal life as beginning before birth. God was actively involved in the whole process of bringing a human being into the world, from the earliest possible moment. The passage is, therefore, significant in our evaluation of the human embryo as well as of the human fetus.

This survey of texts, used by some to support the thesis that the human embryo is a human person, indicates that the poetical nature of these texts precludes them from being used as proof-texts. Equally telling is the fact that none of them was written specifically to investigate the human embryo's status. Nevertheless, it may fairly be argued that the human embryo was seen by some Old Testament authors as being the earliest form of individual personal existence, and that the same personal pronoun could be applied to the embryo and to the subsequent adult. Our investigation to date leads us to favour a view of the embryo which accords it personal status even if the evidence for this falls short of proof.

Texts which suggest a personal relationship with God

The concept of God being involved personally in the development and care of a person even before birth is, as we have already seen in our previous text, one which finds some support in the Old Testament. In the case of the text from Psalm 139, our attention was focused mainly on the implication that personal human development and life could be attributed to the psalmist even before his birth. In this present category our attention is placed on the implication to be found in some texts that God had a personal relationship with individuals even when they were still in their mothers' wombs.

In examining texts which are said to imply that God has a personal relationship with human embryos or fetuses, we will look first at those texts which suggest that God 'called' at least certain individuals to his service while they were still in the womb. Subsequently, we will examine other passages of Scripture which suggest that God deals directly and personally with individuals still unborn. In this group of texts we deal with both Old Testament and New Testament authors and their understanding of God's relationships with the human race.

God 'calls' individuals before birth

In speaking about God calling individuals, more than simple foreknowledge of the path of the individual's future life is involved. We shall examine, in this section of our study, those texts which explicitly state that God actively and unambiguously called individuals to his service before they were born.

> Listen to me, O coastlands,
> and hearken, you peoples from afar.
> The LORD called me from the womb,
> from the body of my mother he named my name.
>
> And now the LORD says,
> who formed me from the womb to be his servant,
> to bring Jacob back to him,
> and that Israel might be gathered to him . . .
>
> (Is. 49:1, 5)

> Before I formed you in the womb I knew you,
>   and before you were born I consecrated you;
> I appointed you a prophet to the nations.
>
> (Je. 1:5)

> But when he who had set me apart before I was born, and had
>   called me through his grace, was pleased to reveal his Son to
> me, in order that I might preach him among the Gentiles . . .
>
> (Gal. 1:15)

These texts all share the theme that their authors were convinced that God had appointed them to fulfil a specific task, and that God's appointment dated not from the time when they became conscious of it but from a time before their birth; indeed, in one case, even before conception. Our task, in the context of our enquiry into the status of the human embryo, is to ask whether these texts really do suggest that God 'called' Isaiah, Jeremiah and Paul in a personal way while they were embryos or fetuses. Alternatively, do they simply affirm that God's plan for each of these individuals was established in his mind and purposes without reference to our limitations of time and space? Biblical teaching on God's eternal purposes can be established from a variety of other texts, but if these texts do suggest a truly personal 'call' to these men while they were still in their mother's wombs, then something new and distinctive has been stated which cannot be found in other biblical passages.

It is none the less true that even if we decide that these texts make statements about God rather than directly about the human embryo, they are still significant for us. We must still decide if it is necessary to attribute a special status to the human embryo, even if it cannot be said to be fully and personally human, if it is the vehicle for bringing into existence a human being whom God has purposed to live his life in a particular sphere of service. What may be said of these men because of their distinctive callings can, it must be presumed, also be said of every individual who may have a more general or less spectacular role to fulfil in God's purposes.

Our first task, however, is to attempt to discover what it is exactly that these texts are saying. As with all the texts we have examined so far, there is no clear consensus on the correct interpretation of these passages. Because the text from Jeremiah expresses the concept of the 'call' of God in the most thoroughgoing terms, it has been seen as the key text in this debate. To some extent at least, the other texts depend upon it for their interpretation. If the Jeremiah text does not, in fact, suggest a truly personal 'call', then we may argue that the other texts need not be interpreted to imply such a call either.

Commentators are divided on the issue of whether or not the only emphasis in the 'call' of Jeremiah is the fact of God's predestined will for his life. While it is true that God calls only individuals and not potential persons, the issue is whether God's personal call to Jeremiah was indeed made while Jeremiah was in the womb, such a 'call' being graphically reinforced by the statement that he was chosen even before he was conceived. The text may claim only that the 'call' of Jeremiah was made by God without reference to our normal limitations of time and space, and so speaks only of God's transcendence rather than of Jeremiah's personhood, or lack of it, in the womb. Even if we answer the problem by stating that the text refers only to God's predestination of Jeremiah as his servant, we are still left with the possibility that even as an embryo Jeremiah was the recipient of God's love, protection and knowledge; without them, Jeremiah the prophet would not have come into existence. Such a relationship with God, however, while it does not argue against the full humanity of the embryo, does not require it either.

The theme of God's predestination is uppermost in the mind of E. W. Nicholson: 'Jeremiah believed himself to have been predestined by God for the solemn vocation to which he was called.'[18] This reading of the text places no importance on the 'consecration' of Jeremiah in the womb and places all emphasis on the theme of predestination. Robert Carroll describes the reference to Jeremiah's call as 'hyperbole which places his formation to be a prophet to the nations before his birth (or even his conception)'.[19] A rather different interpretation of the text is offered by J. A. Thompson: 'Of particular importance to Jeremiah was the awareness that he had been predestined to occupy the prophetic office since his birth, indeed before his birth.'[20] This comment both takes note of the strong element of predestination to be found in the text and hints at the idea of Jeremiah actually occupying the role of prophet, albeit unwittingly, before his birth. R. K. Harrison places even greater emphasis on the antenatal status of Jeremiah: 'There is nothing haphazard about the choice of Jeremiah as a divine messenger to Israel. Indeed, God had formulated each step of the process himself from conception to consecration.'[21]

Commenting on the Galatians text, Alan Cole refers back to the Jeremiah text: 'Like Jeremiah, Paul is one set apart and called from his mother's womb, by the prevenient grace of God. Here too the reference is to unborn children.'[22] Most commentators writing on the Isaiah text interpret it in the light of the 'call' of Jeremiah and are hesitant to state unambiguously whether or not Isaiah was called personally before his birth, being content to express the completeness of God's knowledge of the prophet. Claus Westermann, for example, simply notes: 'His entire life is affected by his call. He is called in every part of his existence.'[23]

Understanding God's 'call'

What then are we to make of these texts? Are they relevant to our study of the status of the human embryo, or are they really speaking about God's will rather than human development? May they, in fact, mislead us if they are used to give biblical support to a particular view of embryonic development? While, as we have already noted, there are other biblical texts which may suggest that the human embryo is to be thought of in a personal manner, these texts have often been used in popular discussion to bolster that opinion. Their rejection as relevant texts does not destroy an argument based on other biblical sources, but their inclusion as texts supporting the personhood of the embryo would certainly strengthen that position greatly.

The crux of the matter is to find an understanding of God's 'call' to human beings which can pre-date their physical existence, whenever that existence may begin. It is surely not enough to state simply that God chooses, before an individual's life begins, that that life will be consecrated to him. This may very well be true, but it hardly exhausts the meaning of the texts we are studying. If this were the only meaning to be found, then the call of God is relegated to an impersonal, mechanistic act of predestination which emanates from the mind of God but which cannot be thought of as being an act of relationship between one personal being and another. Yet, by the very nature of the experience, how can a 'call' from God be anything other than personal? God does not 'call' objects to his service, though it is appropriate for him to set certain objects apart for his use. Similarly, God cannot be said to 'know' an inanimate object, even though it is possible to speak of God 'consecrating' a thing rather than a person. At the same time, we are left with the problem of trying to understand how God can 'know' individuals before they were even conceived, never mind born.

While any suggested solutions to this problem must, by necessity, be speculative and thus of limited value, we are bound to attempt some interpretation of our texts which does more than merely draw attention to God's eternal will. At the same time we also acknowledge that they speak primarily of God's action rather than the individual's response.

For God to 'call' an individual implies not only that God takes the initiative in acting but also that there is an individual who can be 'called'. To state that the individual existed 'only in the mind of God' is not to deny the individual's existence. To exist 'in God's mind' is surely to exist even if that existence is not experienced by anyone (including the individual concerned) other than God. God's thoughts are reality in the fullest sense. We cannot speak of God 'imagining' something, for his thoughts are inherently creative, since whatever is in the 'mind of God' must exist. There is no other ultimate reality to any existence other than its being in the mind of God. If this were not so, then we could ascribe to God an activity which had no reality. If God is the necessary ground of all reality, how can he ever be thought of as doing something which is unreal?

For God to 'know' someone before he was conceived must imply that the person truly exists, albeit in a manner only accessible to God due to the absence of the spatial and temporal limitations which we think of as boundaries for our understanding of reality. This implies that everyone 'known' by God must exist when viewed from an eternal perspective, and that that existence will be present at some time within the confines of our temporal world. This is not to suggest that there are disembodied souls waiting around for embryos to be created to which they can attach themselves. Such a concept would imply that the individual before conception would have some form of semi-autonomous existence apart from God. Our speculation does not demand that such be the case. It does suggest, however, that a person 'known' or 'called' by God must remain 'known' or 'called' by God eternally. Whether as a human adult or as an embryo, or 'in the mind of God', the person must exist in a personal manner, for only as a person can someone be 'known' or 'called'. We may therefore argue that everyone 'called' by God enjoys the status of a human person even at the moment of conception, even though they may not at that time experience the attributes normally associated with a person. This has the important effect of making the ground for assessing the status of the human embryo the purposes of God rather than any functional attribute of the embryo.

This does not necessarily suggest, however, that every embryo is a person, since there is no way of proving that every embryo is 'called', only that every 'called' person must at some time be an embryo. Nevertheless, the idea that there are two distinct types of embryo, those representing 'called' persons and those not, is a highly unlikely suggestion and certainly has no scriptural support.

These speculations are an attempt to do justice to all the possible meanings in the texts we have been surveying. A plausible interpretation of the texts suggests that because God 'called' these men, their humanity and personhood were eternally determined so that at every stage of their development they were human persons. Thus they could be said to be 'called' by God from before their conception or from the womb or at birth. God's 'call' determines how we view them, not our understanding of human development, which cannot determine how we interpret the nature of God's prevenient actions.

These texts, then, may fairly be interpreted to say that some human embryos, at least, should be attributed the status of human beings. This is probably, though not necessarily, the case with all human embryos. We must stress, however, that such an interpretation of these texts is fair but not unquestionably correct. The texts do not prove the humanity of the embryo, but they may be best viewed as supporting it and commending a cautious approach to any possible interference with the developing human embryo.

God distinguishes between people before birth

The story of Jacob and Esau, related in Genesis, is one of personal opposition and competition as well as of God's choice of Jacob to be the one whose descendants would become the nation of Israel. This personal struggle between the two brothers, as well as God's choice of them, is presented as taking place not only during their adult lives but also before they were born. The choice of God is highlighted by the fact that the brothers were twins and that even though Esau was the elder, it was Jacob who was chosen to carry on the patriarchal line from Abraham and Isaac. It was not only the author of Genesis who saw the story as being signific-ant; Paul also viewed the distinction which God made between Jacob and Esau, while they were still in the womb, as of paramount importance.

While the story focuses on God's will for the individuals and their offspring, it is also of significance to us in our study of the status of the human embryo, as it raises the question of the presence of personal characteristics before birth as well as the issue of God's choice of an individual while he was still in his mother's womb. It is true that the story refers to later fetal development rather than embryonic development. Nevertheless, because the main emphasis in the story is God's choice of Jacob before either he or Esau was able to do anything of merit or demerit, it is reasonable to argue that the significance of the text extends to any stage of antenatal development.

> The children struggled together within her; and she said, 'If it is thus, why do I live?' So she went to enquire of the LORD. And the LORD said to her,
>> 'Two nations are in your womb
>>> and two peoples, born of you, shall be divided;
>> the one shall be stronger than the other,
>>> the elder shall serve the younger.'
> When her days to be delivered were fulfilled, behold, there were twins in her womb.
>
> (Gn. 25:22–24)

> . . . when Rebecca had conceived children by one man, our forefather Isaac, though they were not yet born and had done nothing either good or bad, in order that God's purpose of election might continue, not because of works but because of his call, she was told, 'The elder will serve the younger.' As it is written, 'Jacob I loved, but Esau I hated.'
>
> (Rom. 9:10–13)

In the original story, recorded in Genesis, it is unclear if God had decided that Jacob would be the dominant brother or if he is revealing that this will be the case. In his commentary on the passage, however, Paul makes it clear that he views the difference in behaviour between Jacob and Isaac as evidence of God's choice of Jacob which took place while both brothers were in the womb. Of interest to us is not only the emphasis placed on God's 'call', which we have already examined in our previous discussion on God's choice of Isaiah, Jeremiah and Paul, but also the implication in our present texts that God's choice of Jacob resulted in the presence of personal attributes and characteristics in both brothers while they were still in the womb. If our texts do suggest this, then we have an added reason for viewing the human fetus, and perhaps also the human embryo, in a personal light.

Commentators are divided in their interpretation of these texts. Claus Westermann sees no effective significance in the story other than an attempt to portray vividly the choice of God. He views the story itself as being an example of 'extraordinary poetic craft'.[24] Robert Davidson remarks, 'The reversal of roles is attributed to a decree of the Lord prior to the birth of the twins',[25] thus acknowledging the choice of God while the twins were in the womb but not attributing any distinction in character or action to the brothers because of this choice. E. A. Speiser provides the following translation of the relevant passage by way of comment: '. . . who have been drawing apart ever since they were implanted in your womb'.[26] This not only places God's choice of Jacob well before the twins' birth, but also implies that their subsequent conduct was affected by this choice even while they were in the womb. A similar point of view is presented by Gerhard Von Rad: 'Did [Jacob], as an embryo, attempt even then to dispute the birthright?'[27]

Commentators show a similar difference of opinion when they comment on the text in Romans. F. F. Bruce remarks on the phrase 'the elder shall serve the younger': 'This prophecy relates not to the individuals Esau and Jacob, but to their descendants.'[28] From this understanding of the text nothing of significance is said regarding the personhood or otherwise of Jacob and Esau before birth. James Dunn states, 'God made his choice of Jacob and not Esau without reference to their subsequent conduct, whether it was conduct he approved or disapproved of. Since he made his choice before they were born, their subsequent conduct is unrelated to God's choice.'[29] Matthew Black writes:

> The Pauline controversy, faith or works, is determinative of his thought here; it was by a free act of gracious choice that Jacob – and so his descendants, the spiritual Israel – was named: this choice was made by God even before the birth of Isaac's progeny, before they had any 'works' by which they could be judged.[30]

In attempting to reach an interpretation of these texts which takes into account the opinions of the commentators cited, it can be agreed that the main emphasis in both texts is on God's knowledge and choice of Jacob over Esau, even before their birth. In this regard our comments made on the previous group of texts discussed are relevant. We can see our present texts, at the very least, as adding credence to the view that God 'calls' some people personally before their birth. This, however, does not exhaust the meaning of our texts.

Unless we dismiss the prophecy and account of the twins struggling in the womb as poetic licence, we have to examine the implications of that part of the text. Indeed, even if we do view the account as fanciful or dramatic rather than realistic, it does not alter the fact that the author chose to present a picture of the two brothers displaying personal characteristics before their birth. The view that God was speaking of nations rather than individuals may be correct in that Esau never served Jacob but, in the context of our study, it does not answer the question of what was implied by the twins' conduct before birth. Similarly, to say that the brothers' conduct was unrelated to God's choice of Jacob seems to be going beyond the evidence, even if it is correct to say that God's choice of Jacob was unrelated to the relative merits and demerits of the brothers' subsequent actions.

It is possible, of course, to argue that the picture of Jacob and Esau striving in the womb is a fanciful one or that it was based on a wrong understanding of human development. It is difficult to escape the conviction, however, that the author of the passage intended to state that both brothers were displaying personal characteristics which were later to be demonstrated clearly in their adult lives. Without pressing the details of the story too far, it is fair to suggest that these texts may be seen to support the view that some personal characteristics are present before birth. It is true that these texts do not attempt to examine the nature of life before birth, but the Genesis text in particular does indicate that, in the mind of the author, a continuity in personal attributes may be observed which extends even to the later stages of fetal development. This does not give us any direct evidence regarding the status of the embryo, but by attributing personal characteristics to the twin fetuses because of God's prevenient choice of Jacob, it may fairly be inferred that because God's choice would have been an eternal one, the twin embryos were also personally distinguishable. That is to say, one of them was Esau and the other was Jacob, both of whom would develop to display the personal characteristics detailed in the story.

God directs spiritual development before birth

Two texts can be cited which suggest that God is able to direct the spiritual development of individuals while they are still in the womb. If this is so, a degree of personal spiritual development must be considered possible before birth, since we cannot speak of an embryo having a spiritual nature which can be influenced if that embryo is not also personal.

The first of these texts deals with the story of the birth of Samson. It indicates both that he was called by God to deliver the people of Israel from their enemies the Philistines, and that the conditions of his service also reached back to include the period of development in his mother's womb. The second text concerns John the Baptist and relates how he was chosen by God to perform the special task of preparing the way for the Messiah, and that he was filled with the Spirit of God, even while he was in the womb. A later reference in Luke's gospel to the embryonic John moving in his mother's womb when she greets Mary, who has just become pregnant, also suggests the action of the Holy Spirit on the developing embryo. These texts are of particular significance, for they deal with the early period of antenatal development as well as with the later fetal period.

> And the angel of the LORD appeared to the woman and said to her, 'Behold, you are barren and have no children; but you shall conceive and bear a son. Therefore beware, and drink no wine or strong drink, and eat nothing unclean, for lo, you shall conceive and bear a son. No razor shall come upon his head, for the boy shall be a Nazirite to God from birth; and he shall begin to deliver Israel from the hand of the Philistines.'
>
> (Jdg. 13:3–5)

> And you will have joy and gladness,
> and many will rejoice at his birth;
> for he will be great before the Lord,
> and he shall drink no wine nor strong drink,
> and he will be filled with the Holy Spirit,
> even from his mother's womb.
>
> (Lk. 1:14–15)

The text which speaks of John moving in Elizabeth's womb is really a continuation of the above story, but may be reproduced here in the interests of clarity.

> And when Elizabeth heard the greeting of Mary, the babe leaped in her womb; and Elizabeth was filled with the Holy Spirit and she exclaimed with a loud cry, 'Blessed are you among women, and blessed is the fruit of your womb! And why is this granted me, that the mother of my Lord should come to me? For behold, when the voice of your greeting came to my ears, the babe in my womb leaped for joy.'
>
> (Lk. 1:41–44)

Commentators are as much at variance in the interpretation of these texts as they were in our previous samples. Regarding the Judges text, Robert G. Boling writes,

> In this passage, the rule of the Nazirite, formulated for those who will enlist on their own initiative, is delightfully adapted as highly desirable prenatal care. For example, the admonition to stay clear of uncleanness that emanates from a dead body, which is surely beyond the control of the fetus, is displaced by the instruction to the mother to 'eat nothing unclean' like any other Israelite.[31]

John Gray sees more significance in the application of Nazirite ways of life to Samson while he is still in the womb. He comments, 'The dedication of the hero begins in his mother's womb.'[32]

In commenting on Luke 1:15, Joseph Fitzmyer writes,

> In the Old Testament the phrases *ek/apo koilias mētros* can mean either 'from birth on' (Is. 48:8; Ps. 22:11) or 'while still in the womb' (Jdgs. 13:3–5; 16:17; Is. 44:2). That the latter is meant here is evident from 1:41. But the phrase is also used in a broad sense, meaning that John's whole existence will be graced. Later theological speculation will interpret it as the sanctification of John in his mother's womb.[33]

It is interesting to note that Fitzmyer refers to the biblical testimony regarding Samson's conception and birth to prove his point, as well as to the later story of John leaping in his mother's womb. Leon Morris, commenting on the story of Elizabeth meeting Mary, states, 'Movements of the foetus are not, of course, uncommon. But on this occasion Elizabeth was filled with the Holy Spirit and under his inspiration interpreted the movement as the expression of her unborn baby's joy.'[34] E. Earle Ellis takes a less literal approach to the movement of the fetus when he comments:

> As Luke the physician perhaps knew, an emotional experience
> of the mother can cause a movement of the foetus. Elizabeth
> sees in this confirmation of the Holy Spirit and a connection
> with her own pregnancy. She expresses this in the idyllic
> phrase, 'The babe . . . leaped for joy.'[35]

In keeping with his statement, noted earlier, on the prophecy that John would be filled with the Holy Spirit while still in the womb, Joseph Fitzmyer comments on this verse that 'the movement of the unborn child in Elizabeth's womb is intended as a recognition by him of his relation to Jesus'.[36] In this interpretation of the text it is Jesus whom John recognizes, not Mary, implying that personhood should also be attributed to the embryonic Jesus.

This survey of opinions on the relevant texts warns us that we cannot be dogmatic in our interpretation. The balance of opinion, however, suggests that unless we view the texts as employing imagery without attempting to convey any factual information, they do lend support to the view that the human embryo possesses personhood. To argue that the instructions to Samson's mother were merely prenatal health advice misses the point that the instructions were given in the context of Samson's being designated a Nazirite before his birth. At the very least, the text suggests that Samson's prenatal experiences could affect his entire spiritual development. If this were so, it would imply that a personal spiritual aspect of Samson's being existed while he was still in the womb. Similarly, whether the account of John moving in Elizabeth's womb is given an idealized interpretation by Luke or not, it is best to interpret the earlier passage to suggest that John was indeed filled with the Holy Spirit while still in the womb.

The texts in this section of our study again fail to prove that the human embryo is personally human, but they do show that the human embryo is the object of God's love and care and that God knows and calls individuals while they are at an embryonic stage of development. Of most significance, however, is the implication that the status of the human embryo does not depend on its functional abilities but on God's knowledge of it. We have acknowledged that it is not possible to prove that every embryo is 'called' by God, but that all those who are 'called' by God are so 'called' even while still embryos. It is entirely reasonable to argue that all embryos should be treated, not in the light of what they can actually do as embryos, but in the light of God's eternal 'call' of individuals to enter into fellowship with him. This 'call' extends throughout their entire history, including their period as embryos and fetuses.

The incarnation

The incarnation is often cited in Christian circles in an attempt to prove that the human embryo must have full personal status. The argument runs that since Jesus was conceived by Mary, of the Holy Spirit, and since he was the Word made flesh, then that which was conceived had to be a personal entity, for it is not possible to think of the Word of God as ever being anything other than a personal entity. The issue, however, is far from being as simple as this argument suggests.

Theological reflection would indicate that we also need to ask questions such as: when exactly did the Word become flesh? What was the nature of the relationship between the human being Jesus of Nazareth and the eternal Word? After the incarnation, was the Word existing only in the person of Jesus or also existing simultaneously in his eternal completeness? If the latter is the case, it is possible, though not necessary, to argue that even if the human embryo cannot be attributed personal human status, the Word never stopped being a fully personal entity. This is so even if, in his expression of himself as the Word made flesh, he initially experienced a period during which the developing embryo did not enjoy personal attributes and faculties. This argument is, of course, speculative and need not be correct. Nevertheless, it does show that, if we were to argue on purely theological or philosophical grounds that the incarnation demonstrates the personal status of the human embryo, then we must take such arguments into account.

Our task at present, however, is to view the biblical material regarding the incarnation and to see whether it can shed any light on our enquiry.

In doing so, we will examine only those gospel passages which deal directly with the conception or birth of Jesus.

> . . . an angel of the Lord appeared to [Joseph] in a dream, saying, 'Joseph, son of David, do not fear to take Mary your wife, for that which is conceived in her is of the Holy Spirit; she will bear a son, and you shall call his name Jesus, for he will save his people from their sins.'
> (Mt. 1:20–21)

> And the angel said to [Mary], 'Do not be afraid, Mary, for you have found favour with God. And behold, you will conceive in your womb and bear a Son, and you shall call his name Jesus.' . . . And the angel said to her,

> 'The Holy Spirit will come upon you,
> and the power of the Most High will overshadow you;
> therefore the child to be born will be called holy,
> the Son of God.'
> (Lk. 1:30–31, 35)

> And the Word became flesh and dwelt among us, full of grace and truth.
> (Jn. 1:14)

These texts form only part of the story of the incarnation and must be set in their contexts, but they summarize the most important aspects of the biblical material as far as our story is concerned. It is not surprising that most commentators do not remark at all on the implications of the incarnation for the status of the human embryo. It is true to say that such considerations were far from the minds of the gospel writers when they penned their works. Any evidence we may find, relevant to our study, must be viewed in this light. While this does not render such evidence invalid, it does mean that the incarnation is much more important as a theme in theology than as a biblical reference-point for our understanding of the human embryo.

Indeed, it can be argued that as far as Matthew and Luke are concerned, we are not dealing with texts concerning the incarnation at all, but with passages recounting the birth narratives of Jesus. Only

John, strictly speaking, introduces the concept of incarnation, though it is reasonable to read Matthew and Luke with this later theological reflection in mind.

William Hendrikson sees in Matthew's narrative an example of divine and human co-operation in the birth of Jesus, which begins with his conception:

> All have an interest in the birth of the child: (a) The Holy
> Spirit, by the exercise of whose power the child is conceived;
> (b) Mary, who, being the willing instrument of the Spirit in
> conceiving and giving birth to the infant, becomes 'blessed
> among women'.[37]

David Hill takes a similar view in seeing the conception of Jesus as the focal point of the incarnation story. He comments, 'Matthew implies that the creative power and activity of God (Holy Spirit) is inaugurating the New Creation by the conception of the Messianic Redeemer.'[38] E. Earle Ellis, however, commenting on Luke's narrative, takes a different approach and sees the birth rather than the conception of Jesus as being of primary importance: 'The Holy Spirit who was active in bringing the first creation into being is the agency through which the New Creation is born in Jesus the Messiah.'[39] Casting some light on the text from John's gospel, Leon Morris states: ' "Became" is in the aorist tense, and indicates action at a point of time.'[40] The importance of this comment for us is that the Word became flesh not through a process but at a particular point of time, though whether that point was the time of conception or of birth the text does not say.

This survey leaves us in the strange position of knowing that the incarnation must be of significance to us in our study, but that the biblical evidence does not help us to examine the issue in depth. As we noted earlier, the full significance of the incarnation for us is a matter more for theological reflection than for biblical exegesis. It is fair to argue, however, that all that has been said about previous texts in regard to God's choice of an individual and God's care for the developing embryo is also relevant to the story of the incarnation and is underscored by it.

In addition, it is a natural reading of the texts to suppose that the authors saw the conception of Jesus as the point when God acted in creative power to bring the Messiah into the world and hence the moment when the incarnation took place. While this interpretation of the biblical evidence may be preferred, however, it once again stops short of proving that personhood begins at conception rather than at birth or at some stage in the process of gestation.

Exodus 21:22–25

Exodus 21:22–25 stands apart from all the other texts we have examined in our study so far, since, as part of the legal code of the primitive nation of Israel, it provides us with the only scriptural example of the relationship between the law and the embryo or fetus. A few cautionary remarks need to be made, though. The law, at this point, was not attempting to answer the question of the embryo's or fetus's status as a human being. While the text is of great importance for our study, its interpretation is not necessarily binding, since the context is one where the appreciation of the human individuals involved is based as much on the concept of ownership as on intrinsic human value.

Similarly, this text deals with a specific incident which was likely to occur from time to time in the society regulated by the law in question; the author did not engage in a debate on the relative merits and demerits of medical techniques which may affect the embryo or fetus. While a discussion on infertility treatment would, of course, have been impossible, a law on the subject of abortion would not. Consequently, this text is very important for our enquiry, but even it cannot be claimed as a proof-text for any particular viewpoint.

> When men strive together, and hurt a woman with child, so
> that there is a miscarriage, and yet no harm follows, the one
> who hurt her shall be fined, according as the woman's husband
> shall lay upon him; and he shall pay as the judges determine. If
> any harm follows, then you shall give life for life, eye for eye,
> tooth for tooth, hand for hand, foot for foot, burn for burn,
> wound for wound, stripe for stripe.

In interpreting this text in the context of our study, the issue which must be resolved is: does the text refer to harm being done to the woman alone, following the miscarriage, or to harm being caused to either the woman or the child?

Not surprisingly, commentators are divided on the issue. Ronald

Clements comments that the fine 'was clearly intended to represent compensation for the loss of the infant'.[41] A similar approach is taken by J. P. Hyatt: 'If there is no harm to herself, but she has a miscarriage, then the one who hurt her is fined as much as the woman's husband lays upon him.'[42] He further comments, 'These laws show the great importance attached to the causing of a miscarriage, indicating that it was considered almost the equivalent of murder.'[43]

John Durham takes a quite different view:

> If two men in a scuffle inadvertently strike a pregnant woman causing by the trauma of the blow the premature birth of her children, if there is no harm, presumably either to the mother or the newborn child or children, the man who actually inflicted the blow is to pay compensation, fixed by the woman's husband on the basis of an assessment agreed upon by an objective third party. If, however, there is a permanent injury, either to the woman, or, presumably, to the child or the children she was carrying, equal injury is to be inflicted upon the one who caused it.[44]

He further argues that the term translated 'miscarriage' need not mean a fatal premature birth: 'The text, however, is not that specific, referring as it does to "her children going out".'[45] The Free Church of Scotland document, *The Sanctity of Human Life*, argues in a similar way: 'The natural reading of verse 22 is that if the child is born alive and well the culprit is fined, whereas in the case of death or injury of the child or mother, the normal penalty for murder or assault is stipulated.'[46] In a submission to Warnock by the then Chief Rabbi, Sir Immanuel (now Lord) Jakobovits, an attempt is made to steer a middle course:

> While this absolute inviolability – whereby no life may ever be deliberately sacrificed even to save another or any number of others – sets in only at birth (Ex. 21:12, 22–25 and Jewish commentators), the unborn child, too, enjoys a very sacred title to life, in different stages from the moment of conception, to be set aside only in exceptional circumstances, such as a serious hazard to the mother.[47]

This range of opinion warns us not to be dogmatic in basing an argument on this text. The most that can be said is that this text may be interpreted to indicate that the life of the unborn child is a full, personal, human life, but equally it may be interpreted to say that it is not. We may certainly argue that, since the text can be interpreted to mean that the fetus's or embryo's life is equivalent to the life of an adult, we should not do anything which may endanger this life unless another life is also at risk. This line of reasoning will not, of course, commend itself to everyone. Some may argue that since it may also be believed that the human embryo is not given equal status with an adult, to prohibit embryo research may be to rob the human race of medical advances which may benefit large numbers of adults in the future.

Conclusions

What then can we say regarding our survey of biblical texts? First, we must emphasize strongly that no proof-texts exist which determine the status of the human embryo. This can be asserted on three grounds: most of the texts are open to various legitimate interpretations, many of them are poetic in nature and are difficult to assess regarding their significance, and only one text attempts to deal with the human embryo in the context of legislation. The others introduce the subject of the embryo or fetus in discussion of other topics.

Secondly, we can state that, in spite of the above difficulties, it is clear that the Scriptures support a high view of the status of the embryo as well as of the fetus. This status is not defined exactly, but the embryo is seen as being the object of God's knowledge and care, personal language is employed to describe it, and it is seen as being incorporated into God's 'call' of an individual. The Scriptures do not speculate regarding the metaphysical nature of the embryo, nor do they state, in so many words, that the embryo is a human being with the same status as a child or adult.

They do, however, cause us to treat the embryo with profound respect, and they put the onus of proof on those who would argue that the embryo should not enjoy the same status as a child or adult. If the embryo is not to be treated with the same respect as a child or adult, then it must be shown why an entity which is known and loved by God, which is said to be one with the later adult it gives rise to, and which is the object of God's 'call', should be treated in a less than fully human manner. Above all, the Scriptures indicate that the status of the embryo is determined by God's attitude towards it, not by any functional assessment of its capabilities.

The result, then, of our biblical survey is to reject the thesis that the Bible proves beyond doubt that the embryo is a human person, but it also indicates that the burden of proof must rest with those who reject the full humanity of the embryo.

Because the status of the human embryo is of such central importance in the whole debate on human fertilization and embryology, it is necessary for us to pursue the matter further. Our biblical survey has provided us with a foundation, indicating a high view of the embryo as well as of the fetus. We must now also investigate theological, philosophical and scientific opinions before we are in a position to state how we should view the status of the embryo.

4

The status of the human embryo:
a theological approach

Because the status of the human embryo is at the very heart of any debate on human fertilization and embryology, we must be painstaking in our efforts to determine how we believe the embryo ought to be defined. Once again, we need to stress that there are no shortcuts in this process. As others have wrestled with this problem, they have been led into discussions on Christian tradition, metaphysics and the image of God, as well as contemporary medical, philosophical and theological thought.

Some of these avenues of investigation prove to be more fruitful than others. Nevertheless, we must examine all of them if we are to be sure that we have conducted a thorough study into the subject. Only when we are confident that we have looked into every area of the debate can we come to a conclusion regarding the embryo's status.

Christian tradition

Many Christians assume that until comparatively recently the church spoke with one voice regarding the status of the embryo, viewing it as a human person. In fact, a survey of early Christian thought and writing shows the issue to be much more complicated both regarding the status of the human embryo and the reasons given for deciding what status the embryo should have. Such a survey is important for our study, since it enables us to state clearly what the attitude of the church has, in fact, been in different stages of its history. In particular, it will help us to see what type of argument, if any, can be advanced by appealing to Christian tradition.

The primitive church

The earliest extrabiblical material is unanimous in its rejection of abortion and infanticide, often viewing the two acts as one and the same. While little metaphysical reflection is evident in most early statements, a high regard for the human fetus or embryo is proposed.

The *Didache*, probably written around the end of the first century, states: 'Thou shalt not procure abortion or commit infanticide.'[1] The same phrase also appears in the *Epistle of Barnabas*, written around the same time.[2] In responding to pagan charges that Christians practised ritual murder, the second-century apologist Athenagoras asked:

> What sense does it make to think of us as murderers when we say that women who practise abortion are murderers and will render account to God for abortion? The same man cannot regard that which is in the womb as a living being and for that reason an object of God's concern and then murder it when it has come into the light.[3]

Writing at the end of the second century, Tertullian argued:

> For us, to whom homicide has been once for all forbidden, it is not permitted to break up even what has been conceived in the womb, while the blood is still being drawn from the mother's body to make a new creature. Prevention of birth is premature murder, and it makes no difference whether it is a life already born that one snatches away or a life that is coming to birth that one destroys. The future man is a man already; the whole fruit is present in the seed.[4]

Tertullian's near-contemporary, Clement of Alexandria, wrote: 'Women who, in order to conceal fornication, make use of deadly medicines which lead directly to ruin, destroy all humanity along with the fetus.'[5] A lesser-known author, Minicius Felix, writing around the turn of the second century, noted: 'There are women who, by medicinal draughts, extinguish in the womb and commit infanticide upon the offspring yet unborn.'[6]

These comments are unambiguous in their condemnation of abortion and those who practise it. Other less orthodox second-century writings, such as the *Apocalypse of Peter*[7] and the *Christian Sibyllines*,[8] delight in describing in lurid detail the horrors and torments awaiting those who procure abortions and are consigned to hell for their sins.

These early Christian writings demonstrate that following the apostolic period an attempt was made to relate Christian morality to all areas of life. In contrast to the practice of the pagan societies in which they lived, Christians viewed all forms of human life as sacred and deserving of protection. The common acceptance of infanticide was repugnant to Christians, and it is most likely that teaching on abortion arose from a desire to counter this practice. By extrapolation, abortion was also viewed as murder, since no distinction was made between a child's life before or after birth. It is, of course, quite possible that this view was not universal, but the fact that leading Christians argued as they did indicates the probability that their view was the majority one.

It is important that we recognize that these statements propose a personal continuity spanning birth. A person is the same entity before and after birth; no distinctions are made other than the environment in which one lives and the stage of development one has reached. Significantly, no attempt is made to distinguish between the early embryo and the later fetus.

This does not mean that these statements are of relevance only for our understanding of the fetus. Even if the ancients had little understanding of embryology, they did understand the difference between a fully formed fetus, about to be born, and the early embryonic 'seed'. They understood that conception took place nine months before birth and that the early embryo was very different in size and form from the later fetus. The fact that they make no distinction in their arguments, but assert that abortion is murder, indicates that we may view early-church tradition as supporting the view that the human embryo should enjoy a status equal to that of a child or adult.

At this stage in the church's history there was little reflection on the metaphysical nature of the human embryo or fetus; that was to come later. The Jewish view of human life[9] had, no doubt, influenced the early church. Christians were content to adopt what we now may call a 'pro-life' stance without too much philosophical reflection. The opinions of second-century Christians and their first-century predecessors may, of course, be incorrect, but it is, at least, instructive to note the primitive tradition and to acknowledge its influence on the development of Christian thought in this area.

Developments in early Christian thought

If the information available to us regarding first- and second-century Christian thought on the status of the human embryo was uniformly inclined to view the deliberate destruction of the human embryo or fetus as murder, this viewpoint came under challenge in the third and fourth centuries. In clarifying its reasons for prohibiting abortion, the church became increasingly preoccupied with metaphysical arguments regarding the nature of the embryo and fetus. In the deliberations of the third and fourth centuries, unanimity of opinion was lost.

In this period the Septuagint rendering of Exodus 21 was often the basis for discussion. The Septuagint drew a distinction between a 'formed' and an 'unformed' fetus. The penalty for causing the death of a formed fetus was death, while a lesser penalty was proposed for the destruction of an unformed fetus. Not all theologians followed this reasoning, nor was there universal agreement on what it was that distinguished a formed fetus from an unformed one, or when this transformation occurred. Nevertheless, the Septuagint version provided the initial basis for a difference of opinion within the church on the status of the human embryo. It also paved the way for a metaphysical discussion on the nature of humanity, with the question how and when the human soul was formed becoming the real centre of debate.

While the terms 'unformed fetus' and 'formed fetus' do not correspond exactly to our terms 'embryo' and 'fetus', they are close enough for us to view the distinction between the formed and unformed fetus as the ancient equivalent of the modern distinction between the fetus and embryo. The point has been made that formation and animation did not always coincide in Catholic thought, but most authorities agreed that they did, believing animation to take place at forty days for boys and eighty days for girls.[10] The current use of the term 'embryo' to cover the first eight weeks of gestation indicates, therefore, that what we term the 'embryo' would have been included in any general reference to the unformed fetus.

The sharp difference of opinion regarding the status of the human embryo is well illustrated by the opposing viewpoints of St Basil the Great of Caesarea and his brother Gregory of Nyssa. Basil wrote: 'A woman who deliberately destroys a fetus is answerable to murder. Any fine distinction as to its being completely formed or unformed is not admissible amongst us.'[11] Gregory, on the other hand, recorded:

> For just as it would not be possible to style the unformed
> embryo a human being, but only a potential one – assuming
> that it is completed so as to come forth to human birth, while
> so long as it is in this unformed state it is something other than
> a human being – so our reason cannot recognise as a Christian
> one who has failed to receive, with regard to the entire mystery,
> the genuine form of our religion.[12]

Whatever we may make of the reasoning expressed in these statements, one thing is clear: by the end of the fourth century it was possible for leading churchmen to differ fundamentally on the status of the human embryo, if not on the status of the fetus in its later stages of development.

Even though the Christian church in this period was unsure of the status of the embryo, abortion was still universally viewed as a serious offence. The Council of Ancyra, meeting in AD 314, demanded that abortionists must serve a ten-year period of penance and exclusion from communion for their sin.[13] This is a significant ruling, since it demonstrates that it is not necessary to prove the personal humanity of the embryo in order to argue that its life should be treated with great respect.

In spite of the church's prohibition on abortion, pressure mounted throughout the fourth century for theologians to define further the exact status of the embryo and fetus and to provide guidance as to whether or not abortion of an embryo was murder.

The debate in this era eventually went in favour of those following the Septuagint tradition. The rise of asceticism, and the growing belief that sexual intercourse should be encouraged only because of its reproductive potential, meant that the issue was not settled completely in this period. It is, at times, difficult to discern whether an individual's condemnation of abortion was the result of his belief in the personal status of the embryo or whether it was the result of his opposition to contraception. Some of the force of such arguments is lost as a result.

Even though Jerome translated the Old Testament into Latin, using the Hebrew text rather than the Septuagint, the Septuagint tradition was so strong that it remained the accepted interpretation of the Exodus text. This may have been so because it readily fitted in with current philosophical understandings of the relation between the soul and the body and also with contemporary medical opinion.[14] Jerome, however, arguing from an ascetic viewpoint, appears to have equated abortion, or even some forms of contraception, with murder. Considering consecrated Christian 'virgins' found to be with child, he writes:

> Some even ensure barrenness by the help of potions, murdering human beings before they are fully conceived. Others, when they find they are with child as a result of their sin, practice abortion with drugs, and so frequently bring about their own death, taking with them to the lower world the guilt of three crimes: suicide, adultery against Christ and child-murder.[15]

It is not altogether clear whether Jerome is attacking the practice of very early abortion because he views the embryo as a human being, or whether he is thinking of the humanity that would have belonged to an embryo had it been allowed to reach the stage of being 'fully conceived'. It is also not clear what he means by this last expression. Nevertheless, the most natural interpretation of this statement is that he did attribute human status to the embryo.

If this is so, Jerome's opinion was not the one that commended itself to most fourth-century theologians. The *Apostolic Constitutions* followed the Septuagint tradition: 'Thou shalt not procure abortion nor commit infanticide, for everything that is formed and has received a soul from God, if it is slain, shall be avenged, as being unjustly destroyed.'[16] This statement is an interesting example of the primitive church's prohibition on abortion being given a later gloss which served both to weaken the original statement and also to provide theological grounds for its formulation. The idea that it was the reception of a soul which gave the embryo or fetus its true humanity was one which became increasingly acceptable in the church. Inevitably, the discussion became more and more metaphysical in character, as a result.

Perhaps the most important contribution to the debate at this stage of the church's development was made by Augustine of Hippo. Augustine favoured an ascetic view of the Christian life, but also felt obliged to draw a very clear distinction between the respective status of a formed and an unformed fetus:

> If what is brought forth is unformed but at this stage some sort of living shapeless thing, then the law of homicide would not apply, for it could not be said that there was a living soul in that body, for it lacks all sense, if it be such as is not yet formed and therefore not yet endowed with its senses.[17]

Augustine's belief that the human soul could not be present unless the fetus was capable of sense experience and perhaps thought is one which has commended itself to a number of modern theologians. It is also worth noting, however, that Augustine was not completely convinced that even a formed fetus had a human soul, though his logic forced him to acknowledge that such must be the case. Rather tortuously, he commented:

> As for abortions which, although alive in the womb, died before birth, I dare neither affirm nor deny their resurrection . . . I cannot see how I can say that they do not belong to the resurrection of the dead even if they died in their mother's womb.[18]

Augustine, then rejected the personal humanity of the embryo but accepted with reservations the full humanity of the later fetus. We must also recognize, however, that such reasoning did not lead him to accept the practice of abortion; he was attempting to gauge the seriousness of the sin, not to argue that early abortion was morally defensible.

Medieval thought

The view of Augustine was commonly held throughout succeeding centuries. Abortion, even in its earliest forms, was forbidden, as was birth control. This view was held because of ascetic views regarding sex rather than because of any belief in the full personal humanity of the embryo. In the Middle Ages, church canonists were employed in bringing every aspect of life under the church's guidance and discipline. As was to be expected, the question of abortion exercised their minds accordingly. Most of these scholars followed Augustine's thinking, although not all leading churchmen drew such careful distinctions as Augustine.

Gratian, writing in the mid-twelfth century, stated unequivocally: 'Abortion before the formation of the fetus was not equivalent to homicide.'[19] Pope Innocent III, writing in 1211, took a liberal view on the subject, at least as far as his priests were concerned. If a priest was party to a miscarriage he was suspended from his priestly duties. Even this mild punishment was not required, however, if an embryo were involved: 'If the conceptus is not yet quickened he may minister; otherwise he must abstain from the service of the altar.'[20] Innocent's successor, Gregory IX, took a firmer line, seeing artificial forms of birth control, as well as abortion, as murder. While the actual words he used are open to various interpretations, the church understood them to refer to abortion as well as to contraception. His statement on the subject reads:

> If anyone for the sake of fulfilling lust or in meditated hatred
> does something to a man or woman, or gives them to drink, so
> that he cannot generate or she conceive, or offspring be born, let
> it be held as homicide.[21]

It is not clear if this statement was meant to undermine the Augustinian line of reasoning or to show that the punishment for such deeds should be equal to the punishment for murder, but it did not commend itself even to Gregory's contemporaries.

The canonist Raymond de Penafort preferred to follow the reasoning of Augustine:

> If the fetus is already formed or animated that is true homicide
> if because of that blow or potion the woman miscarries, for he
> has killed a man. If, however, it is not yet animated, it is not
> said to be homicide so far as concerns irregularity, but it is
> accounted homicide in regard to penance.[22]

This statement may in fact reflect the sentiments of Gregory, putting the case more accurately, although it may better be seen as a correction to the type of view loosely held by the pontiff and others.

The thirteenth-century church tended to follow the latter line of reasoning, fixing the moment of animation as the distinctive point when the fetus became a human being. This belief became so prevalent that it appears almost as a mark of orthodoxy within debates of the time. In 1216, Thomas of Chobham wrote:

> It is written in the law of Moses, 'If anyone should strike a pregnant woman and she should miscarry, if the fetus has been formed let him give life for life; if however, it is unformed, let him be amerced in money.' From this it is clear that it is a much graver sin to dislodge a formed fetus than an unformed one.[23]

Here again, it is worth noting that the issue at stake was whether or not there was a distinction to be made between an embryo or early fetus and a fetus at a later stage of development. In all circumstances the destruction of an embryo or fetus was viewed as a sin; the enormity of the sin was the subject of debate.

Thomas Aquinas similarly based his reflections on the issue of animation:

> He who strikes a pregnant woman by that act puts himself in the wrong, so that if death should result either for the woman or for the animated fetus he cannot escape the crime of homicide, particularly since it is so obvious that death may result from such a blow.[24]

He fails to say what charge should be laid against a person whose actions resulted in the loss of a fetus not yet animated. Aquinas, following Aristotle, reintroduced the concept of the emergence and development of the soul within the prenatal human being: 'Aristotle says that the embryo is an animal before it is a man . . . so the intellectual soul is not the same as the sensitive soul in man, but presupposes it as the matter it energizes.'[25]

While the language used in this argument is foreign to most modern thinkers, the principles avowed are not. The whole question of the nature of the human soul is still a pertinent one for our enquiry. Even though current theological and philosophical thought is unlikely to speak of an 'intellectual' or a 'sensitive' soul, the nature and development of the human mind is seen by many to hold the key to unlocking the mysteries of determining the status of the embryo or fetus.

Post-Reformation Catholicism

With such names as Augustine and Aquinas following the Septuagint tradition, it is not surprising that the earlier general appraisal of all abortions as the equivalent of murder faded into the background. It was not, however, completely forgotten and from time to time an attempt was made to reintroduce it as the official teaching of the western church.

In 1588 Pope Sixtus V wrote in a papal Bull:

> . . . all henceforth who by themselves or by the hand of an intermediary procure the abortion or the ejection of an immature fetus whether animate or inanimate, formed or unformed . . . and also the pregnant women themselves, who knowingly do the same, shall incur, by the very act, the penalties set forth and inflicted by divine as well as human law against actual murderers.[26]

Such an uncompromising statement was not allowed to stand unchallenged for long. A mere three years later, Sixtus's successor Gregory XIV issued another Bull in which he stated: 'The penalty for procuring the abortion of an inanimate fetus . . . we revoke.'[27]

The battle of the Bulls was settled definitively only in 1869 when Pope Pius IX, with the backing of the new attitude to papal infallibility, proclaimed in unambiguous terms:

> . . . excommunicate all who procure abortion, without distinction either as to the method, direct or indirect, intentional or voluntary, or as to the gestational age of the fetus, whether it were formed or unformed, animate or inanimate.[28]

This statement became the definitive position of the Roman Catholic Church, so that throughout the twentieth century the embryo and fetus have been seen as full members of the human race from conception onwards. In recent years, before the Warnock Report was published, the Roman Catholic Church reiterated its position on a number of occasions.[29] Until relatively recently, almost all Christian churches adopted a similar position, the Protestant churches finding no reason to disagree with the position advanced by the Roman Catholic Church.

What, then, does this brief survey of Christian tradition show us?

First, it is clear that for most of the church's history the embryo was afforded some protection in that performing an abortion was viewed as a sin. At the same time the embryo was not seen as being fully and personally human. It was only in the primitive church, and latterly within the last century or so, that it was afforded full human status from conception.

The second point of note is that for much of the church's history, the issue of whether an embryo or fetus was a human being was settled on the basis of the presence or absence of a human soul within the developing body. If it is decided that an embryo is not fully human because it does not possess a human soul, it does not follow that either abortion or embryo research should be seen as being morally acceptable. But the question of the nature, or even the existence, of the soul is one that we cannot ignore.

What we can say at this stage of our enquiry is that any argument regarding the status of the human embryo based on an appeal to Christian tradition is bound to fail, since no uniform Christian tradition exists. Furthermore, because the church has variously evaluated the status of the embryo throughout history, it is understandable that some should argue that the status of the embryo is a matter for individual interpretation. We cannot accept this argument, however, since our biblical survey indicated a higher view of the embryo than this would admit. We also recognize that much of the church's reflection on the status of the embryo was based on a mistaken interpretation of Exodus 21 and so should not be given as much weight as at first might be suggested.

The debate within the church eventually concentrated on the existence and creation of the soul. If the embryo possessed a soul it was fully human; if it did not it was potentially a human being. For many today the presence or absence of 'mind' is the deciding factor in evaluating the status of the embryo. Examining the concept of the soul is, then, the next step in our investigation. This will lead us into a philosophical and theological maze. It is one we must travel along, though, since many Christians today agree that the existence or otherwise of the soul or the mind ought to be the determining factor in deciding the status of the embryo. Our task, in part, is to see whether or not this is a reasonable argument.

The human soul

In testing the validity of the argument that it is the presence of a soul that makes an embryo or fetus fully human, we must, first of all, recognize that the term can be understood in a number of ways. Both in the Scriptures[30] and in theological and philosophical thought, a variety of uses of the term 'soul' can be found. This means that we must examine a number of different ways of viewing the human soul and attempt to discover what each of them can contribute to our investigation. In so doing we will comment on the reasonableness of various interpretations of the term. Our task, though, is not to prove or disprove any particular theory of the human soul, but only to investigate how various theories affect our enquiry. A full theological and philosophical argument on the existence and nature of the soul is beyond the scope of this study.

Dualism

Traditional Platonic thought regarding the human soul has been expressed in the following terms by Peter Geach:

> Each man's make-up includes a wholly immaterial thing, his mind and soul. It is the mind that sees and hears and feels and thinks and chooses — in a word, is conscious. The mind is the person: the body is extrinsic to the person, like a suit of clothes. Though body and mind affect one another, the mind's existence is independent of the body's; and there is no reason why the mind should not go on being conscious indefinitely after the death of the body, and even if it never again has with any body the sort of connection which it now has.[31]

This summary of dualist thought, which equates the soul with the mind and sees it as the 'real person', quite distinct from the body, represents not only a particular strand in philosophy but also much current popular Christian teaching. While it has been largely abandoned by philosophers and theologians, it is not without its advocates even today, when the general academic environment is unsuited to its survival.

Paul Tournier, for example, restates dualist belief in a striking fashion:

> Life, the ego, the person, are not palpable, analysable realities
> accessible to science. They are a will, a choice, a consciousness,
> an impulse coming from another, metaphysical sphere, of
> which we see only the indirect effect in the
> physico-chemical sphere.[32]

He expands this thought, adding: 'For me it is neither the body which controls the mind, nor the mind which controls the body; rather are both at once the expression of an invisible reality of a spiritual order: the person.'[33] He further draws a distinction between the spiritual and material aspects of human nature: 'The body and mind are only the means of expression of the spirit, which co-ordinates and directs them both at once.'[34]

Hywel D. Lewis defends a type of dualism in more circumspect terms:

> We can in one sense explain a good deal of the way the mind
> influences the body, and the reverse. We can fill out the story
> very fully on the physiological side and are learning more and
> more about it . . . We can likewise discover more about the
> way our thoughts shape themselves and fill out our knowledge
> of logic or psychology in other ways. But this does nothing, on
> either side, to explain why, when the brain is in a certain state,
> we have certain experiences, nor why, when the mind is
> disposed in some way, certain changes in the brain, and
> thereby in the rest of the body, come about.[35]

In further defence of the essentially independent nature of the mind, he asserts:

> It does not follow . . . that the states of our bodies determine
> exhaustively the states of our minds. They condition them, but
> that is a very different thing. The main determinant of the
> course of one's thought's is the nature of these
> thoughts themselves.[36]

Objections to dualism

In spite of such comments and a general popular acceptance in Christian circles of some form of dualism, most modern philosophers reject dualism. Such influential thinkers as Gilbert Ryle, Anthony Flew and Bertrand Russell adopt an essentially materialist viewpoint in which the human soul is thought of as a meaningful term only if it is equated completely with the human brain. Within many scientific circles this is also the accepted position.

In addition to the philosophical problem of how soul and body can interact if they belong to separate independent spheres, the main problem with dualism, for many, is that it runs contrary to a scientific view of the world. The idea that a mental realm of the soul may exist which is not open to scientific investigation, and which in principle is not open to empirical verification, is repugnant to many scientists, theologians and philosophers. We can ally these objections to our experience of everyday life. We observe that changes in our bodies and brains are able to affect, at times dramatically, not only our ability to think or perceive the external world, but also our very characters and even beliefs. This suggests that there is a closer link and greater dependence between our minds and bodies than a traditional dualist position would allow.

If we see the existence of the human mind or soul as being pivotal in our attempt to discover the true status of the human embryo, then it is clear that, if the soul is dependent upon the brain for its existence, we cannot argue that a soul can be present in a very early embryo in which the rudimentary brain has not developed. If, however, the soul exists quite independently from the brain, then it may be the case, though not necessarily so, that the soul is present from the time of conception.

Dualism is certainly out of vogue at the moment in academic circles. In its traditional form it appears to be contrary to much scientific knowledge of how the human brain works. Nevertheless, we have to accept that it is impossible to disprove altogether. The philosophical case against dualism has, indeed, been overstated. It is difficult to see how a soul and a body may interact if they are two entirely different substances, but this difficulty does not mean that such cannot be the case. God is spirit, and while we cannot understand how he interacts with creation, we have no hesitation in believing that he does so. Equally, while a classic scientific view of the world may predispose us against dualism, such a rigid view of the universe would also predispose us against belief in God. If we choose to adopt a classic scientific view as the only means of interpreting reality, then more than dualism will have to be abandoned. This does not mean that dualism is correct; only that it is not as untenable a theory as is often suggested.

The main objection to dualism is a theological rather than a philosophical one. If our souls are the 'real' us, then our bodies and the rest of creation are of secondary importance. If it is the soul that represents the real person, and the body is merely a vehicle for the soul's expression, then all that matters is that our souls survive death and are saved from sin and corruption. This view, however, is contrary to the message of the New Testament. It was in his flesh that Jesus suffered and died for our salvation. The incarnation is central to our salvation; not merely a means whereby the external Word expressed himself to human beings. If all that matters is the soul, then the incarnation, the crucifixion and the resurrection become marginal features in the Christian faith rather than its central events.

Dualism, viewed purely from a philosophical viewpoint, may be correct. We may consist of body and soul, with each component existing in its own right. Our bodies terminate their existence at death and our souls continue to exist eternally. It is impossible to disprove such a theory on philosophical or scientific grounds. As such, dualism remains, for some, a possible solution to the problem of the relationship between body and soul, and is viewed as a possible starting-point for an understanding of human nature. Viewed from a theological perspective, however, dualism is an unacceptable explanation of human nature.

In the context of our discussion, this means that any argument for the full humanity of the embryo which is based on a belief that the soul, understood as mind, is created by God at the time of conception and joined to the embryonic body, is unacceptable. Much popular Christian thought on the status of the embryo is, in fact, based on a false view of human nature.

Materialism and reductionism

One obvious alternative to dualism is materialism. Materialists argue that all that constitutes a human being is the physical organism which comes into existence at conception and which ceases to exist at death. Perhaps this theory is better termed 'reductionism', for in the extreme form stated above, many who would hold to a materialistic view of the human race would also distance themselves from such an uncompromising evaluation of human nature. Nevertheless, there are those who equate the human mind or soul entirely with the human brain in such a way as to make the processes of thought, perception, judgment and belief products of biochemical events in the brain. These events and these events alone, it is argued, determine our characters, personalities and relationships with the external world.

It is the belief that brain-states alone create and determine the human mind that characterizes reductionism. If the term 'soul' is to mean anything at all, on this view, it can only mean a particular way of speaking of the operation of the human brain, a sort of shorthand which we often employ. It does not mean that there is anything actually existing apart from the body, which can be called the soul. In this theory, the human being comes into existence at conception, but the human person exists only when the brain is sufficiently developed to allow thought, self-awareness and the possibility, at least, of relationships with other persons. This theory also allows for the belief that people suffering from extreme forms of brain injury, who are unable to think or enjoy any discernible level of consciousness, are no longer persons.

This viewpoint is advocated by Michael Lockwood:

> What underlies the discernible continuity of memory and
> personality is a continuity of physical organisation within some
> part or parts of a living human brain through time . . .
> Presumably, then, my life began somewhere between
> conception and birth.[37]

Objections to reductionism

Reductionism is attractive to those who espouse a classic scientific view of reality. Because of the philosophical problems of how an extended body can produce non-extended thought, and the difficulty in avoiding determinism if we assume a reductionist stance, materialism, in its starkest form at least, has not commended itself to many who have investigated the question of the relationship of body and soul. If dualism offends scientific sensibilities, then materialism offends our personal view of ourselves. We cannot but think of ourselves as standing to some extent apart from our brains and bodies; we cannot avoid thinking that there is an 'I' observable in principle, as well as in practice, only to ourselves.

The most obvious and most commonly stated objection to reductionism is the problem of how consciousness may be explained in purely physical terms. The objection has been stated in unequivocal terms by F. H. Cleobury:

> It is nonsense to suggest that at some moment matter began to
> exhibit consciousness, for when we use sentences about
> consciousness, 'matter' stands for some object or concept of
> consciousness. To talk about matter beginning to exhibit
> consciousness at some point of time is to mix the two languages
> in the most absurd way.[38]

A more telling objection to reductionism is the fact that it is self-refuting. If my thoughts and the thoughts of all other human beings are entirely the product of biochemical processes in our brains, then our thoughts are entirely determined. I think as I do because that is the way my brain determines my thought. The same is true for all others. If this is so, how can we ever know what is true? The attempt in this study to reason towards a view of the human embryo is then entirely unreasonable, since I cannot but think as I do, and all readers of this book cannot but think as they do. There is no point in persuasion, since all that takes place in discussion is an interaction of stimuli which may cause one brain to react in a manner different from the way it was previously acting. This constitutes not reasoning or persuasion but a complex biochemical pin-ball game where physical forces determine everything. Reductionism may be true but, if it is, there is no way of verifying it. At the same time, it so obviously contradicts our experience of ourselves and our thoughts and relationships that it is correctly rejected by most people.

From a theological viewpoint, this form of materialism is totally unacceptable, since it opposes any concept of free will and individual responsibility and relegates Jesus to the status of an automaton, programmed to die on the cross. He is no longer our Saviour, obedient to his Father's will, but a complex biochemical machine carrying out the function for which he was brought into the world.

For the purposes of our investigation, the twin theories of dualism and reductionism both fail to commend themselves in such a way as to enable us to make a judgment regarding the moral status of the human embryo. On the one hand, dualism is theologically unacceptable, even if it is not quite the 'savage superstition' that Peter Geach would have us believe.[39] On the other hand, reductionism is self-refuting and theologically unacceptable. It undermines the humanity of both the embryo and the newborn, since the brain functions of babies are so far removed from those of adults as to make them susceptible to the charge of being less than fully human if brain function becomes our sole criterion for assessing humanity.

Alternatives to dualism and reductionism

Between the two extremes of traditional dualism and reductionism a number of other theories exist. While each of these theories can be classified as leaning more towards either dualism or materialism, or even being refinements of either of these two theories, they deserve consideration in their own right.

Ian G. Barbour outlines four alternative theories of human nature. Two of these are really amended versions of dualism and reductionism respectively, but they are sufficiently different from the parent theories to merit reference.

Epiphenomenalism, Barbour says, 'asserts that a mental realm exists but has no causal efficacy. Consciousness accompanies but never influences material events in the brain.'[40] This theory does allow that physical events can have a causal effect on the mind, but the reverse is not possible. While this does conform to our common experience of our mental states being affected by the state of health of our bodies, it does not explain how such a causal connection can take place if mind and matter are two distinct categories. At the same time the theory also fails to allow for the fact that our minds can have any direct influence on our bodies. This runs contrary to many people's experience and also to some current medical belief.

In contrast to epiphenomenalism, Barbour cites behaviourism as a means of understanding human nature which does not require us to have recourse to the idea of the soul at all:

> Basic to this view is the conviction that the postulation of
> 'private' events inaccessible to public observation violates the
> canons of science . . . mental phenomena are to be analysed not
> in terms of neural activity in the brain but in terms of the overt
> behaviour of the organism.[41]

This viewpoint is akin to reductionism and is open to many of the same objections. Many who hold to a basically scientific understanding of the world would not adopt a behaviourist position, while it is unreasonable to assert that a scientific view of the world is the only valid view. Reality is too complex for any single approach to furnish us with all the answers we are seeking. A similar and more personal objection to behaviourism, however, is that there are certain thoughts and experiences which we have which are not susceptible to scientific study but which are none the less real. It is unreasonable, for example, to doubt one's experience of personal motivation following a period of reflection or prayer simply because that experience may not be open to scientific investigation in terms of biology or psychology.

Barbour outlines two other theories of human nature under the heading of 'parallelism'. He understands parallelism to indicate that 'There are no mental events without corresponding physical changes. Mental and physical phenomena are concomitant aspects of a single process of activity.'[42] He refines this concept by speaking of universal parallelism (which states that all events are said to have both mental and physical aspects, though in varying degree) and limited parallelism (which states that mental phenomena occur only at higher levels of organization).

The theory of universal parallelism is also outlined by Thomas Nagel. He calls the theory 'panpsychism', and outlines his understanding of it:

> If the mental properties of an organism are not implied by any
> physical properties but must derive from properties of the
> organism's constituents, then those constituents must have
> nonphysical properties from which the appearance of mental
> properties follows when the combination is of the right kind.
> Since any matter can compose an organism, all matter must
> have these properties. And since the same matter can be made
> into different types of organisms with different types of mental
> life, it must have properties that imply the appearance of
> different mental phenomena when the matter is combined
> in different ways. This would amount to a kind of
> mental chemistry.[43]

Towards emergence

Some support for panpsychism is offered by Keith Ward:

> The important point is that conscious states are not just thrown
> up as a sort of irrelevant byproduct of brain activity, which

itself carries on in the same old mechanistic, predictable way. Rather, conscious states will be emergent properties of the physical system, and as such, they will modify radically the nature of the system. They will enter into the pattern of interactions which make up physical reality. Its laws will still, if you like, be physical, but they will not be derivable from the simple general principles of inorganic physics . . . Some people might call this a form of materialism, because we are saying that consciousness and brain are different ways of looking at the same total reality. Where does the soul come in? The conclusion must be that the soul is generated by a particular physical system. At a specific point in time, a subject of rational consciousness comes into being.[44]

Ward further defends this theory against the charge of reductionism:

The truth is that matter has much greater potential, complexity, opacity to quantitative measurement, uniqueness and novelty than can be expressed in any set of scientific models, whether considered singly or together. Indeed, we might say that matter will only be fully understood when it is seen in its innermost tendency towards consciousness and realization of value.[45]

Other writers concerned with the relationship between the human brain and the mind or soul have been less ready to draw the straightforward causal link between matter and mind evident above. Nevertheless, a certain consensus has tended to emerge in contemporary writings. Not only is a dualistic position deemed unacceptable, but it is stressed that we cannot hope to understand the fullness of human nature by scientific study alone.

Donald MacKay has written that we should regard

. . . body, mind and spirit as entities recognizable at three different levels of significance of our mysterious and complex human nature, rather than three different kinds of 'stuff' that have somehow to exert forces on one another . . . This does not mean that these are only three names for the same thing, nor that mental activity is nothing but brain activity.[46]

Druscilla Scott, reviewing the work of Michael Polanyi, has stated the latter's opposition to reductionism in the following terms:

> The brain is on one level a very subtle machine, and it can be studied on that level by physiologists; these studies have made great progress, partly because of abstracting those aspects and looking at them alone. But such study will never see the Mind, which is the experience and activity of the person whose brain it is. The person is dwelling in the bodily process in a relationship not open to anyone else, and using them as clues to an outside reality, the physiologist is looking at them as objects . . . The mind then can be described as the meaning of the brain, as a functioning whole can be seen as the meaning of its parts. Thus it is a different thing from the brain, though not a separately existing thing.[47]

This trend among certain writers to see the soul or mind emerging from the complex organization of matter which comprises the human brain is placed in a wider context by E. L. Mascall. He accepts the basic logic of the position but interprets the process of emergence as being defensible only if matter is seen to exist and evolve within an environment which is characterized by the presence of spirit:

> To suppose merely that men's material body has been spiritualised, in the sense of being endowed with new capacities without being assumed into union with an existant of a higher order than matter, is to make man different only in degree from the beasts and quite inadequate as an interpretation of the great biblical declaration that God has made man in his own image.[48]

He concludes: 'In man . . . matter has reached the point at which, through its assumption by spirit, it has become conscious of itself.'[49] For the theologian it is, of course, essential that belief in the human soul is seen within both the context of biblical revelation and the greater concept of the nature and character of God.

A useful corrective to speculative thought has been supplied by Professor John Montgomery in the symposium *Birth Control and the Christian*.[50] In arguing for an open-minded approach to the whole subject, he writes:

Though there is much scriptural evidence on behalf of the holistic view, there are, at the same time, not only passages in which a 'faculty' approach is taken to man's nature but – even more important – passages clearly showing that the soul can be separated from the body and that it is capable of existence after the body's dissolution.[51]

He also cities a list of biblical references illustrating the points just made.[52] Richard Swinburne, more recently, has put forward a persuasive case for the existence of the soul which may be adapted to support the theory of emergence.[53]

Problems with equating soul and mind

If we argue that it is the presence of the human soul which determines that a human person is present, then we are left with a number of possible answers to the question: when does the soul, and hence the person, come into existence?

Dualists tend to follow a creationist argument and state that God creates souls *ex nihilo* and infuses them into developing embryos either at the time of conception or at some stage during gestation. We have already seen that dualism is unacceptable on theological grounds, and in any case it fails to indicate when the soul and body are united. It is, therefore, of no use in our investigation.

Reductionism is, similarly, a dead end, and endangers the humanity of babies as well as of embryos and fetuses.

A theory of emergence is a better indicator for the creation of the soul, understood as mind, and better reflects the holistic view of the Scriptures regarding human nature. It does, however, provide us with a further problem in evaluating the status of the embryo.

If we argue that it is the mind that makes an entity human, and that the mind emerges from the brain, though it is not the same as the brain, then an embryo cannot have a mind before brainwaves can be detected. Thus, an early embryo cannot have a mind, though some may argue that a later embryo can.

The problem also exists of assessing the quality of embryonic, fetal or neonatal brain activity. In all these cases brain activity is so primitive as to give us little confidence that much if anything in the way of 'mind' exists. A baby cannot talk, think, or relate in a way that

110

is more advanced than many of the higher animals.

This point has been amplified by Peter Singer, who argues that rationality is the hallmark of the human species and that newborn babies and even young children do not possess this faculty. Since this is so, he argues that infanticide is not morally wrong even if the victim is as old as three years, provided that the child has not yet developed a sense of 'self' and a fear of death. Only if others will feel deprived by the child's death is a moral wrong committed. In practice, Singer is prepared to permit a law which prohibits the killing of children over one month old, but he asserts that this is for reasons of law enforcement and prudence rather than morality.[54]

Emergence is a correct understanding of the creation of the mind but it does land us in difficulties if we use the presence of mind to evaluate the status of the human embryo or child.

An alternative view of the soul

One way out of this problem is to assert that the human soul and human mind are two different things. While dualists and some advocates of emergence, such as Keith Ward, effectively equate soul and mind, it may be possible to argue that the mind is distinct from the soul, and so present a case for the existence of a soul in an embryo or fetus before the presence of a mind which emerges from brain function.

This is the position held by the Roman Catholic Church, whose understanding of the soul has been summarized by P. Bristow:

> The Church defines man's soul as 'the substantial form of the body'. The form here does not refer to the shape, precisely because the soul is spiritual, but rather to that which gives unity, as well as life and movement, to the person.[55]

The soul is said to possess the twin faculties of intellect and will, and to be the ultimate explanation of the unity of a human life.[56]

While this doctrine does manage to separate the soul and the mind in so far as the mind may be seen as posterior to the soul, it too is of limited value in assessing the status of the human embryo. Such a doctrine tells us nothing of when the soul comes into existence, a point already noted in our examination of Christian tradition. While it may be argued that the most fitting time for the animation of the body to take place is conception, it may also be argued that an equally suitable time would be the emergence of the primitive streak or even the first signs of brain activity. It may also be argued that we no longer need a concept of soul as the form of the body, since a case can be made for the assertion that what gives human beings their basic continuity and unity is their individual DNA.

This is not to say that the idea of the soul as the form of the body is entirely unhelpful, only that it is inadequate in expressing all that the term 'soul' can mean in Christian usage.

Conclusions

It is best to admit that the term 'soul' is an imprecise one, capable of bearing a number of meanings both within the Scriptures and in Christian thought. For our purposes none of its meanings can help to solve the problem of determining the status of the human embryo.

If, against our arguments, a dualist understanding of soul is adopted, this tells us nothing of when the soul comes into existence and hence nothing of the status of the embryo. If a theory of emergence is adopted and the soul equated with the mind, then we sacrifice the humanity of newborn babies and young children. If we assume that the soul is the form of the body, then we are unsure regarding the time when the soul is created and the body animated. Even if we follow a current emphasis in viewing 'soul and body not as names for two substances, but as referring to two levels at which the human person can be regarded',[57] we are no further on, for this does not tell us when the human person comes into existence.

To find a means of evaluating the status of the human embryo, therefore, we must look beyond the metaphysical argument of the meaning and existence of the soul. In other words, we have been following a *cul de sac* in our entire discussion of the soul. This is, of course, disappointing. It has also been necessary, since many Christians base their understanding of the human embryo on a belief that it is the presence of a soul that makes an embryo a human person. We have shown that such an argument cannot, in fact, produce the goods. It fails to deliver what it promised and so must be dismissed as being of no further use to us in our enquiry.

Contemporary discussion

Even when we turn to contemporary thought regarding the status of the human embryo, we cannot escape completely the issues we have been examining regarding the human soul. Some distinguished writers still attempt to answer the question of the status of the human embryo by referring to the emergence of the soul as the point at which an embryo becomes personally human. Keith Ward, for example, states quite bluntly:

> The soul is the subject of moral and rational consciousness, so it does not exist before consciousness begins . . . Thus it is most natural to say that the soul begins to exist in the human person, between 21 and 42 days after conception, at that point when awareness dawns.[58]

By and large, however, there has been a shift in emphasis away from this sort of metaphysical understanding of the developing embryo. As we have already seen, this is not surprising, since the more one investigates the question of the human soul, the more obvious it becomes that it is not a helpful concept in evaluating the status of the human embryo. It is true that some writers still follow an essentially metaphysical line of reasoning even though they attempt to avoid doing so. Nevertheless, the contemporary debate is concerned less with trying to understand what might be present in a human embryo than with what can actually be observed. The real nub of the present debate is whether we can settle the question of the status of the human embryo by referring to functional aspects of human life, either actual or potential, or whether we ought to view the human embryo in less scientific and more dynamic terms.

This is an important point, for it marks a possible change in the way in which some theologians are beginning to view the whole issue of human development. If we accept that human personhood is tied inevitably to certain functions of either mind or body, then the argument really centres on whether or not the embryo possesses enough of these functions and characteristics to be viewed as a human being. If we reject this line of reasoning, however, different criteria must be found for determining the status of the embryo.

It may be that it is not possible to determine with any degree of certainty whether or not the embryo is a person, if we view the embryo from a functional or metaphysical standpoint. If this is so, we may argue that the status of the embryo is not correctly viewed in terms of personhood, as we experience it, but rather in terms of what it means to be an embryo. In other words, when we speak of personhood we are really using a term which describes us in our present states of consciousness and relationships. Such language may not be appropriate when talking about the human embryo, but that does not mean that the embryo should not be ascribed a status equal to ours. The embryo may not be a person, understood in functional terms, but that does not preclude it from being 'one of us'.

A flaw in much investigation of this subject is that writers have concentrated too much on certain human characteristics which in our minds constitute personhood. There is more, however, to humanity than personhood understood in functional terms. We need to see ourselves united both to the embryo and its humanity before birth, and to the deceased and their humanity after life. If God and his all-encompassing environment of care and love are taken seriously, then it is necessary for us to widen our perspective.

A functional understanding of humanity

Today, many who have abandoned any attempt to understand the embryo in metaphysical terms have chosen to view the embryo from a functional perspective. If we wish to argue that the embryo is a person, when viewed in this way, we must demonstrate that, at a certain point in the embryo's development, it has accumulated enough functional attributes to merit the status of a human person. Equally, we might argue that potential for such functional attributes constitutes sufficient grounds for crediting the embryo with human status from the beginning. If we abandon this line of reasoning altogether, then we can argue that the embryo may not be described as a human person in the same functional terms as an adult, but that it deserves equal status with adults because it is in its own right a personal human being of value and dignity.

Some, who take a functional approach to the subject of human personhood, argue that the embryo becomes a person at that point in its development when brain activity is present. This may be seen as indicating a point some fourteen days into gestation when the primitive streak appears, or a point some six weeks into gestation when primitive neural activity may be observed. Embryos which have not achieved this level of development may be of some moral value, but they do not enjoy the status of persons.

Among those who take such an approach, it has become common to state that the moral significance of the human embryo is not much greater than that of the human gamete. Neither is a person, but both may, in certain circumstances, give rise to persons. In a review of the Warnock Report, Michael Lockwood states: 'There is, to be sure, another sense in which the embryo clearly is a potential person: it has the potential to give rise to a person.'[59] This potential, however, is seen as being no different from the potential inherent within a human gamete.

Among those who argue along these lines, the findings of embryologists are of prime significance. It is understandable that some turn to scientific experts to find the answer to the question: what is an embryo? R. G. Edwards, the Cambridge physiologist, has been responsible for much pioneering work in the whole field of embryology, and his opinions carry great weight. He has stated what has become the standard argument for those who take a purely functional approach to the question of human personhood and who do not believe that potential implies much moral importance. His comments deserve to be quoted at length:

What are the strengths and weaknesses of the absolutist case? The argument implies that 'life' begins at fertilization, but this is not true because life is continuous and patently begun biochemically in the oocyte long before this. This implication is also compromised by parthenogenesis, because ovulatory oocytes can be activated without fertilization, and develop into advanced fetal stages. Absolutists would not accept research on cleaving embryos after fertilization; one reason may be that once fertilization is breached, then there is no obvious point to defend during later embryology. But cleaving embryos are not sentient and are minute, so why should they be defended? Do absolutists fear that studying early human embryos would undermine the value of human life, or lead to abuses in the application of embryo research? The latter situation is the well-known 'camel's nose' argument and applies to virtually every human activity, not only fertilization *in vitro*. There does not seem to be much intrinsically valuable in an embryo being human. It will have a human karyotype and metabolism, but it does not possess any of the higher functions or senses of older fetuses, and could only make a biochemical response to other biochemical stimuli. An embryo is an embryo, not a fetus or a child. Another related defence offered by absolutists is the need to respect the individual genotype as established at fertilization, the basis of individuality. But this argument cannot be accepted either, because genotypes might be established long after fertilization, for example in twins, mosaics [where cells differ in their chromosome content] and chimaeras [organisms composed of genetically different tissues, formed as a result of cell mutation]. Moreover, a hydatidiform mole [a degenerative mass which forms in the womb, leading to the death of the embryo] or a choriocarcinoma [cancer of a fetal membrane] has a unique human genotype, but no-one can give any value to such a genotype or to the embryo before it transformed into these conditions. The absolutists' arguments are a full stop: they block any further reasoning of the balance between benefits and problems, so leaving serious clinical problems uncured.[60]

In spite of applying the less than fair appellation 'absolutists' to those who oppose his views, Edwards does present a strong argument against attributing human personhood to the human embryo on the basis of actual functional abilities.

Apart from dualists, who may argue that the fertilized ovum does have certain spiritual powers and functions, however, most people who argue for personal status for the embryo do so on the strength of the potential for functional abilities which the embryo has from its earliest moments. Usually, care is taken to state that this makes the embryo a person with potential rather than a potential person.

The issue has been presented concisely by Kevin Kelly:

> The question can be stated as follows: From the point of view of its intrinsic dignity, does a being with potency have the right to exactly the same level of respect and reverence as a being whose potency has been actualised?[61]

Those who follow Dr Edwards' reasoning would clearly answer negatively, but there are many who would reply in the affirmative.

The embryo's potential

J. Foster, in an essay entitled 'Personhood and the Ethics of Abortion', argued that potential is enough to secure actual personhood for the embryo. He states:

> A baby qualifies as a person in the morally relevant sense, in virtue of its potential to develop, mentally and/or spiritually, in a certain way. But this will commit us to recognising the fetus as a person right from conception. For since the fertilized egg has the potential to develop into the newborn baby, it has the potential to acquire whatever characteristics the baby has the potential to acquire.[62]

This argument shows the weakness in Edwards' approach, since it is difficult to argue from the actual mental or spiritual functions of a baby that it enjoys what we tend to think of as the important aspects of our existence which make us persons.

It may be countered, however, that this argument shows that we attribute personhood to babies not because of scientific reasoning, but because of sentiment or moral pressure. If we argue on purely scientific and functional grounds, then the actual personhood of the baby may be in question. The fact that most people recognize that it would be a monstrous thought to treat babies as less than persons indicates that this whole approach from science alone, which sees personhood as being the sum of certain functional attributes, is seriously flawed. Nevertheless, it is the approach that is taken most often both by those who wish to argue that the embryo is not a person and also by those who attempt to show that the human embryo is a person.

Peter Byrne allows that the argument from potential is necessary to safeguard the personhood of the newborn infant, if personhood is to be understood in functional terms. At the same time, he seeks to escape the conclusion reached by Foster above. He takes as his starting-point the medically fit human adult and argues that personhood should be attributed to such an individual. He then allows that this person in all stages of his development, regardless of temporary periods when certain functions normally associated with personhood may be absent, should be seen as the same person and hence credited full human status. This, he argues, is true of the person as a baby, as a comatose patient and as a fetus, but not as an embryo. The embryo is disqualified because

> If we consider the possibility that up to about fourteen days
> after fertilization the embryo can split and even re-unite again
> it is plausible to conclude that it is not yet the historical being
> that a person by definition is. There is not sufficient stability in
> the early embryo to count it as a human being.[63]

The argument is persuasive at a first reading, but on closer inspection it merely confirms the difficulties we encounter in constructing our arguments of personhood on a functional basis. Byrne agrees with Foster's argument, that potential is sufficient to attribute personhood to the human being at all stages of his development, but disagrees with him that the early embryo is the same human entity as the later person. In doing so, he leaves his case vulnerable to anyone who wishes to argue on the fundamental level that genetic correspondence is sufficient to guarantee both continuity of person and potential for personal attributes.

An approach based on the genetic constitution of the embryo is advocated, among many others, by G. B. Bentley:

> The embryo is genetically complete from the time of
> conception; the potentialities are all there from the beginning;
> and there is no break in the continuity of its subsequent
> development. All attempts to locate within the continum a
> point of transition from a pre-human to a human condition
> have been unconvincing.[64]

At this stage in the discussion we have returned to the point where we begin to determine the status of the embryo on purely scientific terms. But, as we have already seen, such an approach is fruitless since, when we view personhood in such functional terms, we cannot justify the personhood of the newborn child. It is only when we assume the personhood of the infant that we can begin to argue for the personhood of the fetus or embryo, but once we fall back on purely scientific arguments we become aware that this assumption is not scientifically valid. For this reason we have to look beyond the findings of science and beyond the functional approach to personhood to determine the status of the embryo.

We have already seen, however, that a purely scriptural approach does not provide us with all the answers we need. Discussions on Christian tradition and the existence of the soul have not resolved the issue. We need to find an approach which takes us beyond both science and metaphysics.

A *dynamic understanding of humanity*

Richard Higginson has expressed the issue we are grappling with in the following terms:

> The question of when life begins is susceptible of a straightforward factual answer. What is present from the moment of fertilization is unquestionably alive. It is an organism in the process of growth and development. And it is alive in a significantly different way from the pre-fertilization sperm and egg because (unlike either of those separately) it has the potential to develop into a creature whom we would all describe as a human person. Whether personhood should already be ascribed to the early embryo is a more open question, but it is not so much a moral judgement as an evaluative one . . . The word 'personhood' itself eludes precise or generally agreed definition. But what is fundamentally at stake is whether the embryo commands a status and deserves a respect comparable to that given to human persons outside the womb. In short, is status linked to attainment of a particular stage in the developmental process?[65]

Neither science nor metaphysics is able to provide us with an acceptable definition of personhood. Following Higginson's line of thought, however, it is possible to come to an understanding of the embryo which more accurately describes its status without first having to prove that it either is, or is not, a person understood in functional terms.

Professor Gareth Jones, as a scientist, argues for the human embryo to be evaluated not in terms of its actual or potential personhood alone but rather on the basis of what it is:

> A fetus is never 'half a person' any more than a child is 'half an adult'. Just as the child is on its way to adulthood, so the fetus

is on its way to actual personhood. In the same way as a child is not of less significance than an adult, although it is certainly different from an adult, so the fetus is not of less significance than the child (or adult).[66]

He continues his argument and evaluates the status of the human fetus in the following terms:

Fetuses are one of us; or perhaps more accurately they are the earliest versions of ourselves . . . Fetuses, therefore, have a value in, and of, themselves, just as we have a value in, and of, ourselves.[67]

This argument suggests that it is possible to view the human fetus, and by implication the human embryo, as being historically continuous with the adult it later becomes. We recognize that the embryo does not enjoy the same functional abilities as an adult. Nevertheless, its status as 'the earliest version' of the adult, who is accepted by all as being a person, is enough to assure it equal status with the adult. This argument also ensures that children are given the same status as adults. Here we are presented with an argument which upholds the personhood of the child without doing so on a purely functional basis. It also upholds the status of the embryo as being equal with that of a child or adult, without attempting to prove that the embryo is either the functional equivalent of the adult or the metaphysical union of body and soul which, for some, would guarantee its personhood.

The humanity of the embryo

This line of reasoning is brought to its logical conclusion by Oliver O'Donovan, whose thought displays a frustration with the functional approach to ascertaining the status of the human embryo. In 1973 he wrote:

At the point when the ovum is fertilized there is established an individual 'genotype' which controls all that is hereditary in the future child's career. From that point on, the loss of the embryo or fetus by any means is the loss of one who would have had a natural talent for doing things with his hands or for speculative

120

thought, would have been liable to hereditary disease at the age
of forty, or would have inherited grandmother's longevity.[68]

Writing eleven years later, O'Donovan emphasized the link between
the embryo or fetus and the later adult. Not only was the embryo the
forerunner of the adult, but both together constituted a single historical
entity: 'To speak of a person, then, is to speak of "identity"; that which
constitutes sameness between one appearance and another, and so makes
us beings with histories and names.'[69] He continued:

> A person is a substance, and a nature is the 'specific property' of
> a substance; it is not the case that to every nature there
> corresponds a person. In other words, the distinctive qualities of
> humanity are attributable to persons, not persons to the
> qualities of humanity.[70]

As a moral philosopher, O'Donovan was still unable to state that the
fetus or embryo was unambiguously personal, on purely philosophical
grounds. Rather, God's purpose in calling the embryo into being is the
determining factor; ultimately it is God who underwrites the personhood and status of the embryo:

> Unless we approach new human beings, including those whose
> humanity is ambiguous and uncertain to us, with the
> expectancy and hope that we shall discern how God has called
> them out of nothing into personal being, then I do not see how
> we shall ever learn to love another human being at all.[71]

In 1985 O'Donovan further argued that the status of the human
embryo could not be determined on functional grounds, but rather that
it should be treated as a person because personhood was essentially a
dynamic concept. This concept has meaning only when it is viewed in
terms of relationship either with other human persons or with God. His
arguments deserve to be examined at some length.

Central to O'Donovan's concept of the person is the idea that
personhood defies all attempts to pin it down and define it. As we have
already seen, we tend to accept our own personhood and the personhood
of others without really understanding what it is that we are accepting.
Once we try to define personhood in scientific or functional terms we

inevitably run into trouble. It is impossible to think of a functional definition of personhood which does not either sacrifice the personhood of the newborn infant, the comatose or the senile, or reduce personhood to the level of genetic investigation with the associated notion of reductionism. In pursuing a functional approach to personhood, we either deny personhood to children because they are incapable of rational thought, or we safeguard the personhood of the embryo at the cost of making human beings nothing more than expressions of biochemical structures.

O'Donovan attempts to escape from this impasse by reverting to a much simpler approach to personhood. We know ourselves to be persons and we accept others as persons because we identify in them and in ourselves a sameness or similarity which causes us to relate to others in a manner that suggests that we are equals. While ultimately it is God who guarantees that such is indeed the case, in most instances our natural responses indicate that we are encountering other persons. In the case of the embryo or fetus, O'Donovan's thought suggests that it is possible to argue that, in spite of appearances or even feelings to the contrary, we should accept the embryo as a fellow person. In the embryo we encounter something which is the same as ourselves, although at a different stage of development. The God-given sameness is there if we are prepared to discern it.

He could, perhaps, also have stated that the same vocation is given by God to the embryo as to the mature adult: to share in his life. We cannot think of God calling us in any way other than in a personal way, or to consider that there may be a time in our personal history when we were outside the call of God. Equally, we cannot accept that there is any distinctive discontinuity between ourselves as we are now and as we were in the womb. If God calls us into fellowship with himself from all eternity, then within the confines of our human existence there was never a time when God was not calling us. If he calls us, as the Christian faith asserts, then he must have called us, as well as the Old Testament prophets, while we were still in our mothers' wombs. This may be going further than O'Donovan, but it is the corollary of O'Donovan's thought.

Before moving on to view the implications of these suggestions, it is necessary to allow O'Donovan's views to be presented in his own words. Three extracts from an essay on personhood should suffice to indicate the train of his thought. He writes: 'In the first instance, then, there are no "criteria" of personhood by which a person could be recognised independently of, or prior to, personal engagement.'[72] In order to underline the failure of the functional or scientific approach, he goes on to assert:

> It is a category mistake to say that a new conceptus cannot be a person until there is brain activity; it is a category mistake to say that it must be a person because there is an individual genetic structure . . . For whatever criteria we take, we end up by reducing the notion of personhood to that one constituent of human functioning.[73]

Finally, in order to safeguard the status of the child and fetus from the earliest moment after conception, he argues from the evident continuity that exists between the embryo, fetus, child and adult:

> The scientific evidence about the development of the unborn child does not prove that the unborn child is a person because that cannot in principle be proved. We cannot accept any equation of personhood with brain activity, genotype, implantation, or whatever for that is to reduce personhood, which is known only in personal engagement, to a function of some observable criteria. However, what the scientific evidence does is to clarify for us the lines of objective continuity and discontinuity, so that we can identify with greater accuracy the ' beginning' of any individual human existence. It is, of course, a purely 'biological' beginning that biology discloses to us. How could it be otherwise? In adapting it as the sufficient ground of respect for the human being, we are not declaring that personhood is merely biological. We are, rather, exploring the presuppositions of personal commitment. The only ground we have for risking commitment in the first encounters with the new human being is biological appearance.[74]

As already mentioned, O'Donovan could have introduced the purely theological argument of human personhood being a gift from God, centred on God's call to us to enter into a life of fellowship with him, but he chose to rest his case.

Review of the debate

At this stage of our investigation it is useful to review briefly what we have established so far. Our analysis enables us to make a number of statements.

The Bible, while asserting the continuity between the embryo and the adult, and while speaking of God's call to those in the womb, cannot be used to settle the issue in a straightforward manner. The Bible passages normally used in this debate were originally not concerned with this issue and they are often of a poetical or ambiguous nature. Nevertheless, they do lend support to a view of the human embryo which sees it as personally human.

The evidence of Christian history indicates that the church has always upheld a high view of the embryo's status and has consistently opposed abortion, but the embryo, as distinct from the later fetus, has not always been ascribed personhood.

Any attempt to settle the issue on the metaphysical ground of the existence of the human soul is fraught with difficulties. None of the various interpretations of the term 'soul' helps us in deciding the status of the embryo. Either they are unable to indicate when animation takes place or they fail to view the soul or mind apart from the human brain which gives rise to it. If the latter is made the basis of personhood, however, the personhood not only of the embryo, but also of babies, the comatose, the senile and the mentally handicapped is at risk. In addition, the concept of the image of God, which must be central to personhood, is reduced to one attribute, namely rational thought.

Scientific and functional approaches to the issue either reduce human personhood to mere biology, and perhaps ultimately to absolute reductionism, or make rational thought the basis of personhood, with all the problems mentioned above coming once more to the fore.

The best approach to the problem is to take a more dynamic view of personhood. Personhood is a gift from God. It is based on God's call to us to enter into fellowship with him and can be discovered in others and in ourselves when we identify a common humanity among us. Because of the continuity between the adult and the embryo, there is no reason for assuming that, even from the earliest moments of human existence, we are dealing with anything other than an embryonic person who, given the right environment, will become the adult human person whom all will acknowledge as fully and personally human. God's call to fellowship, rooted in eternity, must extend to every moment of this individual's life; even to the earliest moments following conception. For this reason, even though the embryo is not a person in the same way as is an adult, he or she is still a person as an embryo and is deserving of the same respect, dignity and sanctity as any other member of the human race.

It may be objected that such an approach can appeal only to those of a religious disposition, and that Christians can have no hope of persuading others of the status of the human embryo by using this argument. In a sense this is true, but two further arguments can be made which strengthen the case for treating embryos as human persons.

In the first instance, the emphasis on continuity between the embryo and the later child or adult will be persuasive for some, even if the theological arguments are not accepted. Secondly, even if some wish to view the embryo as having only the potential to become a human person, understood in terms of a normally functioning human adult, they would view the human baby in the same way. An argument from potential, as long as a continuity is perceived between the embryo, the fetus, the child and the adult, is by no means to be dismissed out of hand. While this is a second-line argument from a Christian perspective, and should be used only to support the more important theological argument, it does, none the less, provide a useful point of agreement with some who would espouse a secular approach to the subject.

The image of God

Before attempting to apply these conclusions to the practical issues raised by the Warnock debate, it is necessary to take into account more fully the important biblical assertion that humanity is made in the image of God. While the Bible does not say how, or when, the image of God is given to individual human beings, it is important to examine whether anything in this doctrine either undermines or strengthens the conclusions we have reached. In a largely secular society, few are likely to be attracted to any conclusions based on the premise that human beings are made in God's image. For Christians, however, this belief is central to an understanding of the dignity of the human race. Consequently, it is important for us to explore the meaning of the term in some detail.

The Old Testament

The key verse in the Old Testament which gave rise to the distinctively Jewish and then Christian concept of humanity is Genesis 1:26: 'Then God said, 'Let us make man in our image, in our likeness, and let them rule . . .'[75] The Old Testament does not attempt to define this image, nor does it try to make a clear distinction between 'image' and 'likeness'. This is borne out in the Septuagint, where the translators usually translated ṣelem (image) by eikōn, but were also able to use morphē, homoioma or typos. 'Likeness' was translated homoioma or homoiosis.[76] Certainly, for the Greek writers, the terms 'image' and 'likeness' were interchangeable.

While no attempt to define the image is made in the Old Testament, there are indications of the implications of the term for Hebrew anthropology. It is clear from the Genesis passage both that the image separates humanity from other creatures and that it is the source of the human race's dominion over the rest of creation. Equally, because of the Hebrew belief that body and spirit were interjoined, there is truth in the idea that the author of Genesis 1:26[77] believed that the image was more than a spiritual likeness, but also was indicated in some visible, physical way.[78] The human body has a dignity of its own, akin to that of the human mind and spirit.

From Genesis 9:6, 'Whoever sheds the blood of man, by man shall his blood be shed; for in the image of God has God made man',[79] it is also clear that the image is universal and that it existed after the fall. It has also prompted one author, R. S. Anderson, to make the following reflection regarding the status of human life (an important point for us):

> Why is murder such an affront to both God and man? Because it is an affront to the *imago Dei* which is present as embodied humanity. God does not pronounce a judgement on murder because it involves the killing of a creature, but because we encounter the *imago Dei* in other persons in any act which affects their own existence in the world.[80]

He continues: 'My abstract obligation to humanity as a moral responsibility is primarily determined by my concrete and specific encounter of the *imago* in the other.'[81]

This concept of the dignity and status of humans being fundamentally determined by the image of God is an important one in our attempt to evaluate the human embryo. If it can be demonstrated that the image is to be found in the human embryo, then any destruction of it or experimentation on it ought to be opposed.

The New Testament

The teaching of the New Testament regarding the image of God has been summarized as follows:

> The word 'image' is used in three main senses in the New Testament: firstly to describe Christ's singular dignity and divine sonship; secondly to describe the likeness of God into which believers enter through faith in Christ; and thirdly to describe man's humanity. The third is marginal in the New Testament, and the second is the central one.'[82]

The first meaning may be found in such passages as Colossians 1:13–18 and Hebrews 1:3. Examples of the second usage include Romans 8; 2 Corinthians 3:18 and 1 Corinthians 15:49. The third meaning, which corresponds most closely to the Old Testament use of the term, is found in James 3:9 and 1 Corinthians 11:7. As can be seen from these references, not only does the New Testament use the term in different ways, but St Paul is quite happy to employ different meanings of the term depending on the context in which he is writing.

We are presented, therefore, with a dual understanding of how the image of God is to be found in humanity, alongside the assertion that Jesus is the image of God in its fullness. The twin ideas that the image is something which every human being has and that it is something to which believers are conformed by their union with Christ do not easily conflate into one coherent theology. In order to examine the concept further, we must now turn to theologians' treatment of the term and the dual way in which it is presented in the Bible. Of particular interest to us will be whether or not theologians have seen the image as something spiritual, something mental or something which is known only in relationship with God and others who bear his image.

Irenaeus, Clement and Athanasius

Reviews of the doctrine of the image of God customarily begin with Irenaeus. He was the first theologian to develop the concept as a central part of his understanding of humanity and his understanding of salvation. He also made a sharp distinction between the ideas of 'image' and of 'likeness'.[83] As we have already noted, the biblical evidence does not favour this distinction, but Irenaeus set in motion a train of thought which was to be pivotal in the church's understanding of the human race. For Irenaeus, the likeness was lost at the fall, but the image remains in all human beings. The image of God was viewed in two ways: as rational free will and as physical body.[84] All human beings share these things and so have the image of God. Likeness means spiritual likeness and is imparted by the indwelling Spirit who creates or activates our spirits.

In this theology Irenaeus safeguarded the idea that all human beings are made in the image of God. He did so, however, by interpreting the image as rationality expressed in a human body. Equally, he made an artificial distinction between image and likeness at the expense of ignoring the dual way in which the image is spoken of in the Scriptures.

Clement of Alexandria used the terms 'image' and 'likeness' in an unsystematic manner. At times, he made no distinction between the two, and seems to have held that both were universal in the human race. At other times, without distinguishing image from likeness, he argued that they were not universal, but rather were to be found only in Christ. At still other times, he indicated that a Christian receives the image at baptism and assumes the likeness of God during the process of sanctification. On some occasions, however, Clement approaches Irenaeus in his treatment of the terms by suggesting that the image is to be equated with rationality and is universal, while 'likeness' is a character resemblance to God and is found in Christ and in union with Christ.[85]

Athanasius marked an attempt to return to a discussion of the image rather than a discussion of the distinction between image and likeness. His understanding of the term suggested that it meant more than rationality, but he also believed that it was lost at the fall. Only in Christ may the image be restored, since he is the image of God and we share in his life.[86] Only Christians had the image of God. This not only ignored Genesis 9:6, but also removed the fundamental distinguishing feature between human beings and the rest of creation.

Augustine and Aquinas

Augustine sought to find a definition of the image of God which took as its starting-point the nature of God rather than the nature of humanity. The definitive feature of God's nature which he chose was God's trinity of one essence, three equal persons. If humanity was made in the image of God, then it too must be able to display an immortal trinity within its nature. Augustine found this trinity within the human mind. 'The mind remembers, understands, and loves itself; if we discern this, we discern a trinity, not yet indeed God, but now at last an image of God.'[87] Once more the image has become a universal element in the human race, though it has become associated with the human mind and its rational powers.

Augustine also wrote that the human soul was 'made in the image of God in respect to this, that it is able to use reason and intellect in order to understand and behold God'.[88] Reason is again to the fore, though it is worth noting that a new element has been introduced: the idea of relationship. The image is not so much an abstract quality as something which enables a person to have a meaningful relationship with God. In introducing the concept of relationship, he opened the door to an understanding of the image which moved away from the centrality of rational thought and towards the soul in communion or relationship with God. In this respect Augustine anticipated much modern thought.

Aquinas represented the culmination of the church's first millennium of theological reflection. He built on the thought of Augustine and viewed the image as being essentially rational in character, but rational in relationship with God. On reflecting on the nature of the image of God, he wrote:

> Some things are like God first and most generally inasmuch as
> they exist, some inasmuch as they have life, and a third class
> inasmuch as they have mind or intelligence . . . it is clear,
> therefore, that intellectual creatures alone, properly speaking,
> are made in God's image.[89]

Aquinas underscored the importance of rationality for an understanding of the image of God in humanity. In so doing he made the image universal, or almost so, since it is not clear how much 'mind' a person has to have before he can properly be said to possess the image of God.

In the context of our investigation into the status of the human embryo, it is clear that, if the image of God is equated with rational thought, the human embryo cannot bear God's image and so is less than human. This would contradict our argument so far and would undermine the view of the embryo gained from our biblical survey. The understanding of the image as possession of rational faculties was most prevalent in the first millennium of Christian thought. Importantly for our study, other interpretations began to displace it.

Luther and Calvin

For Luther, the concept of the image was not artificially divorced from the idea of the likeness of God. Luther did not define the image as such, but he did argue that 'this likeness [universal image] remains under sin up till now; the Fall did not take this likeness from Adam; that likeness, goodness and justice, sin did remove.'[90] A universal image safeguarding man's dignity and divine destiny was thus preserved by Luther but this was a shadowy thing without any real effect on man's moral or spiritual character.

Adam and Eve's original knowledge of God was the real context for the image of God in humanity. With that knowledge gone, until it is restored in Christ, the residual image is powerless to promote ethical or spiritual good.

> We have only the blunted, and as it were dead, relics of their knowledge. Other animals lack it entirely . . . Thus though that image is almost wholly lost, there is a very great difference between man and other animals.[91]

Luther believed strongly in the need for the image to be restored in Christ, but he could not bring himself to argue that the image was entirely lost in the unregenerate. What was lost was the substance of the image, that which gave it its spiritual and moral content.

Luther, then, gave humans a status which was above the animals, and insisted that the grounds for this exalted status was the image of God, but he also argued that the image should have a moral and ethical quality which did not belong universally to the human race.

Calvin approached the topic of the image of God in humanity from a perspective similar to Augustine's. He began with God rather than humanity, and saw the image of God first in terms of God's endowment of humanity rather than as a universal attribute of the human race. For Calvin, the image of God cannot be said to be present in a person unregenerated by the Holy Spirit. He expressly states: 'Since the image of God has been destroyed in us by the Fall, we may judge from its restoration what it originally had been.'[92] He goes on to say that the image may be understood only in terms of our characters being transformed in relationship with God into something akin to God's own character.

Calvin was insistent that the image of God was lost at the fall, and so the natural status of humanity is no better, indeed it is even worse, than the status of other creatures.

> When man is considered in himself and his nature, what can we say? Here is a creature cursed of God which is worthy of being rejected from the ranks of all creatures, worms, lice, fleas and vermin; for there is more worth in all the vermin in the world than in man, for he is a creature where the image of God has been effaced and where the good which He has put in it is corrupted.[93]

Again he writes: 'When I say that all mankind is polluted, my meaning is, that we bring nothing from our mother's womb but mere filthiness in our nature.'[94]

At the same time Calvin did believe that humanity was more important than the rest of the animal kingdom: 'But scripture . . . tells us that we are not to look to what men themselves deserve, but to attend to the image of God in them.'[95] This apparent contradiction in Calvin's thought may be eased by a brief examination of his treatment of Genesis 9:5-7. In this passage he argues that human beings do have a special dignity unique in creation, but that this dignity is not a ground for moral boasting, but is rather a gift from God. This gift cannot depend upon a human response to God's creation or love, and so must be related to the image of God in humanity. The standpoint of Calvin may be summarized as stating that only regenerate human beings have the image of God actually within them, but since humanity was created in order to bear the image of God, all are to be afforded a special dignity. This is so, since it cannot be known who may or may not bear the image at a subsequent stage in their lives. The image is restored only to the elect in Christ, so that for some the Old Testament image is a prelude to salvation, while for others it is only a prelude to damnation. From a human perspective, however, it cannot be ascertained who is elect and who is not, especially before God's Spirit makes a person regenerate. Thus, all are to be treated with the same special dignity by fellow human beings.

Calvin removed the universal nature of the image but he did not remove the moral implications of the belief that the image is universal. What is more, he managed to expand the idea of the image beyond the powers of rationality, making it both an ethical and spiritual image which is found only in relationship with Christ.

Twentieth-century theology: Brunner and Barth

The seminal figure in the development of the concept of the image of God in humanity, this century, was Emil Brunner. This is so both because of the merit and scope of his own work, and also because of the influence this work had on the thinking of Karl Barth.

Writing about the Old Testament image of God and its echo in the New Testament, Brunner argued that

> . . . the original image of God in man is destroyed, that the
> *iustitia originalis*, and with it the possibility of doing, or even
> willing what counts before God as good, and consequently the
> freedom of the will, is lost.[96]

He also recognized that the most common New Testament interpretation of the image of God in humanity refers to humans being conformed to God's character:

> The presupposition of this, New Testament, *imago* doctrine in
> contrast to the Old Testament doctrine, is that man's existence
> in the image of God is lost, that man must be restored to it, so
> that the whole reconciling and redemptive work of Christ can
> be comprehended in this central concept of renewal and
> perfection of God's image in man.[97]

If there seems to be a contradiction here (that Brunner is implying that the Old Testament image is destroyed but not completely lost), his thought is more clearly expressed when he writes:

> Even as a sinner, man can only be understood as one created originally in God's image – he is the man who lives in contradiction to that image. We must not forget that when we speak of an image of God and its destruction we are using a figure of speech. What we can say in clear terms is this, that the relationship to God which determines the whole being of man is not annihilated by sin but perverted. Man does not cease to be a being responsible to God, but his responsibility is changed from a life of love to a life under the law, a life under the wrath of God.[98]

Brunner is close to the old idea of a 'relic' of the image remaining in man while the substance of the image can be seen only in the lives of those who are in Christ. He does, however, manage to introduce a new concept: that of the image as responsibility, initially to God but also to others. This responsibility is known only in relationship, and it goes beyond the mere attainment of rationality.

Brunner's reconciliation of the dual aspect of the biblical understanding of the image of God may be discerned in the following reflections:

> We make a distinction of category; formally the image is not infringed upon even in the least degree – whether he sins or not, man is a subject and responsible. Materially, the image is completely lost, man is a sinner through and through, and there is nothing in him which is not stained by sin.[99]

Unable to relegate humanity completely, however, he also wrote: 'No one . . . can deny that there is such a thing as a point of contact for the divine grace of redemption. This point of contact is the formal *imago Dei* which not even the sinner has lost.'[100] This attempt to salvage something of the image of God in all human beings led Brunner to clash with Barth, who pursued his own understanding of the term.

Like Brunner, Barth viewed the image very much in terms of relationship. He saw the nature of humanity, expressed in both male and female, as being pivotal in an understanding of the image. The image is seen in terms of 'I and Thou' in confrontation.[101] It did not consist 'in any particular thing that man is or does. It is constituted by the very existence of man as such, and as a creature of God. He would not be man if he were not God's image. He is God's image inasmuch as he is man.'[102]

Barth's reasoning is not easily followed, but he appears to be saying that Jesus is true humanity, and in him we see the image of God; now that we know what the image of God is, we can ask: does humanity have this image? Barth saw every human being as belonging to God and as the object of Christ's redemptive act wrought in history.[103] Humanity is elect in Christ to be human. It is because of this election in Christ, and not because of any 'natural' endowment or moral characteristic, that humanity has the image and so may be a recipient of God's grace. In agreement with Calvin, it is Christ's work in humanity that is the important factor. Barth, however, believes in an actual image present in all because of humanity's universal election in Christ to be human. He rejects Calvin's concept of treating people as if they bear the image even though time may prove that they have not.[104] For Barth, sin may hide the true nature of humanity, as elect in Christ, but it cannot destroy it. God's grace reveals the true God-given nature of humanity and brings it to perfection.[105]

Barth's understanding of the image restores it to all people as an actual reality, but only because of their election in Christ, not because of any 'natural' quality enjoyed by human beings in their own right. The image of God is discerned in relationship with God and with others who bear the image. It manifests itself as we recognize our neighbours as real human beings, as we engage in real dialogue with them, as we help them and as we do all this gladly.[106] Barth developed the concept beyond the mere appropriation of a rational nature. He gave all people equal status as God's image-bearers, and argued that this image is known in relationship.

The image of God and the status of the human embryo

What, then, are the implications of the doctrine of the image of God for our study? The main issues can be stated briefly as a series of related questions.

Fundamentally, are all persons made in the image of God or may this be said only of Christians? Is the image of God really to be equated with our minds and, consequently, is it dependent upon brain function? Is it a spiritual endowment which results in persons being transformed into the ethical and personal likeness of God? Is it to be understood in terms of human beings' ability to relate to God and each other in a personal and meaningful way? Some of these possibilities are not, of course, mutually exclusive, but much depends on where we place our emphasis.

The scriptural evidence does suggest that all persons are made in God's image, but it also asserts that it is the work of the Holy Spirit to transform those in Christ into the image of God. Any theology which denies that all are made in God's image ignores part of the biblical evidence. Equally, any concept which states that all are not made in God's image, but that we should treat them as if they are, is not quite honest or rigorous enough. The idea of a relic of the image remaining in human beings is not helpful, since it is the image of God which gives human beings their particular status; a relic of the image is insufficient to do this.

We are left with two choices. Either the term is used in two (or three) quite separate ways and there is little point in trying to harmonize them, or Barth is right in seeing all humanity as being elect in Christ in order that they may live as human beings and so share God's image. Either way, we must hold to the belief that all are made in God's image. Barth's understanding of the term therefore deserves closer examination.

If we follow Barth's line of reasoning that Jesus is the image of God incarnate, then it is surely logical to argue that the only way of defining the nature of the image is to look at the person of Jesus. In particular, we must look at those aspects of his human nature which made him definitive humanity.

The possession of a rational nature is an important part of most people's lives, but how is this to be defined or measured? People are more than the sum of their rational faculties, while rationality differs widely from individual to individual, to such an extent that some persons are barely more rational than the higher animals. In any case, it is not in his rationality that Jesus impresses us as being definitive humanity, even though he possessed perfectly good powers of reason.

It is in Jesus' relationship with God that we see his distinctiveness. It is in his call by God to be the Suffering Servant, the Messiah, the obedient Son, the Lord of the church, that his distinctiveness is shown and the image of God made plain. This is the source of his human ethical and spiritual likeness to God. This relationship with God necessarily involves relationship with others. If our possession of God's image is dependent upon Jesus and our election as a species in him, then the image can only mean an endowment by God of a relationship with him and with others. This relationship is given by God even though it may be ignored or nurtured or even twisted and abandoned wilfully by those who choose to reject their election.

Wolfhart Pannenberg writes: 'From the theological perspective "to be like God" describes not only the striving proper to sin but also the divine destiny by which human beings are to participate in God as his images.'[107] He continues:

> The Bible uses the concept of image of God to describe this human destiny; in the belongingness to God, which sets human beings apart, it sees the special dignity which makes human beings inviolable and grounds the prohibition against taking their lives (Gen. 9.6). The invocation of God's rights as the divine Majesty makes the inviolability of human dignity immune against human caprice.[108]

What all this means for our investigation is that all humans are made in God's image. This image is not to be found in the development of brain function, but is rather to be discovered in a God-given relationship with himself and with others, in his call to humanity to enter into fellowship with him. The essential nature of humanity depends on God, not on human development.

Our investigation into the use of the term 'image of God' serves to underline our opinion that embryos owe their distinctive status to God's calling of them into fellowship with himself. The call of God to humanity embraces all humanity and, as we have seen, embryos are human even if they do not enjoy many of the functional attributes enjoyed by adults. Embryos are, therefore, bearers of God's image, the ultimate status any creature can be given, and hence must be treated with the same respect and dignity as any other members of the human race.

Conclusions

Our examination of the status of the human embryo has led us to argue that the embryo must be treated in principle in the same way as a fetus, a child or an adult. The status of the embryo is dependent upon the nature of God and his call of the human race into fellowship with him. Functional abilities and metaphysical speculations are not deciding factors in our assessment of the embryo.

This means that Christians have an essentially theological basis for their understanding of the human embryo and that their ethics regarding its treatment are also theologically based. How then does this affect a Christian evaluation of the Warnock debate?

First, there is nothing wrong in saying that Christians think theologically and that the human embryo is defined, as are all things, primarily in a theological context. We do not expect all to accept this reasoning, but we should hold to it regardless. We ought to emphasize that the human embryo is to be treated, in principle, with the same respect as a human child or adult.

Secondly, our insistence that the embryo is the earliest form of us, and that it is continuous with the later child and adult, is one which many who do not share our theological convictions find acceptable. This insistence can be made into an argument based on the shared potential of the embryo, fetus and child to become a human adult. Here is one source of common ground with others in society.

Thirdly, our emphasis on a dynamic understanding of humanity rather than a functional or metaphysical understanding will be welcomed by others also. The failure of functional arguments to safeguard the humanity of the newborn, the comatose, the senile and the mentally handicapped is important even if the theological basis for our argument is not accepted. Presenting people with a challenge to recognize humanity in the weak, the shattered, the unformed and the malformed will strike a chord with some where arguments based on scientific measurements will fail.

This is not to say that all will accept our position. It is, none the less, defensible, it is worth promoting and in it we can find common ground with the rest of society. Unfortunately, in the Warnock debate Christian submissions seldom prepared the ground sufficiently regarding the status of the embryo, but rather were too hasty in stating their opinions and making various recommendations regarding the activities under review.

5

Sexual ethics

The status of the human embryo is undoubtedly the central issue in any debate on human fertilization and embryology. There are, however, other important concerns that we must not overlook. Under the general heading of sexual ethics, we can explore a range of related topics.

We must examine the important issue of fertility. Is fertility a blessing from God, a basic human right or a command which God expects us to obey? Our answer will help us to determine what controls, if any, there should be on the treatment of infertility.

Equally important is the question of the place of the family in the treatment of infertility. In particular, what is the role of sexual intercourse within the marriage bond? It may be the case that certain treatments for infertility, while being successful at a medical level, are likely to cause injury to the family unit as a whole or to the place of the family in society. It may also be the case that certain infertility treatments create an environment in which the marital bond is compromised, or at least weakened. If so, this will have implications for the way in which the family and marriage are likely to evolve, at a legal level at least, within our society. An investigation of these topics will also help us to see which treatments should be subject to legislation and which should be left to individual moral choice.

The Old Testament

The pivotal scriptural reference here is the creation decree that the human race was to 'be fruitful and multiply'.[1] There is little doubt that this statement constitutes a command of God to the human race. Indeed, within Judaism, this saying is deemed to be the first of the 613 commandments of the law.[2] It is also clear that the command is given to the whole human race.

This does not mean, however, that God intends every individual to procreate, since it is God's will that certain people should remain single. Such people, including Jesus, can hardly be said to be breaking one of God's commandments! The Genesis command is certainly a statement of God's will for the human race, but it need not be seen as a command for every individual. What it does indicate is that God expects humans to survive and prosper as a species, and that within that plan most people will be involved in procreation. We would be overstating the case, therefore, to suggest that fertility is an absolute command given to every person or even to every couple.

It makes even less sense to speak of fertility as a basic human right. On what theological basis can such a statement be made? While it may be acceptable for us to speak of certain rights regarding the way in which we expect humans to treat one another, how can we speak of God owing us anything?

It is reasonable to believe that God wishes to give the gift of fertility to every married couple. We can argue with conviction that God intends every member of the human race to be healthy and to enjoy the gift of life to the full. We may also contend that it is a necessary duty of the medical profession to attempt to alleviate infertility, but all of this falls short of saying that every human person can demand fertility as a basic human right. Such language is foreign to Christian theology, since it runs counter to the essential Christian position that all that is good in life is a sign of the grace of God.

If then, the creation command in Genesis is neither to be interpreted as a commandment applicable to every individual or every couple, nor to be seen as sanctioning the belief that fertility is a basic right, how should we view fertility?

One answer is that it is a gift from God. This view finds support in the scriptural statements that children are given to us by God and that fertility is a reward from God.[3] While this statement need not mean that

God chooses certain individuals and rewards them with the gift of children because he favours them more than others, it does place the whole issue of fertility in a new context. Children are God's gift to the human race and can be seen as part of the blessings which stem from being his special creation made in his image. Even though many people in the Old Testament world saw fertility as an indication of God's particular favour, and infertility as an indication of God's displeasure, this need not be seen as the basic principle behind the Old Testament view of fertility.

This idea of fertility as a gift from God, which couples were expected to accept positively, runs throughout the Old Testament. The importance of childbirth is evident as is also the distress of couples who were unable to have children. The stories of Sarah and Abraham, Rebecca and Jacob, and Hannah and Elkanah all show the pain caused by infertility as well as an acknowledgment that fertility was a gift from God and not something which was theirs by right.[4] The fact that some of the women in these stories believed that God had chosen to make them infertile should not detract from the essential point that all fertility is a gift from God. We may disagree with their belief that God caused illness, while accepting that in enabling them to have children God was giving them the gift of fertility which he always intended them to enjoy.

The New Testament

In the New Testament the same basic attitudes are evident. The birth of John the Baptist has similarities with the stories cited above.[5] The same anguish caused by infertility is evident, as is the belief that in giving a son to Elizabeth and Zachariah, God was bestowing on them the gift of fertility. Again, we should note that while this gift was given as part of God's plan for the coming of the Messiah, this does not mean that it is any less a gift when it is given more usually as part of normal health. Equally, God's desire to restore fertility to Elizabeth and Zachariah indicates that it is a correct thing for medical science, within ethical limits, to attempt to restore fertility to couples today. What those ethical limits are is, of course, a matter for further discussion.

The teaching of Jesus on celibacy does not alter the impression already gained from other scriptures.[6] Voluntary celibacy, as part of a vocation, does not undermine the fact that fertility is a gift. Paul's exhortation that in some circumstances celibacy is preferable to marriage does not change the principle either.[7] At the same time the curious statement that women will be saved through child-bearing[8] shows the importance of the gift, but it cannot mean that those unable to exercise the gift of fertility are beyond salvation!

The overall impression gained from the Scriptures, then, is that, while fertility is not a God-given command to every individual, it is a command given to the human race as a whole. Only God can give the gift of fertility, which he normally does as part of his blessings to all members of the human race. Where, because of genetic or other illness, an individual or a couple is infertile, they should not think that a basic right has been denied them, but that God's gift has been compromised by medical or other circumstances. Because fertility is a gift and not a right, it is correct to seek to alleviate infertility within Christian ethical limits. Had fertility been a human right, then it could be argued that the alleviation of infertility should have little or no limits. Such is the importance of fertility, both as an expression of God's will for the human race, and as an expression of an individual's personal aspirations, that enabling couples to enjoy the gift of fertility should be high on the list of priorities in Christian medical and social concern.

Contemporary issues

The biblical principles outlined above are relatively easy to grasp. It is much more difficult to see how we ought to apply these principles to the myriad of real-life situations which face scientists, doctors and counsellors as well as individuals or couples seeking treatment for infertility. Fortunately, others have walked this path before us and we can turn to them for help.

In the course of the debate on human fertilization and embryology certain pivotal Christian documents have emerged. These documents, or the arguments they express, come to the fore again and again. Three in particular deserve our attention. They are important not only because of what they say but also because of the influence they had on the debate which surrounded the Warnock Report. The documents, representing respectively the Roman Catholic Church, the major Protestant churches in Great Britain, and the Church of England are *Humanae Vitae* (1968), *Choices in Childlessness* (1979), and *Personal Origins* (1985).

Humanae Vitae

Even though this document was written in 1968 before the immediate concerns of the Warnock debate were evident, it is still of fundamental importance. It mapped out the basic Roman Catholic position not only in regard to the status of the human embryo[9] but also in regard to that church's understanding of fertility, marriage and the essential relationship between parents and children. All subsequent official papers presented by the Roman Catholic Church in Great Britain have been careful not to go beyond the boundaries set by this important document.

The first thing to strike a reader of *Humanae Vitae* is that it is not an academic, theological treatise. It is addressed primarily to pastors, teachers, medical staff, politicians and married couples.[10] Its language is straightforward and its arguments direct and simply stated. Nevertheless, it represents the single most important document to have been produced by the Roman Catholic Church this century in the field of fertility and the transmission of life.

Fertility

Fertility is seen as being both a gift from God and also something which is necessarily part of married love. Quoting from the Second Vatican Council, the document states: 'Marriage and married love are by their character ordained by the procreation and bringing up of children. Children are the outstanding gift of marriage, and contribute in the highest degree to the parents' welfare.'[11] It recognizes that not all married couples are able to enjoy the gift of fertility, but this does not alter the God-given character of marriage and the relationship between marriage and procreation.[12] It is God's will that married couples should seek children as part of the order of his creation,[13] and it is unlawful to attempt to preclude procreation using artificial methods.[14]

It is the task of scientists to assist the natural laws which God has ordained. This means that a better understanding of the body's rhythms and cycles will help some couples to limit the size of their families by natural birth control. It does not indicate that there is any conflict with the church's teaching that artificial means of contraception are unlawful. Again, *Humanae Vitae* echoes the Second Vatican Council: 'There can be no contradiction between two divine laws – that which governs the transmitting of life and that which governs the fostering of married love.'[15]

Procreation, then, is a gift from God. *Humanae Vitae* also comes close to seeing it as a divine command given to every married couple. Because of the problems of infertility, the responsibility to have children is not an absolute law, but it is clear that the Roman Catholic Church expects every married couple to intend to have children. Marriage and procreation are, together, a central part of God's plan for the human race.

The sacrament of marriage

Humanae Vitae affirms that marriage is a sacrament. Through it, God speaks to the world of his love. Marriage is also a principal means by which God establishes his loving design in the world. God is the Father of the human race 'from whom every family in heaven and on earth is named'.[16] Therefore, married couples are to reflect God's love and help to bring God's design into the world. This means that

> . . . as a consequence, husband and wife, through the mutual gift of themselves which is specific and exclusive to them alone, seek to develop that kind of personal union in which they complement one another in order to co-operate with God in the generation and education of new lives.[17]

The relationship between marital love and procreation is based not on personal desire or expediency but on principle. Because God has given marriage as a gift, he alone orders how the gift is to be used. This principle is spelt out in unmistakable terms:

> This particular doctrine, often expounded by the Magisterium of the Church, is based on the inseparable connection, established by God which man on his own initiative may not break, between the unitive significance and the procreative significance which are both inherent to the marriage Act.
> The reason is that the marriage Act, because of its fundamental structure, while it unites husband and wife in the closest intimacy also brings into operation laws written into the actual nature of man and woman for the generation of new life.
> And if each of these essential qualities, the unitive and procreative, is preserved, the use of marriage fully retains its

143

sense of true mutual love and its ordination to the supreme
responsibility of parenthood to which man is called.[18]

In other words, the union between the unitive and procreative aspects of
sex is absolute.

Marriage and contraception

The most controversial aspect of the above argument is not so much the
principle itself as its detailed application. *Humanae Vitae* notes the
proposition that this principle should apply not to every act of sexual
union, but to married life as a whole,[19] yet it dismisses it as being
inadequate.[20] It does acknowledge that God has ordained naturally
infertile cycles so that it is not medically possible for every sexual act to
lead to procreation. Nevertheless, it argues that the intention of every act
of sexual union should be to enjoy both the unitive and procreative gifts
of marriage.[21] To do otherwise is to fail to use the gift of marriage in
accordance with the wishes of God. This is forcefully argued:

> . . . an act of mutual love which impairs the capacity to
> transmit life which God the Creator, through specific laws, has
> built into it, frustrates his design which constitutes the norms
> of marriage, and contradicts the will of the Author of Life.
> Hence, to use this divine gift while depriving it, even if only
> partially, of its meaning and purpose, is equally repugnant to
> the nature of man and woman, strikes at the heart of their
> relationship and is consequently in opposition to the plan of
> God and his holy will.[22]

Following on from this view of the proper use of the gift of sex, *Humanae
Vitae* also stresses the need for 'responsible parenthood'.[23] This term is
used to describe the conditions under which Christian parents may
properly exercise their parental duties. The 'objective moral order
instituted by God'[24] is to be the reference-point for Christian parenthood.
This means that duty to God, themselves and human society is part of
parental responsibility.[25] This has obvious implications for DI and other
techniques dealt with in the Warnock debate.

Responding to Humanae Vitae

The issues raised by *Humanae Vitae* are of the utmost importance in our investigation of human fertilization and embryology. We can certainly agree that marriage is a gift from God and that Christian married couples must exercise their privileges and responsibilities under his guidance and direction. Other aspects of *Humanae Vitae* are, however, more controversial.

The belief that marriage is a sacrament and plays a sacramental role within the created order is an attractive one. Christian marriage and family life are, by virtue of their God-given nature, a means whereby God expresses and expands his rule of order and discipline in the world. We must be careful, though, that we do not isolate marriage from other ways in which God speaks to society. While Christian couples and families must play their part in forming the basis of an orderly society, it is putting too much stress on marriage to claim that it is the chief means whereby God communicates his rule to the world.[26]

As we shall see in our examination of the other documents under review, not all Christians believe that all married couples are called to become parents. While it is undoubtedly true that this has been the orthodox position of the church through the ages, it can reasonably be argued that the very thought of voluntary childlessness is such a modern one that the church has never before had to examine the subject in any depth. The validity of this argument is diminished, however, by acknowledging that the Roman Catholic position is based not on matters of expediency or culture but on the central principle of the indivisible union between the procreative and unitive aspects of sex.

Humanae Vitae interprets this principle to mean that every act of sex must, in the intention of the couple involved, be an act in which both the unitive and the procreative aspects of marriage are present in an unimpaired fashion. While this view certainly does give children and the gift of fertility a very high status, it also gives sexual intercourse a central, if not in fact controlling, role within marriage. This is significant in two regards.

First, if every act of love must be both unitive and procreative, then fertility becomes an essential part of married life. This must mean not only that voluntary childlessness is an un-Christian mode of living, but also that those who are involuntarily childless are in some sense incomplete in regard to their marriage. While *Humanae Vitae* does not, of course, imply any moral censure on such couples, it must surely be interpreted to mean that a marriage without children is a marriage that has to some extent failed in the role God gave it. While the couple involved may not be morally guilty of any misconduct, it is difficult to see how such a couple could feel free of such feelings of guilt. If fertility is a necessary part of marriage, rather than a desirable part, then infertile couples are inevitably going to feel less than fully married, if they take this particular view of Christian marriage to heart. It is better to see fertility as an important and desirable part of marriage which, in the normal circumstances of life, most married couples will be able to enjoy and should feel a responsibility to enjoy. In this way, if a couple is infertile their marriage is not seen to be compromised. The impression gained from *Humanae Vitae* is that this is the pastoral position the Roman Catholic Church would wish to espouse, but its teaching on the essential role which fertility plays within God's design for marriage contradicts this stance.

Humanae Vitae does allow for the use, by a Christian married couple, of the natural cycles of infertility which are part of God's created order. These, however, are to be seen as part of the normal cycle of fertility which is at the heart of marriage. The document prohibits any extension of these naturally infertile periods; it does not suggest that they form the basis for any belief that an infertile marriage is not a compromised marriage.

The second implication of the essential link made between the unitive and procreative aspects of marriage is that a sexual act must also be a unitive act as well as a procreative act. This has great relevance for some of the infertility treatments now available. DI, as currently practised, for example, is clearly not an act which can be seen as having any unitive aspects. To make every sexual act the focus of both the unitive and procreative aspects of marriage is also as unrealistic as it is unnecessary.

The stress placed on responsible parenthood in *Humanae Vitae* also militates against many infertility treatments such as DI, egg transfer and surrogacy. Given the Roman Catholic Church's attitude to the embryo and fetus, even IVF, with its corollary of spare embryos, is possibly deemed to be an irresponsible act. All Christians welcome responsible parenthood, but it cannot be guaranteed by making every sexual act both unitive and procreative. Equally, responsible people may be excluded from becoming parents by a blanket rejection of all the infertility treatments discussed in the Warnock debate.

Choices in Childlessness

Choices in Childlessness is the report of a working party which met under the auspices of the British Council of Churches and the Free Church Federal Council. It first met in 1979 and published its report in 1982. While in some respects it anticipated the concern of the Government in establishing the Warnock Committee, its brief was essentially pastoral rather than philosophical in character. Accordingly, many areas which became the concern of the Warnock Committee were not dealt with by the working party. Nevertheless, *Choices in Childlessness* examines some salient principles and makes a number of relevant recommendations.

Choices in Childlessness does not, of course, enjoy the status of *Humanae Vitae*. Unlike *Humanae Vitae*, it is not an authoritative document. Its goal is simple, being 'presented for the consideration of the churches in particular and of society in general'.[27] The report examines the whole area of infertility in some depth, but begins by recognizing the real human suffering caused by involuntary childlessness. This strong pastoral concern is evident throughout.

The report recognizes the Genesis command to be fruitful and multiply as being one of the first divine commands mentioned in the Bible, but places this statement in the context of an infertility rate in each generation of some 8%.[28] It also makes clear that any complete treatment of the subject of fertility must come to terms with voluntary childlessness, which has emerged in recent years as a very real option for many couples.[29] In this respect *Choices in Childlessness* reflects a change in the mood of society since the publication of *Humanae Vitae*. In 1968 the question of voluntary childlessness was not one which commanded great attention, since it was likely to affect only a fringe group within society. By 1982 society in Britain had changed markedly. Consideration of this topic was essential.

Wants, needs and rights

The report asks this pertinent question:

> If, morally speaking, wanting a child is thought to be a necessary condition for bringing a child into the world, might it also be a sufficient reason? If a couple, or even an individual, want to have a child, ought society to encourage and assist them

to have a child? Have they some sort of right to have a child? If there are good moral grounds for saying that those who do not want to have children ought not to have them, might there also be good moral grounds for saying that those who want to have children ought to have them?[30]

Choices in Childlessness begins, then, by acknowledging that many people make decisions on the basis of either their real wants or their perceived wants. It also argues that wants are notoriously subjective things, liable to change. It is doubtful if such a basis can form the foundation for a proper ethical code of conduct in the alleviation of infertility.

In trying to show the inadequacy of wants as a moral basis for action, the report contrasts the wants of an individual or a couple with the interests and needs of children. These needs are simply stated: 'Children need a basic care and protection if they are to grow up into mature and responsible human beings. They need fathering and mothering within a stable and reliable environment.'[31] This change from the wants of prospective parents to the needs of children is a crucial one. It moves us from the subjective area of want to the more objective area of need. It also illustrates the wider context in which decisions regarding fertility are to be made.

The report anticipates the obvious question: what about the needs of couples wanting to have children? Needs, it argues, are divided into primary needs for food and shelter and secondary needs for health, communication, responsiveness, responsibility and love.[32] All of the above are universal needs which determine either the continued existence of a person or that person's meaningful existence. Such needs must be met, if at all possible, by society. The deep-seated desire which many people evince to have children cannot be seen as a basic need. Such desires may indeed be deep and cause great misery to individuals if unsatisfied, but they are too variable and too unevenly distributed throughout the population to warrant any moral obligation on society.

If then neither wants nor needs can be used as a basis for Christian action in regard to the alleviation of infertility, can the concept of rights prove more useful?

Choices in Childlessness is initially rather sceptical regarding the whole issue of rights. Nevertheless, it accepts that certain rights may exist in so far as they are closely related to the basic human needs expressed above. Furthermore, they must be considered in the context of a complex social environment in which others have interests, needs, and perhaps conflicting claims to rights. In essence, rights should refer to those things which belong to the very nature of what it means to be a human being, living a meaningful life. The discussion is summed up in a clear and uncompromising statement:

> If, as we have suggested, it is implausible to speak of an individual's basic 'need' for children, it is surely even less plausible to speak in the abstract of an individual's inherent 'right' to have children. Such an alleged right could be established only on the basis of an inalienable right to individual self-fulfilment, isolated from and elevated above all other interests. A claim to such a right as this can find no moral justification. It should certainly never be argued in isolation from a child's 'right' to good parenting.[33]

The working party goes on to assert that it is only in the context of Christian commitment that an answer to the various dilemmas which face couples can be found. Even then the correct path to follow is not always obvious or easy, but at least a method for discovering the way ahead is promised:

> Human beings are made in the image of God, redeemed by the sacrifice of Christ and called to an eternal destiny . . . Thus from a Christian point of view wants, needs, interests and rights are brought together, ordered and transformed by reflection on what God calls man to be.[34]

The dual aspects of sex

Choices in Childlessness makes a carefully worded statement regarding the relationship between the unitive and procreative aspect of marriage. It argues that in the past these two aspects were seen as being necessarily joined because having children was believed to be the more or less inevitable consequence of sexual intercourse. Now, the widespread use of contraceptives and the increasing trend, in certain sections of society, to opt for voluntary childlessness, has meant that a practical and not a merely theoretical distinction must be made between the two obvious aspects of sex. The report's statement is worth quoting at length:

In the past sociological orthodoxy has always argued that the institution of marriage is rooted in the needs of the family. This view, however, has recently been questioned and its opposite suggested, namely, that the needs of the family are secondary to the needs of the husband and wife. That is, the primary function of marriage is for husband and wife to give to each other a stable personal identity in an unstable and impersonal world. It may be suggested that theological reflection has been moving in a similar direction. Certainly, there would be few, if any, Christians today who would argue that a marriage without children somehow fails to achieve the essential purpose of marriage. The relationship of love and fidelity between husband and wife is at the heart of marriage. The relationship between parents and children is subsequent. Each of these relationships may be enriched by the other. Consequently, the unitive and procreative aspects of marriage are still closely interrelated. Nevertheless, it may be suggested that, whereas the relationship between husband and wife is of the *esse* of marriage, the relationship between parents and children is of the *bene esse* of marriage. Children can deepen and enhance a marriage but a marriage without children may be no less of a marriage for being childless.[35]

While this statement has been couched in careful and unassertive language, it does introduce into the debate quite novel and challenging arguments which question the foundations of much of the church's position through history. If it is true that a childless marriage is not in any way essentially diminished, though it may be somewhat impoverished, then it cannot be argued that the alleviation of infertility is an essential element in a Christian understanding of medical care and provision. Equally, if the procreative aspect of sexual union can be separated from its unitive aspect in the sense that it is appropriate for a couple to enjoy marriage for its unitive rewards alone, then it may be argued that there is no reason why a couple may not engage in sexual activity only in order to have children. At the very least it may be argued that any form of artificial insemination, or of egg or embryo transfer, would be permissible without its implying any unitive relationship between the parties involved. On the other hand, to relegate children to the *bene esse* of marriage is to run the risk of making them less important than the adults who gave them life, and consequently to provide an environment in which children are seen as commodities which are created primarily for the benefit of their parents.

The report provides further guidelines on the subject of fertility and its place within marriage. Having suggested that procreation is not an essential part of marriage, and that the intention to procreate does not necessarily form part of a Christian marriage, the report suggests a more symbolic meaning and significance for procreation. Children, it is argued, are 'pledges of the love and fidelity of God'.[36] We trust our children to become the means whereby God will bring his blessings into the world in succeeding generations. While it is accepted that this may be a rather unrealistic way to view procreation, in that most couples do not have children with this purpose in mind, *Choices in Childlessness* argues that it is important to set a Christian agenda for our discussion of procreation, and that this cannot be done unless we view having children as a calling of God.

The vocation of parenthood

The report's argument culminates in the statement that procreation is a vocation which is both a gift from God and a service rendered to God. This gift must be exercised with deliberation and planning, and it must not be used as an excuse for refusing to exercise responsibility regarding the number of children to be brought into the world. Children are not possessions but gifts, not only to their parents but also to the whole community. Children are of fundamental importance in and for the Christian community, but are the result of a vocation given by God to their parents.

The language used in discussing procreation must be the language of vocation, not the language of law. In this regard, the report emphasizes once more its belief that the concept of vocation means that only some are called by God to exercise a certain role within society, and that it is by no means an automatic conclusion that all married couples are called to the vocation of child-rearing: 'In speaking of a vocation to having and rearing children, we must emphasise again the fact that not all Christians are called to procreate.'[37] The possibility that God calls certain married couples to a vocation of childlessness, and that it is perfectly appropriate for them to enjoy the unitive aspects of sexual union without ever enjoying its procreative aspects, is a real one. This also means that certain couples who are involuntarily childless may be called to accept their condition rather than to seek to overcome it. Alternatively, some who are involuntarily childless may be called to parenthood and should seek the alleviation of their condition of fertility.

This report certainly moves well beyond the position evident in *Humanae Vitae*, both in its scope and in its suggestions. Its insistence that it is necessary to view the whole subject within the context of God's will and God's calling is important and commendable. Its suggestion that the unitive and procreative aspects of sexual love may not be separated not only in practice but also in principle is a significant departure from previous orthodoxy. The further suggestion that parenthood is a specific vocation to which only some married couples are called provides another basis for the rejection of the necessary link between marriage and procreation. We will examine these propositions after we have reviewed the third of the central documents in our present discussion: the Church of England's report, *Personal Origins*.

Personal Origins

Of the three reports we are considering, only *Personal Origins* had its genesis in the Warnock debate. Understandably, the working party which produced the report was concerned primarily with the problems presented by new scientific techniques. Consequently, the section of the report which deals with the principles which underlie a Christian understanding of marriage, fertility and sexual union is quite brief. Nevertheless, a treatment of the theology of marriage was felt necessary in so far as it was relevant to the issues raised by these new scientific and medical techniques.[38]

Marriage

The report notes the three traditional 'goods' of marriage as elaborated by Augustine: offspring, fidelity and sacrament. Drawing from this and the *Book of Common Prayer*, the report states:

> The union of two people in the completeness of marriage,
> involving sexual, social, emotional and relational aspects, is
> seen as promoting three central goods of human life: namely,
> the transmission of life in the human community, a disciplined

structure of living in which the individual may grow to moral maturity, and a strong and enduring relationship between them. In short we may speak of the 'procreational', 'moral' and 'relational' goods of marriage.[39]

From this analysis of marriage, *Personal Origins* argues that the alleviation of infertility should play a part in any Christian approach to fostering good marriages. Procreation is one of the natural ends of marriage, and while it is accepted that a childless marriage is perfectly valid, it is none the less one in which a couple are deprived of a good which is proper to them. This statement is balanced with the caution that this does not mean that every possible treatment for infertility is acceptable; each treatment must be judged on its own moral merits.[40]

In examining the issue further, the report makes it clear that the 'goods' of marriage are given by God and are not merely a description of the purposes which we have found for marriage within our society. Consequently, these goods do not change from society to society or from time to time. Furthermore, Christians have always attempted to hold the goods of marriage together.[41]

Marriage and children

The issue of how exactly the procreational, moral and relational goods of marriage are to be held together is central to the present discussion. The report rejects the belief that every act of intercourse should be allowed its full potential for procreation. It equally rejects the common assertion that it is entirely up to a husband and wife to decide how many children, if any, they intend to have. Marriage and its goods are gifts from God and are not to be treated simply as human possessions. Nevertheless, in marriage there should be a measure of responsible planning. As a result, it is not necessary to hold together the relational and procreational goods of marriage on every occasion. Indeed, in practice, these goods will not be held together on most occasions.[42]

Personal Origins is at pains to point out that it is not reversing the traditional view that in marriage all the stated goods should be held together. While rejecting *Humanae Vitae*'s understanding of the unitive and procreative aspects of sexual union within marriage, the report goes to some lengths to argue that the traditional principle should still be accepted.

In asking how the goods of marriage may be kept together, *Personal Origins* offers this argument:

> One may say that the procreation of children is not just an optional matter of choice for Christians. It is a proper good of marriage, intended by the ordinance of the Creator himself. It is one of the proper purposes of marriage. So, except for very good reasons, every Christian marriage should seek to fulfil itself by the procreation of children. And such procreation should not take place outside the marriage bond. Similarly, that mutual companionship, help and comfort, for better or worse, which the couple promise at their marriage to give and accept one from the other, is not some sort of optional extra to marriage. It, too, is a proper good, ordained by God. Its proper locus is marriage. In saying that these goods should be held together, one may be saying that the intention to have children – even when it is responsibly planned, and therefore very much brought under human control – and the intention to maintain lifelong fidelity, for better or worse, should positively inter-relate . . . In other words, the important points are: that procreation should not occur entirely outside the loving relationship; and that the loving relationship should issue in the good of children, unless there are strong reasons to the contrary (like genetic defect of a grave kind).[43]

This argument is instantly attractive to many Christians. It allows for the unity of the various aspects of marriage without insisting that contraception is contrary to a Christian understanding of marriage. We must ask, however, whether the working party has simply accepted a fairly standard view of marriage without fully examining the basis for this assertion. While it is clear that marriage is the only correct place for both sexual union and procreation, and that an act of sexual love has the potential for both procreation and strengthening the bond between a married couple, does it necessarily follow that in marriage, procreation must be a good that is sought? Equally, is it necessarily the case that in every marriage, sexual union should be the way in which a couple display and share their feelings of love and intimacy?

While it is to be expected that many or even most marriages will result in the birth of children, and that most married couples will wish to be joined in sexual union throughout their married lives, is this necessarily the way marriage has to be? Is it an abuse of the gift of marriage for a couple to decide not to enjoy the good of children or to decide not to enjoy the good of sexual union after a certain stage in their marriage? We may wish to argue that to refrain from enjoying these goods is to decide to impoverish a marriage, but is this the same as saying that the gift of marriage has thereby been abused?

The argument can be turned round the other way. If it is permissible to divorce the relational and procreative aspects of marriage, may it also be permissible for children to be born within marriage but without any sexual union taking place?

Personal Origins anticipates this question and provides an answer within the framework of the general principle that the various goods of marriage should be held together in the marriage as a whole. Artificial means of reproduction are acceptable within a marriage as long as the marriage, when viewed as a whole, can be said to display both relational and procreative aspects and that the act of artificial procreation is an extension of the life of love and union of the couple. The argument is summed up in a few sentences:

> The technique is offered as an aid to the restoration of a good proper to the marriage which through some handicap has been impeded. So it is calculated to strengthen the relational good, and the bond between the various goods which go together to make a proper Christian marriage. It seems, then, that the use of assisted fertilisation by a couple who cannot, or who are advised on medical grounds not to, have children is acceptable, since it may be said to hold together the procreational and relational goods within the marriage as a whole.[44]

The role of sex within marriage

The argument advanced by *Personal Origins* serves to emphasize the way in which the focus for the relational and procreative goods of marriage has been shifted from the act of sexual union to the marriage as a whole. Traditionally, sexual union has been seen as the focal point where the relational and procreative aspects of marriage find their full expression. In this report there is no single point of focus, but rather a belief that the whole marriage may be viewed as a single act in which relational and procreative goods may be enjoyed. Sexual union forms an important but not exclusive part of the way in which a couple may find their relational and procreative needs met.

This view has great implications for our understanding of the role of sex within marriage. If sexual union is not the only means whereby the unitive and procreative aspects of marriage are held together, then there is no need to insist that either relational goods or procreative goods of marriage must be focused on sexual union. Marriage may still be the correct environment for intimate union and procreation. Sexual union will normally play a central role in effecting this. In certain cases, however, other means of expressing personal union or of procreation may be enjoyed without abusing the gift of marriage.

The question that has to be asked, though, is whether the act of sexual union is as inessential as this implies. Could it be the case that sexual union has been designed specifically by God to be the only means whereby the goods of marriage may be kept together? Alternatively, may we argue that just as contraception is a method by which human beings use their God-given knowledge to help them to exercise responsibility within nature, so too are artificial means of reproduction? We will return to these issues presently.

Donor insemination and egg donation

Personal Origins argues that it is necessary to separate the numerous practical difficulties associated with gamete donation from certain moral principles which underlie them. As a result of its investigation, the report states that it is wrong to equate gamete donation with either adoption or adultery. Some advocates of donor insemination have, indeed, argued that what is really taking place is a form of antenatal adoption. Others, opposed to DI, have claimed that such a procedure is the same as adultery, since a third party has intruded into the marriage relationship.

Against equating DI with adoption, *Personal Origins* defines a clear difference between a couple who voluntarily accept a child into their family and a couple who consciously decide to bring into being a child who is at most only partly their own genetically. The distinction is obvious enough. In one case an existing child is offered a good which he or she has been previously denied. In the other case a child is brought into existence in order to provide a good which has previously been denied a childless couple. There are similarities between DI and adoption, but there is an essential moral difference.

Overall, the working party which produced *Personal Origins* was divided on the appropriateness of gamete donation:

> There are two differing points of view held among us. One is that if donation takes place within a stable marriage relationship, it still has the status of a good, though not, of course, one which should become a norm; the other believes that the perils to marriage, as understood by Christians, are so grave that the extension of gamete donation should be strongly discouraged and [DI] dislodged from the established position it now holds among the techniques of aided fertilisation.[45]

Personal Origins also rejects the argument that DI is a form of adultery. It accepts that a genetic union which is extrinsic to the marriage does take place. This alone, however, does not constitute adultery. Since there is no physical infidelity involved, or even personal relationship with the donor at any level, the marriage bond is not broken. This is not to say that the report sees no problems in gamete donation for a married couple's relationship, but these cannot be equated with adultery.

As mentioned above, the working party was divided on the question of whether DI is an acceptable form of infertility treatment for Christians:

> We differ . . . depending on whether we see the genetic as the most basic manifestation of the personal and find the alienation of genetic parenthood from marriage a development which undermines the Christian understanding; or whether we judge that, although everyone is fundamentally influenced and limited by his or her genetic endowment, nevertheless the overriding factor is the social context which can assure proper love, respect and care. To this extent the question of genetic origin is not of fundamental moral importance, when compared with the question of how the child will be loved and cared for.[46]

This statement brings us back once more to the relationship between the different goods of marriage. The secure environment which marriage is intended to provide for children is a good of marriage which may, of course, exist in the case of adoption, and is a necessary condition for responsible parenthood. While it is clear, therefore, that a stable marriage should be provided as the environment for child-rearing, it is not correspondingly clear that a child born through artificial means of reproduction will suffer as a result of this experience. Indeed, as the report points out, because such a child is likely to be strongly desired by its social parents, it is assured of a greater chance of a loving environment than are many children born under more normal circumstances. The report tentatively suggests that some scientific studies carried out on children born after DI provided evidence that such children were, as a whole, better balanced emotionally and socially than other children.[47]

Conclusions

How, then, can we build on these documents to promote a coherent Christian view of marriage, sex, fertility and the family? How can we decide which, if any, infertility treatments represent a threat to marriage and family life?

We can begin by looking at the fundamentals of family life. It is often assumed that the family enjoys a pivotal place in Scripture and within Christian tradition. In one sense this is true. Paul gave certain instructions regarding the ways in which members of families should treat one another,[48] and he also taught that all families have their ultimate origin in God.[49] We must also accept, though, that there is no attempt in Scripture to defend or define the institution of the family as such. This does not mean, of course, that the family is not a good and necessary institution. It does mean, however, that we have to accept the institution of the family as something of a presupposition in Christian thought, in much the same way that the existence of God and the fact of creation are offered in the Scriptures as foundation beliefs which are neither proved nor defended.

If this is so, then the assumption behind *Humanae Vitae*, that the family is God's instrument for exercising his order in the world and that it has a sacramental role to play within society, is essentially correct, though somewhat overstated in the document. This means that in defending the Christian understanding of a family, we should have as a priority a desire to ensure that the family is not compromised in its God-given task. Where the family unit is seen to be at risk, the basic fabric of society is also at risk and legislation would be appropriate.

When we ask what the central roles of the family are, we agree with the authors of *Personal Origins* that these may be discerned from a careful study of Scripture and Christian history. The unitive and procreative aspects of marriage are clearly promoted, as is the creation of a secure environment in which children may be nurtured. It is surely correct, also, to agree with *Choices in Childlessness* in its assertion that the Christian family has something of a prophetic role to play in the world and that we cannot view the importance of either the family or of child-rearing in purely clinical terms. We must further agree that it is God's intention to speak to the world, through the Christian family, about love, order and children. In order to preserve responsible parenthood, to safeguard children and to give society a stable order, the family unit constituting both parents and children, with a wider network of relatives, should be promoted and made the object of protective legislation. This desire to preserve responsible parenthood should include an insistence that the genetic parents of a child are deemed to be its legal parents unless, as in cases of adoption, they waive their legal rights, a course of action to be considered only in extreme circumstances.

It is much more difficult to find a way through the detailed problems of infertility and the nature of the link between the unitive and procreative aspects of marriage. On one hand, we are tempted to leave the discussion by stating simply that nothing should be allowed to compromise the basic principles which govern marriage, outlined above. On the other hand, this would leave too many practical problems unsolved, offering little real guidance to those considering infertility treatments.

On balance, the argument regarding the nature of the link between the unitive and procreative aspects of marriage does not support the position proposed by *Humanae Vitae*. As is accepted there, only a few acts of sexual union within a marriage result in children. It is reasonable to argue from this that God signifies that it is not his intention for every sexual act to be open to the possibility of procreation. It is not necessary, therefore, for us to intend every act of sexual union to be open to that possibility either. We should reject any insistence that every sexual act should be allowed its full potential for procreation. Our position is an extension of the order that God has created; *Humanae Vitae*'s is a deliberate decision not to engage God's creation in relationship with science and social responsibility.

How, then, are the unitive and procreative aspects of marriage related? Although, as we have already said, it is logically possible to argue that these are quite distinct gifts and that they may be enjoyed without reference to each other, this fails to do justice to God's design in giving both these gifts to be enjoyed only in the context of marriage. Even if there is not a strictly logical link, there is, at least, an apparent one. It may be correct, in certain unusual circumstances, for a couple to join together in a marriage based on duty rather than love. It may also be the case that in certain circumstances it is right for a couple to decide not to enjoy the gift of children. This, however, is not how God intends normal marriage to be. The traditional view that marriage should result in children, where this is possible both physically and socially, mirrors more accurately God's design, even if we cannot prove the point logically.

This means that couples who are infertile, or for whom children would be quite inappropriate, may be assured that their marriage is valid and fully Christian. But couples who choose to avoid having children, without thinking about their use of the gift of marriage, should be encouraged to ask themselves whether or not they are misusing God's gift.

In all of this, we must try to find not only what is logically permissible, but also what is most in keeping with God's design for marriage and the protection of that design within society. This leads us to say that infertility is a condition that, where possible, should be cured by medical and scientific techniques, but these techniques must not endanger marriage as a God-given gift. A childless couple must be assured of the validity of their marriage while at the same time encouraged to seek treatment of an appropriate kind. They need further assurance that if treatment is available which may be effective, but which may endanger their long-term relationship or undermine the status of the family in society, then it would be correct to choose childlessness.

As we come to the end of this chapter it may be useful to list clearly the key points in our discussion on marriage, sex and infertility.

1. Fertility is a gift, not a right.

2. God intends this gift to be used only within marriage.

3. Every married couple should be able to enjoy this gift and, normally, should seek to enjoy it.

4. Where a couple face the problem of infertility, a remedy should be sought, but not one which would endanger their marriage.

5. In marriage, sexual union has a dual role: to unite husband and wife in love, and to bring new lives into existence.

6. Not every act of sexual union need have potential for procreation, but within the environment of a marriage, sexual union should be allowed this potential unless there are undeniable medical or social reasons why this must not be so.

7. Not every act of procreation need result from an act of sexual union, but any act of procreation should occur only between people who are married and as such enjoy a shared life of sexual union.

8. Sexual union and procreation must be kept together in the context of married life, even though each individual act either of procreation or of sexual union need not express this dual role.

9. Children are not commodities to be created for the pleasure of their parents or even to meet their parents' needs; they are to be sought for their own sake and are to be treated with dignity and respect. To safeguard the status of children and to strengthen the degree of personal commitment invested by adults in their children's welfare, legal and genetic parenthood should not, normally, be separated. Adoption is an allowable exception, where the genetic parents have either died or have relinquished their parental responsibilities.

It is now time to move to the sharp end of the debate on human fertilization and embryology. How do we put our principles into practice? We need to find real and practicable solutions to the problems facing doctors, counsellors and couples as they grapple with issues of the deepest importance.

6

Artificial insemination by husband (AIH)

Before we begin a detailed discussion of AIH, a few words are necessary regarding the method employed in this and the following chapters. We will examine each subject, first of all, by looking at the original Warnock proposals and initial Government responses. Next, the eventual legislation, found in the 1990 Human Fertilization and Embryology Act, will be outlined. Following this, we will survey the contributions made by churches and Christian groups during the Warnock debate. Finally, with our own principles in mind, we will give a detailed analysis of each technique. This will include looking at what legislation, if any, ought to be in place.

This is quite an exhaustive process, in keeping with our approach throughout. It necessarily involves some repetition, especially when detailing church responses. At the expense of seeming pedantic, or at least pedestrian, this method is essential if we are to gain an accurate and comprehensive picture of each issue. Some readers, however, may wish to leapfrog over the detailed reports of submissions in order to get to the analysis at the end of each chapter. In this case, the earlier parts of each chapter may still prove useful as additional resource material for future study.

Survey

The Warnock Report and subsequent Government papers

The Warnock Committee was aware of the objections of some groups to AIH, namely, that such a practice separated the unitive and procreative aspects of sexual intercourse, and that it frequently involved the practice of masturbation. Such objections did not cause the committee to believe that AIH was morally wrong or that it should be prohibited by law.[1]

They were concerned, however, about the possibility of a widow wishing to be inseminated with sperm donated by her late husband. The committee did not wish to encourage this possibility, nor did it feel that it had the right to prohibit it. In the end they made only two recommendations. The report stated that a five-yearly review should be made of all donated gametes; in the case of the donor's death the right of disposal should fall to the storage authority. Furthermore, any child resulting from posthumous AIH should be debarred from any inheritance rights.[2] In their framework for legislation the Government upheld these recommendations, with the added proviso that gametes should be stored for a maximum of ten years[3] after donation.

The Human Fertilization and Embryology Act 1990

The Act upholds the recommendations of the Warnock Report. AIH treatment does not require a licence where freezing and storage are not concerned.[4] Where storage is required, the regulations for storage of gametes dictate that if the husband dies and his sperm is used to inseminate his wife, he is not to be treated in law as the father of any resulting child.[5] Such use of a husband's sperm is permissible only if he had consented to it when his sperm was being stored.[6] The woman in question could be inseminated with her dead husband's sperm only after counselling, which must include a thorough investigation of all the likely implications of such a procedure.[7]

Christian submissions

So widely accepted was the practice of AIH that a number of churches failed to include it in their responses to various infertility treatments. Of those churches and groups which did state their opinions regarding the practice, none was entirely hostile, while most were firmly in favour of the practice as long as it was used to aid fertility within marriage. Problems were seen to increase, however, if AIH was employed using frozen sperm following the death of the husband.

Unfavourable responses

The most cautious approach to AIH was taken by the Roman Catholic Church. In evidence submitted to the inquiry by the Catholic Bishops' Joint Committee on Bio-ethical Issues on behalf of the Catholic Bishops of Great Britain,[8] the view was expressed that to sever procreation from the 'central marital act' would be to open society to a range of 'undesirable and scarcely reversible changes'.[9] They did not specifically condemn AIH, but it is clear that the Roman Catholic bishops were far from convinced that artificial insemination should be employed even within marriage.

A more liberal approach was taken by the National Board of Catholic Women, an umbrella organization for Roman Catholic women's groups in Great Britain. They acknowledge the problem of separating procreation from sexual intercourse and allowing medical practice to 'intrude . . . into the relationship of the couple'. Nevertheless, the Board also affirmed that some of their members felt that these considerations were outweighed 'in some circumstances by the joy given to married couples previously thought to be incapable of having children'.[10] The acceptance, by some, of artificial insemination within marriage was guarded but none the less real.

In their response to the Warnock Report the Free Presbyterian Church of Scotland also took a guarded view on the subject of AIH. While agreeing that masturbation was not, in theory, necessary for AIH, they argued that current practice dictated that this was the usual way in which semen was collected. The church found this practice unacceptable and consequently placed a question mark over the practice, if not the theory, of AIH.[11]

Favourable responses

Those Anglican churches or groups which included AIH in their submissions to Warnock were uniformly more positive in their attitude. The Church of England, through its Board for Social Responsibility, indicated its agreement with the Warnock Committee's acceptance of AIH. The Board stated that even though AIH involved artificial interference in the process of reproduction, since they accepted contraception, they should also accept AIH. The use of masturbation was noted, but the Board was prepared to accept that practice for the purposes of AIH, since they supported 'the intention of the act, the nature of the act and its consequences'.[12]

The Mothers' Union, an organization with some 200,000 members and a high profile within Anglican churches, stated in their response to Warnock that they welcomed AIH as 'a genuine relief of suffering'.[13] The Children's Society, a voluntary society of the Church of England and the Church of Wales, was equally positive in its acceptance of AIH. As with the other Anglican submissions, the society welcomed AIH, stating that AIH was 'a very positive and constructive technique', and that it should not be regulated by law except when the question of storage and disposal of frozen sperm arises.[14]

The Methodist Church in Great Britain summed up its opinion of AIH in a terse statement. Its Division of Social Responsibility commented that the technique was therapeutic for the individuals concerned and supportive of family life, and that 'it does not raise any serious moral or ethical issues for the majority of Christian people'.[15] In an even terser statement the Methodist Church in Ireland expressed its opinion by stating: 'AIH does not present us with any problem.'[16]

The Church of Scotland, through its Board of Social Responsibility's response to the Warnock Report, commented that it had no objection to AIH when fertilization was either difficult or impossible through unaided means.[17] The Free Church of Scotland, similarly, accepted AIH, noting that it did not raise the question of the sanctity of life, since the insemination takes place prior to fertilization and has fertilization as its objective.[18] The Presbyterian Church in Ireland submitted evidence and responded to the Warnock Report through the deliberations of an *ad hoc* group, which also reported to that church's General Assembly. In their report they stated that, while there was a danger of AIH leading to a 'purely mechanical treatment of sexual activities and relationships', the more positive aspects of the technique may be found in the assistance given to men with medical disabilities.[19] Thus a guarded welcome was given to the technique by the *ad hoc* group, and this viewpoint was upheld by the Church's General Assembly.[20]

Two statements by umbrella groups are also worthy of note. A number of churches, in their submissions to Warnock, referred to the report *Choices in Childlessness*. The report stated that it was the opinion of the working party that there is no moral or legal objection to the practice of AIH.[21]

The evangelical organization CARE, formerly the Nationwide Festival of Light, also voiced its support for AIH in certain circumstances. A note of caution was sounded, however. In their evidence to the Warnock Committee they stressed that the need for AIH to produce offspring should not be allowed to compromise in any way the continuing normal sexual relationships of a married couple. AIH, they pointed out, should not replace normal marital intercourse 'even though fertility was not expected to result from sexual union'.[22]

Analysis

The main arguments we have encountered against AIH, from Christian submissions, indicate that the separation of the unitive and procreative aspects of sexual intercourse and the usual practice of masturbation are the main foci of concern for some groups. The principles we have suggested do not agree with these criticisms of the practice of AIH. The unitive and procreative aspects of marriage, as distinct from every single act of sexual intercourse, are not compromised by AIH. In the context of a shared life of sexual experiences, both the unitive bond in marriage and the procreative aspects of sex are honoured. It is true that AIH cannot be accurately described as sexual intercourse, but in the context of marriage it is a mutually agreed use of the sexuality of both partners, applied exclusively within the marriage for procreative purposes. While the actual experience of insemination cannot be said to fulfil any unitive function, nevertheless the whole experience of deciding to try this form of treatment, and the subsequent shared nature of its operation, would in many cases strengthen the bond between a husband and wife. As long as neither partner views his or her sexuality as being compromised by the technique, it is acceptable for Christians to use it after appropriate counselling.

The issue of masturbation is not a major concern here, since, regardless of one's opinion of the practice, it may be seen as a medical technique rather than as a matter of personal sexual gratification. Alternatively, the collection of sperm does not necessarily have to be done in a strictly clinical setting outside the context of sexual experience within marriage. We may view AIH as a means of furthering the desire of a couple to fulfil the procreative aspect of their marriage; in this instance the actual technique is not of prime importance.

Posthumous AIH

The posthumous use of a man's sperm to inseminate his widow is a more complex issue, which goes beyond the practical consideration of the legal status of the offspring. It is a relatively easy matter to ensure that the will of an individual may not be changed after his death by the introduction of any new offspring through the use of posthumous AIH, but that is not the central moral issue. From the perspective of Christian morality and understanding of marriage and the family, is such a use of AIH acceptable? In this regard, it is disappointing that while some Christian responses objected to posthumous AIH, they failed to indicate precisely why.

The main issue here is to what extent, if any, a person may be said to be married to a deceased partner. It is clear that, legally, the marriage ceases to exist at the time of the death of either partner, even though by virtue of the marriage which did exist the surviving partner is able to claim certain rights. It is also clear that the emotional bond cannot be severed instantly at the time of a partner's death, if at all. Nevertheless, the surviving partner of a marriage can no longer be said to be in a marriage. The bond of love may be as strong as ever, and it may even be the case that there is an expectation of meeting with one's loved one again, and of continuing a relationship of love, but these feelings and hopes do not constitute marriage. An act of posthumous AIH is, in fact, not AIH at all but donor insemination, even though the donor is one who used to be the woman's husband.

This argument does not minimize the bond which a surviving partner may continue to feel exists between her and her deceased husband, but it does acknowledge that marriage is a relationship which is proper only to the living, and that at the death of a partner the marriage ceases to exist even though the bond of love may continue. Consequently, the question becomes whether a widow may be eligible for DI, knowingly using the sperm of someone she loved and for whom she continues to feel an emotional bond. We can answer this question only after we have examined the practice of DI.

167

In failing to categorize posthumous AIH as DI, Christian groups failed to address the issue in the correct light, thus enabling the Warnock Committee and Parliament to come to the opinion that it was better to leave it as a matter of choice. If it had been viewed as a special case of DI, the 1990 Act may have been more rigorous in the provisions it made, and Christians could have given clearer guidance regarding the essential moral nature of the activity.

With the exception of posthumous AIH, the technique is morally acceptable, subject to individual choice. Since there is no evidence of likely harm to individuals, society or nature, it should not be a matter for coercive legislation.

7

Donor insemination (DI)

Survey

The Warnock Committee and subsequent Government papers

DI (then known as AID, artificial insemination by donor) provided the Warnock Committee with a wider range of ethical and legal problems than did AIH. The committee recognized that there was still strong opposition to the practice, mainly from church and religious bodies, even though general public opinion had shifted in favour of the technique since the Feversham Report. In particular, the committee took note of the opinion that DI represents an intrusion of a third party into what many consider to be an exclusive relationship. Quoting the case of MacLennan v. MacLennan,[1] however, the report also stated that, in law, DI did not constitute adultery and hence is not legally an intrusion into a marriage.[2] Nevertheless, Warnock recognized that DI did pose a possible threat to a marriage if the husband felt either inadequate or excluded as a result. The common fears of genetic illness being transmitted to a DI child were also noted, as was the fear of a DI child becoming unwittingly involved in an incestuous relationship with another child from the same donor.[3]

In spite of these objections, the committee was of the opinion that, subject to careful licensing arrangements, DI should continue to be made available to suitable couples. To avoid the problems of genetic illness, incest and cultural mismatching, the committee recommended that it should be a criminal offence to provide a DI service without the relevant Government licence.[4]

In addition to this essentially positive response to DI, the Warnock Committee further recommended that children born as a result of DI should be treated under the law as legitimate children of the woman and her husband.[5] As a consequence of this, semen donors should have no parental rights or duties, and a consent form signed by both partners should be a prerequisite of DI treatment. Where a husband has not signed such a form, the burden of proof should be on him to show that he did not consent to DI if such a procedure leads to marital problems.[6] It is also worth noting that the Warnock Committee envisaged the possibility of DI being offered to single women.[7] A further radical departure from the Feversham Committee's opinion was the recommendation that, if desired, the husband of a woman receiving DI should be allowed to register himself as the father of the child. This would not affect the child's right, at the age of eighteen, to receive basic ethnic and genetic information about his donor father, whose identity would remain secret.[8]

These far-reaching recommendations caused some concern on the publication of the report. In their subsequent consultation document, the Government requested further submissions on this whole area.[9] Following these submissions the Government decided in their *Framework for Legislation* White Paper to uphold the Warnock recommendations, though they did allow for the anonymity of the donor to be removed by law at a future date if public opinion should change. Such a change in law would not affect existing donors.[10]

The Human Fertilization and Embryology Act 1990

The Act clarifies the situation regarding the legal status of DI. It stipulates that DI should be practised only in pursuance of a licence[11] and states that anyone contravening this regulation is guilty of an offence.[12]

The Act does not specify that a woman wishing to be provided with treatment services must have a male partner. It does state, however, that account must be taken of the welfare of any resulting child and that this should include the child's need of a father.[13] The Act, however, stops short of making this need an absolute one. Consequently, certain women who do not have a partner, or who have a female partner, may argue that they are able to meet a child's needs without any paternal involvement. Rather weakly, the Act simply stipulates that in these and other circumstances, counselling is necessary before treatment may be given.[14] To ensure that appropriate donors are used in each case of DI, and that a minimum risk of genetic disability is assured, screening of donors is also commended.[15]

The vexed subject of paternity is also addressed by the Act. While, in purely biological terms, it is clear that the genetic father of a DI child is the donor, the Act makes provision for social parenthood to be recognized as being more important than biological parenthood. Except in cases of adoption, or where common law dictates that a child is the legitimate child of another marriage, the legal father of a DI child is the husband of the woman receiving treatment.[16] If the woman is not married but presents herself for treatment with a partner, then he is the father of the child.[17] In both cases, if the husband or partner does not consent to such treatment, then he is not the legal father of the child.[18] This applies even if a couple subsequently divorce, as long as they were not legally separated at the time of treatment.[19] If the marriage is subsequently declared void, the supposed husband is still the father of the child as long as one partner, at least, believed that the marriage was valid at the time of receiving treatment.[20] This paternity is legally binding in all situations.[21]

Negatively, the Act states that the donor in DI is not to be considered as the father of any resulting child[22] (AIH is considered to include a couple living together but not formally married), and that in no circumstances can a deceased person be the father of a child if his sperm is used after his death.[23] Titles of honour and any property rights associated with them are to remain unaffected by these various provisions.[24]

The Act is also concerned to ensure that all adequate provisions are made to keep a full record of all donors, recipients and any children born. It states that records must be kept of all gametes used, children born, persons receiving gametes, and all instances of mixing gametes, all of which may be practised only under licence.[25] The identity of the legal father will also be known, but there is no requirement that a birth certificate of a DI child should indicate that the legal father is not the genetic father of the child.

The Act also deals with the rights of the DI child regarding access to information about his or her genetic father. Following counselling, a DI child may, at any stage after his or her eighteenth birthday, apply for information regarding whether or not he or she is a DI child[26] and whether any intended spouse is genetically related.[27] While other information may be given at the discretion of the Human Fertilization and Embryology Authority, this information would not usually include the identity of the genetic father.[28] Where there are paternity disputes,[29] or where an action is being taken against a parent under the Congenital Disabilities (Civil Liability) Act 1976, the identity of the genetic parent may be made known to a court.[30] This Act does extend to DI donors even though they are not legal parents, as we have already noted.[31] In the case of a minor wishing to marry, the Authority will give information regarding whether or not the minor is or may be a DI child[32] and whether there is a genetic relationship between the minor and the intended spouse.[33]

Christian submissions

In general, churches were favourably disposed towards AIH, within certain limits. By contrast, DI presented the churches with a much more difficult set of ethical problems to resolve. Understandably, a much wider range of opinions and attitudes was expressed. While the predominant attitude to DI was negative, this was not uniformly the case. Not only was there much less agreement between Christian groups regarding DI, but even within individual churches disagreement was evident. Clearly, this confusion within and between churches contributed in some measure to the Warnock Committee's argument that while DI would be unsuitable for some because of their moral or religious beliefs, there was no reason to allow those beliefs to dictate to others what their response should be. Consequently, Warnock accepted the practice of DI, subject to certain controls.[34] This was so even though a number of churches and individuals argued that they had the right to state what practices should be acceptable to the society in which they lived, as well as stating their personal moral codes and standards.

In many of the Christian responses to Warnock, a double position was maintained. Many groups argued that their preferred opinion was that the practice of DI should not be allowed within the United Kingdom. Nevertheless, they recognized that it was so common that they did not expect their view to be accepted by the committee. As a result, they also maintained a secondary position which sought to introduce safeguards into the practice in order to reduce the likelihood of legal and personal problems in the future. In the end, the preferred position of some groups was similar to the fallback position of others; an indication of the complexity of the debate within Christian circles regarding DI.

Favourable responses

Three submissions were favourable to the practice of DI where the husband was willing, with full knowledge of the facts, to seek this remedy, with his wife, for their infertility problem.

The Children's Society stated specifically that DI should not be available to any woman not in a stable relationship with a male partner. Such a partner did not have to be a husband, though this would be preferable.[35] With this caveat, and with the understanding that future DI practice would be closely monitored, the society stated that, as a majority opinion, DI was acceptable even though disquiet about the practice was common in Christian circles.[36] The society commented that all due care should be taken to ensure that incestuous relationships did not occur as a result of DI offspring marrying at a later date. It was declared that, if desired, DI offspring should have access to a 'genetic identity kit' of the donor, although the donor's name should always remain anonymous.[37] The society was also of the opinion that the 'receiving male' should be named as the child's father on the birth certificate, without any further code or comment attached.[38] A central register of DI births would, it was argued, keep track of any DI offspring wishing to marry. Good counselling should ensure that the social parents of the DI child would reveal at a suitable stage the true circumstances of the child's conception.

The Scottish Episcopal Church took an even more positive approach to the practice of DI. They argued that there should be no assessment for suitability for prospective parents seeking DI, that full legitimacy should be accorded to all DI offspring and that the social parents of the child should be recorded on the child's birth certificate as being the child's father and mother.[39] The Church, however, differed from the findings of the Children's Society by arguing that DI offspring should not have access to genetic information regarding the donor, since many children in one-parent families do not have access to this information.[40]

The Methodist Church in Ireland favoured strict screening of donors and prospective parents. They argued that counselling ought to be mandatory and that two obstetricians should give their consent before a couple may take part in a DI programme. Any resulting offspring should be recorded as the child of the social parents, and the child, as an adult, should not have access to information regarding the donor.[41] If these conditions were met, they viewed DI as an acceptable form of infertility treatment for suitable couples.

Mixed responses

A number of contributors to the Warnock debate were unable to reach a clear and consistent consensus in their contributions on DI.

The Methodist Church in Great Britain balanced the therapeutic benefits to the childless couple with the moral problems of separating the unitive and procreative elements in sexual intercourse and the introduction of a third party into a marriage. The church accepted that many Christians find DI unsupportable, while some Christians do allow for its use in limited circumstances.[42] The matter was left unresolved, with an appeal to the report *Choices in Childlessness* for further insight.

This report was, itself, uncertain in its conclusions on DI. It recognized that DI 'is open to moral and legal questions in a way which AIH is not'.[43] It also accepted, however, that DI was a common practice which was likely to continue, regardless of any argument to the contrary. As a result, the report decided to recommend strict controls and guidelines for the exercise of good practice in this respect. The report recommended that all DI agencies be registered, that DI donors should be screened and registered and that the mixing of semen should be made illegal.[44] The report also stated that in the event of a birth following DI, the child should be legitimate, and that access to his or her medical history should be forthcoming, with the proviso that the donor's name remain anonymous.[45]

The report *Choices in Childlessness* provides us with an example of a Christian body grappling with the consequences of DI even though it was unsure of its essential attitude to that practice. In so doing, the report attempted to be realistic regarding its possible influence without wishing to prejudice the arguments of many who believe that DI is unacceptable on moral and religious grounds.

The Church of England, in its original evidence to the Warnock Committee, stated that at that date of writing, the essential Anglican position was not to accept DI.[46] In saying this, they were following the line taken by the Archbishop of Canterbury's Commission in the 1948 report *Artificial Human Insemination*, and by the Lambeth Conference of 1958 which claimed that 'the committee cannot see any possibility of its acceptance by Christian people'.[47]

In addition, the Board for Social Responsibility went on to list a number of problems regarding the management of DI, concluding that even though some may argue to the contrary, DI and adoption are quite distinct concepts. In DI the alleviation of childlessness is the primary concern, while in adoption the care of the child is to the fore. They argued that to equate DI with adoption is to relate the child to the status of a commodity which can be brought into existence solely for the alleviation of a couple's problems.[48]

In their response to the Warnock Report, however, a significant number of the Board's members had either changed their minds or had felt that the time had come to state their personal beliefs. In this response the Board stated: 'The majority of us agree with the report that "those engaging in [DI] are, in their own view, involved in a positive affirmation of the family" and hence [DI] may be regarded as an acceptable practice.' The Board also welcomed the Warnock proposals that DI children should be declared legitimate, and that at the age of eighteen the child should have access to basic genetic information regarding the donor.[49] This acceptance of DI was assumed to be within the context of a code of good practice which would include central registration of donors, recipients and all offspring.

The Mothers' Union was another Anglican body which found great difficulty in grappling with the issue of DI. In their submission to the Warnock Report, the Mothers' Union said: 'By far the majority of our members think that [DI] . . . is ethically and morally wrong and a wrong use of the advancement of medical science.'[50] The Mothers' Union was uncertain regarding the rights of access to information that a DI child should have, and whether or not the husband of the woman giving birth should have his name recorded on the birth certificate.[51]

In their response to the Warnock Report, however, a shift in opinion is noticeable: 'While a sizeable minority of members are not prepared to consider the practice of [DI], whether regulated or not, the majority accept the inevitability of the continuation of the practice and therefore welcome the proposed controls.'[52] This fell short of active support for DI but it does show a change in attitude. The response to the Warnock Report also stated that the majority of Mothers' Union members remained opposed to the introduction of a third party into the marriage relationship, but a majority of members were prepared to accept that this moral stance had to be modified in the light of current practice.[53] In its response to the Government's consultation paper, the Mothers' Union clarified its position by stating that it still opposed DI but that it was also prepared to offer guidelines regarding its practice, as a second line of argument.[54] Having accepted the inevitability of the continuance of DI, the Mothers' Union stated that DI children should be legitimate and that the husband of the woman giving birth should be registered as the child's father, providing he had given his consent to DI.[55]

This debate within the Mothers' Union illustrates well the difficulties involved in adopting a dual approach: stating a preferred moral position and also a second line of argument on the assumption that the moral position does not gain acceptance. A degree of confusion is likely, though it may be argued that in the long term some influence is still exerted over the practice of a technique which otherwise may not be regulated in an acceptable manner.

The Presbyterian Church in Ireland also showed some signs of a shift in opinion as the Warnock debate progressed. In the *ad hoc* group's submission, judgment on the practice of DI was suspended. It was noted that DI affects not only the relationship of the adults involved, but also that of any resulting children with those adults. At the same time, it was accepted that evidence suggested that good practice in the area of DI was common and that counselling was a usual precursor to the technique being employed. The *ad hoc* group noted that the law required changing in order to address the subject of legitimacy, and that tighter controls on the practice of DI would be necessary in the future.[56]

Following the report of the *ad hoc* group, the General Assembly of the church debated the subject and passed a resolution which took a much more conservative line on DI. The church stated that it 'rejects under all circumstances the employment of any procedure which involves the intrusion of a third party into the one flesh union of marriage through the use of donated sperm'.[57] This debate is noteworthy, since it shows, contrary to the debate within the Church of England, a shift to a more conservative position as the topic became more widely discussed within the church.

Unfavourable responses

The remainder of the correspondents to the Warnock Committee were united in their rejection of DI on moral grounds. While most recognized that DI practice was well established, they still voiced their opposition to it and added that if DI was to be practised against their recommendations, strict guidelines should be adhered to.

The Salvation Army recorded that DI was 'contrary to our view of what is morally acceptable or socially desirable'.[58] Nevertheless, they also recognized that DI was an established practice and that its continuance was more or less guaranteed. In the light of this realization, they proposed the establishment of a system of control, registration and monitoring of the work of all medical practitioners active in this field. They also recommended that DI offspring should be considered as the legitimate offspring of the mother and her husband, provided that the husband had given his consent to the procedure.[59]

The Church of Scotland was also strongly critical of the practice of DI. In their response to the Warnock Committee's report, they argued that DI represented 'the unwarranted intrusion of a third party in the marriage relationship'.[60] The church was also unhappy with the current law regarding illegitimacy, but it believed that simply to change the registration practice on a child's birth certificate did not in itself address the underlying issue of paternity.[61] The church felt strongly enough on these matters to write to all Scottish Members of Parliament, outlining their position, which was that while sympathy must be shown to those with fertility problems, such profound feeling must not lead to an acceptance of DI.[62]

The Free Church of Scotland showed equal disquiet at the practice of DI. While not committing themselves to the belief that DI involves adultery, the members of that church's Public Questions, Religion and Moral Committee argued that it constitutes 'an invasion of the divinely sanctioned unity and exclusive "each for other" relationship in marriage'.[63] They reiterated this position in their response to the Government's consultation paper, in which they also argued that a change in the law regarding legitimacy would be inadvisable. They argued that the law relating to illegitimacy served a useful function in that it preserved the status of marriage and of children born within marriage. Any changes in the mode of registration of a child's birth would, they argued, be merely a legal fiction.[64]

The Free Presbyterian Church of Scotland took the toughest line of all Christian groups on DI. In response to the Warnock Report the church submitted that DI was by its nature an adulterous act and prejudicial to the family and society. In addition, they also argued that DI children are not born as a result of proper sexual relations within marriage and hence ought to be declared illegitimate. The church stated that to 'abolish the illegitimate status of the DI child is morally wrong and will not be beneficial to society'.[65] In its recommendations to the Government, the church stated that DI should be made an illegal practice, thus going further than previously noted Christian opinion.[66]

The Baptist Union of Great Britain and Ireland was also critical of DI practice, but, while arguing strongly against its acceptance by Christians, the Union did not believe that DI constituted adultery. In their evidence to the Warnock Committee they argued that one of the causes for concern in DI practice was that the act of procreation was divorced from responsibility, in the context of a continuing relationship between the person donating sperm and any resulting offspring. They argued that such a practice not only leads to the view that genetic material is merely a commodity to be bought or sold, but that the whole concept of responsible parenthood is weakened. DI, they suggested, did not constitute marital unfaithfulness but it did disturb the principle of 'one flesh' within marriage. They concluded that DI should not be used as 'a normally available method for overcoming infertility'.[67]

The Church in Wales also highlighted the problem of allowing a third party to enter the marriage relationship, particularly when that party did so without any subsequent responsibility for his actions. The church, however, was adamant that where a married couple had agreed on DI, adultery was not an issue. Indeed, the church stated that

> When [DI] is undertaken out of such a freely-given mutual
> consent, when it is decided on as an act of love expressing the
> inner meaning of the marriage covenant, when it expresses the
> desire for a child of the wife's own flesh who will be the child of
> the parenthood covenant of the husband as well as the wife,
> then DI hardly constitutes adultery. To the contrary, it may
> well express the very opposite: fidelity in the richest sense of the
> term.[68]

This statement is quoted at length because it shows an argument not commonly approved by Christian groups. Nevertheless, the Church in Wales remained opposed to the practice of DI, not least because of the problems which a husband may face in being made to feel inadequate. The church also recognized the problems which the mother of a DI child has to face in dealing with her own emotions, the needs of a child and the emotional and psychological effects of DI on her husband.[69]

The position of the Church in Wales can be contrasted with the approach taken by the Church of Ireland. While a similar conclusion is reached, the Church of Ireland merely stated:

> Any solution of infertility problems by means of [DI] . . . is wrong and no amount of confidentiality can ever make it one hundred percent anonymous or right, and will in any case make for more misery, fear and suffering than it is meant to cure.

While not stating that DI is an adulterous act or that it should be made illegal, it is clear that the Church of Ireland was strongly opposed to the practice and that it did not consider that in any circumstances DI could be seen as a positive statement by a married couple regarding their fidelity to one another.[70]

Roman Catholic opinion on DI was uniformly opposed to the practice. While allowing that DI is commonly practised, and that it did alleviate infertility for some couples who act in good faith, the technique was condemned on moral and religious grounds. The Catholic Bishops' Joint Committee on Bio-ethical Issues argued, both in its evidence submitted to the Warnock Committee and in its response to the Warnock Report, that DI was not an acceptable practice, since it takes as its starting-point the alleviation of infertility rather than the welfare of the child. It was argued that this is a fundamental flaw in the whole concept of DI. In its evidence to the Warnock Committee the Bishops' Committee stated that 'the rights and interests of the prospective child should systematically prevail over the understandable desires of men and women who want a child'.[71] This opinion was reinforced in the later response to the Warnock Report. The bishops stated:

> Children have the right to be born the true child of a married couple, and thus to have an unimpaired sense of identity. Society should not countenance procedures which deliberately

set out to generate children whose biological parentage or 'identity' differs from their parentage and 'identity' of upbringing . . . As always, the inquiry has viewed the matter exclusively under the aspect of 'a treatment for the alleviation of infertility', and not from the viewpoint of the child proposed to be generated as the means of this alleviation.[72]

The Catholic Union of Great Britain also took issue with the practice of DI, on the grounds that it severed the donor from his parental responsibilities. In replying to the Government's consultation paper, the Union stated that it repudiated the belief that the donor had no obligation to the child who, it was argued, was his by nature. In particular, they contended that where there was no husband, or where a husband refused to care for a DI child, the donor should be expected to fulfil his parental duties. In any case, the Union also proposed that DI children should have the same rights of access to genetic information as children who have been adopted.[73]

The National Board of Catholic Women drew attention to the emphasis in DI on infertility treatment rather than on the welfare of the child. The Board also felt that the intrusion of a third party into the marital relationship upset the spiritual as well as the physical unity within marriage, and that DI would not necessarily deal with feelings of inadequacy within the marriage, particularly for the husband.[74] In its response to the Warnock Report, the Board argued that DI should not be made officially available, and that the mere fact that the practice had been common for some years did not make it acceptable. If, against their wishes, DI was officially sanctioned, then the Board regarded a licensing body as being essential.[75]

Our survey of Christian groups' attitudes to DI concludes with a brief examination of two umbrella evangelical groups: CARE and the Christian Medical Fellowship. CARE, under its previous title of the Nationwide Festival of Light, stated that while extramarital sexual relationships were not necessarily criminal in English law, they were always unlawful in the strictest sense. Consequently, they argued that couples using DI connived in an unlawful act, by allowing the intrusion of a third party into the marriage relationship. The end result of such a process would be the undermining of marriage and the family within society. While it was acknowledged that sexual intercourse would not occur in DI, a woman would have to accept semen into her body. This

should only come from her husband's body. DI, they claimed, constituted marital unfaithfulness.[76]

The Christian Medical Fellowship voiced its opposition to DI,
although it did admit that a small minority of its members did approve
of the practice in limited circumstances. It recognized, however, that DI
was an established practice, and consequently the Fellowship's main
concern was to see it regulated.[77] Such regulation must include
counselling, assessments of prospective parents, and a central record of
all donors and recipients. The DI child should have access to basic
genetic information regarding the donor, but not to the donor's identity.
They also proposed that DI children should be declared to be the
legitimate offspring of the marriage and that there should be two birth
certificates issued; a full one which would state the true nature of the
child's conception, and a shorter one which would simply state that the
husband of the woman giving birth was the child's father.[78]

Analysis

This survey of Christian thought has necessarily involved a good deal of
repetition. Nevertheless, it helps us to identify the major issues that need
to be resolved. Time and again, the same concerns surfaced in the
submissions made by churches and other Christian groups.

For us, the main issues to be resolved here are the intrusive nature or
otherwise of DI into marriage, the question of the separation of genetic
and legal paternity, and the practice of offering DI to those who are in a
heterosexual relationship but who are not married, or to those who are
single or in a homosexual relationship.

DI and marriage

In addressing the core question of the intrusive nature or otherwise of DI,
we must state, first of all, that there can be no question of DI constituting
adultery, as some Christian groups suggested.[79] In DI there is no personal
contact between the individuals involved and the identity of the donor is
unknown. The contact is at the purely clinical level of the transfer of
genetic material from one person to another. While this is not without
significance, it bears no resemblance to adultery where personal contact
and, very often, emotional attachment are at the centre of the act.

This being said, it is true that in some successful cases of DI a married woman will have a child without her husband's physical involvement. There is a strong possibility that her husband will feel that she has abandoned him with his infertility problem. This feeling may well be exacerbated by the fact that his wife has turned to another man, albeit a stranger with whom she will have no personal or sexual contact, in order to have a child. Consequently, while we cannot equate DI with adultery, there are still serious moral and personal issues to be resolved.

That there is an intrusive element in DI is evident from the fact that a solution to a couple's infertility is found by recourse to a third party who has to contribute his sperm in place of the sperm of the infertile husband. While different couples will react to this prospect differently at an emotional level, our task is to find whether or not such a practice is, in principle, wrong or inadvisable. It may be the case that because of the danger of an adverse effect on a couple's marriage, they should be advised against DI, but this risk would not make it morally wrong in all cases. At the same time, if DI is wrong in principle, then no matter how well a couple may react to it, it would be wrong for them to accept this form of treatment.

The question we need to answer is: does DI so separate the unitive and procreative aspects of sex that it compromises the use of the gift of sex within a marriage and so risks compromising the marriage itself? We have already seen that it cannot be proved that the unitive and procreative aspects of sex must always belong together. In the Christian tradition, based on the Scriptures, however, it has been understood that in giving sex this double function, God designed it so that procreation and the unitive relationship of marriage should belong together. Seen in this light, DI does compromise the gift of sex within a marriage, even when both partners are in agreement that DI is acceptable, since there is no unitive relationship whatever between the woman and the donor.

The question of levirate marriage is sometimes introduced to suggest that the principle of third-party intrusion is acceptable. This does not follow, however, for in levirate marriage the husband of the woman was already dead and the brother of the deceased would have been allowed more than one wife in any case. The laws regarding levirate marriage[80] are of some relevance regarding the question of genetic and legal paternity, but they should not be used to support the principle behind DI.

Our approach, then, views DI as an unacceptable intrusion into a couple's marriage, even though this intrusion may be acceptable to the people in question. On principle, rather than on the basis of how individual couples may feel, it has to be said that DI compromises the Christian understanding of sex and marriage. Because God has given us the gift of sex both for procreation and for building a unitive relationship between a man and a woman, both these aspects of this gift should be held together unless through illness or age it is not possible.

This does not mean that infertile couples may not enjoy the unitive aspects of sex or that sexual experiences should end at menopause. Equally, every sexual act does not have to be potentially a procreative act. It does assert, though, that where it is possible, a couple ought to experience both the unitive and procreative aspects of sex in the course of their marriage. In DI, a couple accept that they are unable to do this, but attempt to overcome the difficulty by introducing a third party into their experience of life together in such a way that the third party fulfils one of the functions normally fulfilled by the husband. A woman accepts from another man the means of fulfilment of one aspect of her sexual life without any unitive relationship with him, and he donates sperm and engages in procreation without experiencing any unitive relationship at any stage with the mother of his child. The happiness of the woman, and even of her husband, at her being able to bear a child should not be minimized, but the price to pay is too great for the practice to be accepted.

As scientific progress continues, advances in IVF techniques are likely to result in DI being used less frequently than at present. Where this is not possible, due, for example, to an impossibly low sperm count, then, with regret, we must accept that a marriage is better served in the sharing of infertility than in looking beyond the marriage for a fulfilment of one aspect of a couple's experience of sex. To argue otherwise is to allow a complete separation of the two aspects of sex and thus, in principle, to endorse procreation without love or responsibility.

Legal and genetic parenthood

We need to look in some detail at the issue of the separation of legal and genetic paternity which was enshrined in the 1990 Act. It is best to begin by refreshing our memories regarding the basic position in law. Where two people, married or not, come to a treatment centre for artificial insemination of the woman by the man's sperm, that man will be the legal father of the child. In this case, legal and genetic fatherhood are the same. In cases of DI where a woman seeks treatment with her husband's or partner's consent, then he, not the anonymous donor, is the legal father of the child. In cases where a woman presents herself for treatment without a male partner, or where her partner refuses consent, then any resulting child will be without a legal father. In no circumstances will the anonymous donor become the legal father of the child. If the woman's partner has not in fact given his consent, the onus is on him to prove that that is the case; in the absence of such proof it will be assumed that he is the legal father of the child.

The first question which faces us here is whether legal and genetic fatherhood should be separated in this way. It is true that the separation of legal and genetic fatherhood is an established practice in certain circumstances. In adoptions such a separation exists, and, as we have seen, in the biblical instance of levirate marriage such a separation was actually commanded. Adoption, though, is very different from DI, since in adoption a child is not deliberately conceived with a view to such a separation. The intention behind the two processes is quite different: in adoption a father is provided for a child who in all probability would have grown up without the presence or perhaps even the knowledge of a father; in DI a transfer of paternity is an essential part of the arrangement from the outset. The example of levirate marriage is also different from DI, since in that case the legal father is deceased, while the genetic father would have had responsibility in nurturing the child even though the child would have borne the legal father's name. In any case, the cultural environment is so different that any argument from levirate marriage to present-day circumstances carries little weight.

While it is understandable that couples opt for DI, we must express concern over any automatic transfer of paternal rights and responsibilities to the husband of a woman who accepts DI. While it may be said that the husband of a woman accepting DI deserves to be the father of any resulting child, if he has given his consent to such treatment, the fact remains that he is not the genetic father of the child. The woman could have had the same child without his consent. Furthermore, the child will always be hers in a way that it can never be his.

Having said this, there should be no barrier placed against a man applying to become the adoptive father of such a child, after the child is born. But it is living out a legal fiction to give automatic parental rights to a man who has had no genetic input into the child's life. The 1990 Act further confuses the issue by saying that the same man, had he not given his consent, would not have been the father of the child. To make fatherhood a matter of such subjective processes does not advance the status of parenthood or of the family.

Paradoxically, however, under the present law, the refusal to allow a donor any parental rights is clearly correct. While he may be the genetic father of a child born following DI, he will have no personal relationship with the mother of the child and will take no part in deciding which woman should be inseminated with his sperm. This is not to deny the principle that the genetic parent ought to be the legal parent. Rather, it indicates that DI is, in essence, an unacceptable practice. Being realistic, though, we must recognize that DI will continue. In these circumstances, damage limitation is called for. To allow the genetic father any parental rights would make matters worse rather than better. This serves to underline the unacceptable nature of DI, since it can only work at the cost of separating legal and genetic parenthood. This endangers the development of responsible parenthood as well as threatening the stability of the family unit within society.

DI *outside marriage*

For single women, or women in homosexual relationships, or women wishing to be inseminated with their deceased husband's sperm, DI is not acceptable. To separate reproduction from marriage is to undermine the status of the family and to denigrate to a large extent the role of the father in a family. While babies will continue to be born to single women or to women whose husbands have died during their wives' pregnancies, these are to be viewed as unenviable circumstances which should evoke compassion and support. To bring about similar circumstances deliberately is a different matter. This suggests that marriage is not the correct environment for procreation. Fatherhood is seen as an optional extra. In the case of a woman in a homosexual relationship, the dual aspects of sex are totally separated. All of this runs counter to the principles we have suggested, drawn from biblical and traditional Christian teaching.

We need to emphasize, though, that the pastoral responsibilities of the church do not end with such a statement of principle. They must extend to the care and acceptance of people involved in any DI arrangement. Children born as a result of DI should never be stigmatized. This is, of course, the case with children born in any circumstances we might care to imagine.

DI *and the law*

Summing up the discussion so far, we can say that those Christian groups which opposed the practice of DI were right, though those which argued that DI constituted adultery were wrong. We must, however, answer a further question: were some Christians right to state that DI was wrong, but then to go on to propose guidelines for its practice in acknowledgment that it was unlikely that it would be made illegal? To answer this question we must recall our earlier discussion on morality and law. There we said that in order for a practice to be made illegal, it must not only be immoral but also pose a threat to society, individuals or the environment.

We have argued that the correct Christian approach to DI is to reject the practice as immoral. In spite of feelings of compassion towards those who are infertile, the most loving and just course of action is to safeguard the nature of sex within marriage and also the essential link between genetic and legal parenthood. We accept that the nature of sex within marriage is often compromised and that genetic and legal parenthood are often separated, sometimes because of human selfishness, and sometimes, in the case of adoption, through human compassion. Nevertheless, to advocate DI as an acceptable practice is to endorse the separation of genetic and legal parenthood as a matter of principle. It also places the nature of sex within marriage, and hence the family unit, under institutionalized threat.

Real harm to individuals may well follow DI arrangements, especially where the husband is not involved in the decision and the children so born learn of their origin. The family unit as an essential part of society is placed under threat and, even though the place of the family has already been greatly eroded, any further erosion can only bode ill for the stability of society in the future. All of this would suggest that DI ought to be made an illegal practice, and that Christians should argue for a change in the law, as well as advising couples against adopting DI as a solution to their infertility problem. Certainly, making DI available to unmarried women, be they heterosexual or homosexual, is a direct attack on the place of the family in society.

The one consideration which would cause us to question this conclusion is that those married couples who do opt for DI do so in order to strengthen their marriage and to create a new stable family unit in society. This means that we are faced with a paradox. Even though DI attacks a Christian understanding of the nature of marriage and the family, in principle it is difficult to prove that the actual practice of DI has, on balance, led to any greater marital disharmony or placed marriages under any greater strain than has infertility. Consequently, it cannot be proved, from statistical evidence, to threaten social order or to cause harm to others. This means that while we will continue to see DI as a threat to marriage and to the role of the family in society, the point cannot be proved sufficiently to demand that the practice be made illegal.

We conclude, therefore, that DI is always to be rejected on moral grounds, but that it should not be made illegal for a married couple to seek DI if both partners consent to the practice. DI for unmarried women, for widows and for women whose husbands object to the practice should be illegal, for its use in these situations represents an unmitigated threat to the family unit within society.

If it is argued that on that basis, all childbirth to single women should be made illegal, it must be pointed out that DI is different in that it represents medical intervention with the specific purpose of creating a child. It is a deliberate, medically controlled example of intervention, very different from the circumstances and intentions which give rise to single-parent families. Similarly, divorce should not be made illegal, even though it weakens the place of the family unit within society. Divorce is a legal acceptance that a marriage has broken down; it is not the cause of the breakdown. It is impossible to legislate for marital harmony. Thus, while divorce is not a means of settling marital problems it is, at times, necessary.

8

Egg and embryo donation

Survey

The Warnock Report and subsequent Government papers

In its sixth chapter, the Warnock Report dealt with the question of egg donation. In genetic terms, egg donation is the female equivalent of DI, though, as yet, it has not been possible to freeze eggs for future use. In addition, the extra problem of possible risk to the donor's health must be taken into consideration.[1]

The arguments in favour of the use of egg donation were similar to those suggested in DI. Egg donation has one advantage over DI, however, in that it offers the chance of both parties to be actively involved in the pregnancy. While it is true that the child cannot be the genetic child of the woman, it is still possible for the woman to experience every other aspect of pregnancy normally.[2]

Since the Warnock Committee had already accepted DI in principle, it was only to be expected that, within the framework of medical good practice and supervision by a licensing authority, egg donation was also found to be an acceptable form of infertility treatment.[3] In line with their statement on legitimacy and parental rights in regard to DI children, the committee members also recommended that the donor in egg donation should have no parental rights or responsibilities and that the carrying mother should be considered the legal mother of the child.[4]

In their subsequent consultation document, the Government noted that they had received a number of objections to egg donation on the ground that it was not appropriate for the woman giving birth not to have donated the egg.[5] Nevertheless, in its White Paper the Government recommended that egg donation be accepted subject to regulation by a statutory licensing authority, although the previously noted restrictions on the storage time of gametes would also apply.[6]

Embryo donation is a natural extension of DI and egg donation using IVF techniques. While this form of treatment is suitable only where both partners are infertile or carry known dominant or recessive genes, or where one partner is infertile and the other carries a dominant gene, a small number of couples have found this technique their only hope of the woman giving birth to a child they consider to be their own. While genetically the child cannot be considered to be theirs, psychologically, couples seeking this type of treatment are likely to consider any resulting offspring as belonging completely to their family.

All the combined objections to DI and egg donation were noted by the Warnock Committee as well as objections to the use of IVF techniques. The committee also noted the added objection that where the lavage method of embryo collection was used, the donor faced the possibility of pregnancy or infection. They also recognized that in cases of embryo donation the eventual parents will have no genetic link with the child.[7]

Against these arguments, the committee considered the evidence that embryo donation represented a form of prenatal adoption, and that in this form of treatment the woman and child enjoyed the experience of bonding during pregnancy.[8]

The Warnock Committee's recommendations were that embryo donation should be allowed under regulation only where fertilization took place *in vitro*, and that the same conditions should apply in regard to legitimacy and the rights of donors and parents as in DI and egg donation.[9] In the consultation document some reservations were expressed since division of opinion was likely in this area,[10] but in the White Paper the Warnock proposals were accepted with one amendment: embryos were to be stored for a maximum of five years, not ten as Warnock recommended.[11]

The Human Fertilization and Embryology Act 1990

The 1990 Act recognizes the many similarities between DI and egg or embryo donation. The regulations which apply to DI consequently apply also, where relevant, to egg or embryo donation. The obvious difference between DI and egg or embryo donation is that in the former case the woman is the genetic mother of the child as well as its social mother, while in the latter case there is no genetic link between the woman carrying the child and the child itself. In keeping with the principle that genetic parenthood is not a primary consideration, the Act states that in all cases the carrying mother is to be recognized as the legal mother of the child.[12] This provision does not, of course, affect any subsequent decision to have the child adopted, when another woman would then become the legal mother of the child.[13]

Christian submissions

It should not surprise us that many of the arguments presented in the debate on DI also surfaced in the debate on egg donation. Indeed, while there were certain refinements in the arguments used, no church or Christian body which made submissions during the course of the Warnock debate took an essentially different approach to egg donation from that taken in regard to DI.

Favourable responses to egg donation

The churches and groups most positive in their acceptance of egg donation were the Methodist Church in Ireland, the Church of England and the Children's Society. The Methodist Church in Ireland suggested that similar controls should be exercised in the practice of egg donation as in DI, but, with this condition noted, no other obstacle was advanced to question the technique.[14] The Church of England, in addition to noting that the same moral and legal difficulties applied to egg donation as to DI, recognized that there was a certain health risk to the donor in the process of collecting the egg. Nevertheless, in principle the church recommended that, as a majority opinion of the members of the Board for Social Responsibility, egg donation should be accepted as an acceptable form of infertility treatment in appropriate cases.[15] The Children's Society recorded that a minority of its members rejected egg donation on the grounds that the genetic mother would not be the same person as the physiological mother, but that as a majority opinion egg donation was acceptable.[16]

The report *Choices in Childlessness* did not attempt to reach a definitive position on egg donation, but concerned itself with noting that, in principle, moral objections to the practice did exist. No clear recommendation was advanced, however, as to whether or not egg donation should continue to be practised. Equally, it did not determine whether the moral objections to the technique were such as to preclude acceptance on the grounds of a Christian ethic.[17]

Unfavourable responses to egg donation

In submissions to the Warnock Committee or subsequently to the Government, those churches and groups which opposed egg donation did so on the grounds on which they opposed DI. In some cases the opposition was even more keenly felt. CARE, for example, found the removal of an egg from its natural environment a totally objectionable practice. The natural process of conception necessitates the male gamete being expelled from a man's body, but this is not the case with the female gamete. Thus, an additional degree of interference is introduced in egg donation contrasted with DI.[18] The Church of Scotland expressed the view that egg donation may lead to the treatment of women, in certain circumstances, as little more than incubators. The severing of gestation from conception in such a radical way as practised in egg donation, would, they argued, lead to a demeaned status for women.[19]

Embryo donation

As was to be expected, those churches and Christian bodies which rejected DI and egg donation also rejected embryo donation, although some extra arguments were advanced to support this position. Only one church accepted the technique, while one other group gave its tacit support to the technique without discussing it in detail.

The Methodist Church in Ireland stated that it had no objection to embryo transfer (in this context embryo donation) provided certain basic guidelines were observed. These were quite extensive and included the stipulations that the potential mother should be unable to become pregnant in any other way, that her health would not be impaired by the pregnancy, that the potential parents should enjoy a stable relationship, that a conscience clause should be involved for medical staff who found such a technique morally objectionable, that the programme should be available on the National Health Service, and that it should not represent an unnecessary drain on public money.[20]

The Children's Society did not discuss embryo donation in any detail, but in discussing egg donation they also stated:

> The donation of an egg must be on the same basis as the donation of sperm, i.e. the rights and responsibilities of parenthood pass to the recipient with the donation, in return for an acceptance of the anonymity and unapproachableness of the genetic parent. Sperm or embryos can only be given to a third party and never loaned.[21]

This statement gives tacit support to the technique of embryo donation, even though the matter was not discussed more fully in its own right.

In its evidence to the Warnock Committee, and again in its response to the Report, the Salvation Army stated that it disagreed with egg and embryo donation. In its response to the Government's consultation paper, however, the Army reported that 'a pragmatic, second order view suggests that the practice cannot be eliminated and we thus favour formal control, such control to be included in the role of the Statutory Licensing Authority'.[22] This statement certainly did not denote an acceptance of embryo donation on moral or religious grounds, but it did conflict with those bodies which insisted that embryo donation must never become acceptable in any event.

One church did shift its position in responding to the subject of embryo donation compared with its stated position on DI and egg donation. The Church of England's Board for Social Responsibility stated that by a small majority its members could not accept embryo donation as a means of alleviating infertility. In so doing, the Board raised the theological issue of how far nature was 'given' by God and how far humans are to co-operate in perfecting or correcting nature. While acknowledging that the principle of genetic intervention in procreation had already been granted in the acceptance of DI and egg donation, the Board nevertheless felt that complete intervention, in which 100% of the genetic material involved had come from outside the bodies of the potential parents, was unacceptable. The Board was aware that it could be accused of arguing on the basis of pragmatism or emotion rather than on principle, but it nevertheless held to its stated view. It felt that a child whose genetic origins had to be kept entirely anonymous would be unfairly treated by a society which allowed such an occurrence, and that such a child would have begun its life more as a product or a commodity than as a human being deserving dignity.[23]

Other churches and Christian groups which opposed embryo donation did so by referring to their statements on DI or egg donation, with the exception of the Catholic Bishops' Joint Committee on Bio-ethical Issues, which added a further argument to its previous statements. In particular, the committee voiced concern at embryo donation by lavage. The specific issue raised was that the Warnock Committee had accepted embryo donation in principle but had rejected this particular method of donation because of risk to the egg donor. The Bishops' Committee stated:

> The risk the inquiry has in mind is primarily the 'risk of pregnancy' for the egg donor (para. 7.2). In truth, the egg donor does become pregnant but her pregnancy is interrupted after three or four days by the washing out of the embryo before implantation. The whole procedure is one in which the body of the donor, like the embryo itself, is instrumentalised, i.e. used as a mere means to the ends of other people.[24]

One interesting comment on embryo donation was made in this regard by the Catholic Union of Great Britain. While rejecting embryo donation, they did not wish to see the practice made illegal in case a woman wished to offer her womb in order to give continued life to an embryo which would otherwise be discarded or destroyed.[25]

Analysis

Because of IVF, the number of women who may be helped by egg donation is small, and the number who would make use of embryo donation is smaller still, but the techniques have been used. This discussion is, therefore, not merely of theoretical interest. Some of the arguments in a discussion of egg or embryo donation are the same as for a discussion of DI, in particular the separation of legal and genetic parenthood in a deliberate manner. There are, however, differences in the argument regarding the intrusive nature of these techniques compared with DI.

As we have seen, in DI, the sperm of a third party is used to inseminate a woman in order to fulfil a function which her husband is not able to fulfil. In accepting such treatment, a woman or a couple must accept a degree of intrusion into their relationship, even if this cannot be equated with adultery. In the case of egg donation, a third party must also be used, but in this case the woman accepts from another woman something which she is unable to provide for herself: a healthy ovum. In this instance there is, at most, minimal intrusion into the marital relationship, for what is happening is not something which can ever be mirrored naturally within marriage. The woman is not accepting something which in a natural way she could have received from her husband as part of their sexual life together, while, of course, the husband is not receiving anything. In some ways it may be suggested that egg donation resembles organ donation more than it does DI, for there are no sexual overtones in receiving an egg from another woman as there are in receiving sperm from a man.

Having said this, other problems do remain. The sperm of the woman's husband must be mixed *in vitro* with the donated egg. In this way the separation between the dual aspects of the gift of sex which we noted in DI still occurs. The problem with deliberately separating legal and genetic parenthood is also present, though it may be argued that because the woman receiving the egg will be the only woman implanted with the embryo, she has something of a claim to motherhood.

In the case of embryo donation, the separation of the unitive and procreative aspects of sex is total, as is the separation of legal and genetic parenthood. The argument that embryo donation is an antenatal form of adoption is valid only at a genetic level for, as we have already argued, the intention behind adoption and the intention behind deliberately creating a child in this way are different.

As DI failed to meet with approval, neither egg nor embryo donation can be viewed positively. Once again, though, we ought to extend sympathy and understanding to those couples who would wish to use the technique. While the invasive techniques necessary to collect ova need not constitute a moral objection to the practice of egg or embryo donation, they may constitute practical problems for some.

As with DI, egg donation is always morally unacceptable, though it should be made illegal only in cases where unmarried women wish to be the recipients.

Embryo donation is also morally unacceptable and there are good grounds for arguing that it should not be a lawful practice. It allows the creation of embryos without any parental responsibility on the part of either genetic parent, thus encouraging society to view embryos and children as commodities. This is a direct assault on the status of embryos and children which represents a real harm being done to them and a real threat to society, and should properly be the subject of prohibitive legislation.

9

In vitro fertilization (IVF)

Survey

The Warnock Report and subsequent Government papers

In discussing *in vitro* fertilization, the Warnock Committee followed its customary procedure of examining arguments for and against the use of the technique. Practical limitations inherent in the technique were recognized, as were moral objections. The committee took note of the objection that the procreative aspect of sex should not be separated from the act of sexual intercourse. It also accepted the reality that, since most IVF treatments require the creation of more embryos than can be subsequently implanted in the woman undergoing treatment, many unwanted embryos will be destroyed. Some respondents also objected to IVF on the grounds that, as a highly technological method of treatment, it was too expensive and hence took too much money away from other more widely needed forms of health care.[1]

Against these arguments, the committee recorded only one basic argument in favour of the use of IVF: that for some couples IVF represents the only chance they will ever have of becoming the parents of a child that is genetically theirs.[2]

This argument was sufficient to sway the mind of the committee. While recognizing the current low success rate of the technique, and the resulting problem of extra embryos being left either to die or to be frozen for possible future use, the committee recommended that IVF treatment, under licence, should be made available as widely as possible within the National Health Service.[3] Subject to IVF treatment being offered only by agencies licensed by a proposed independent statutory licensing authority, the Government, in its White Paper mapping out a framework for legislation, upheld the Warnock opinion.[4]

The Human Fertilization and Embryology Act 1990

Following Warnock, the 1990 Act accepts IVF as an acceptable form of infertility treatment, subject to certain conditions.

Because IVF is important both for certain types of infertility treatment and for embryo research, the Act recognizes that the distinction between these two uses of IVF is a central one. The Act stipulates that IVF may be practised only under licence, even in cases where the gametes used are those of a woman and her partner who wish to have a child using techniques which require the application of IVF.[5] In all cases consent must be given regarding the use of any IVF embryo, and this consent must state clearly whether or not the embryos created are to be used for implantation into the woman giving consent, for implantation into another woman, for embryo research, or for a number of these uses.[6] Without exception, consent must be given by the donors of gametes to allow their gametes to be used in an IVF programme.[7]

Christian submissions

In contrast to DI, egg donation and embryo donation, IVF was, in principle, acceptable to most, though not all, Christian groups which made submissions to the Warnock Committee or which responded to later Government papers. A few churches were critical of the technique in principle, although most of the groups which stated that IVF was an acceptable form of treatment for infertility also stated that certain conditions had to be met in practice before they could give the IVF programme their full support. As we shall see, some of the conditions suggested were so strict that in practice few if any IVF practitioners would be prepared to accept them.

Objections in principle

The Roman Catholic Church had difficulty in principle, as well as in practice, with IVF. The principle involved is one that we have already encountered in our discussion on AIH: the severing of procreation from sexual intercourse. The core of the problem is that in IVF the natural unity of procreation and sexual intercourse is disrupted in such a way as to make procreation no longer dependent on an act of intercourse between spouses. This was keenly stated in the evidence submitted to the Warnock Committee by the Catholic Bishops' Joint Committee on Bio-ethical Issues:

> In procreation by sexual intercourse, one and the same act of choice, made by each spouse, governs both the experienced and expressive sexual union and the procreation of the child. There is one intentional act, and its intention remains governing even when procreation depends on supplementing the act of intercourse by some technical means. But in IVF these are irreducibly separate acts of choice, all indispensable, and all independent acts of different people.[8]

They further argued that in IVF the child tends to be viewed as a product which is brought into existence solely for the benefit of the parents involved. Not only can the child not say that it had its origin in a single act of love between its parents, but it is also deprived of 'the status which the child of sexual union has, a status which is a great good for any child: the status of radical equality with parents, as partners like them in the familial community'.[9]

In addition to these objections in principle, practical problems were also recognized. The committee rejected any IVF programme which made use of embryo research or experimentation which might cause damage to the embryo or delay its implantation. Similarly, any procedure which used multiple fertilization, but then chose only the healthiest embryos for implantation, was discounted. The equally problematic question of multiple implantation, used frequently in many IVF programmes, was cited as an obstacle to acceptance of the technique.[10] Underpinning all of these objections was the Roman Catholic Church's belief that the embryo should be treated with full human rights from the time of conception.[11]

In spite of these grave misgivings, the Roman Catholic Church did allow for the state to provide IVF, as long as it was available to married couples only and that no intentional killing of embryos resulted from the technique. This was a concession to public law rather than an opinion based on theology or Roman Catholic ethical teaching. In practice it may not be possible to construct an IVF programme which does not necessitate the likely destruction of at least some embryos.[12]

The National Board of Catholic Women echoed the bishops' views in its submission to the Warnock Committee, voicing grave concern over many practical aspects of current IVF programmes.[13] In response to the Warnock Report, the Board recommended that IVF should be available only to married couples and that no destruction of embryos should be involved.[14] Given the widespread use of superovulation and multiple fertilization, few IVF programmes would meet these criteria.

Objections in practice

The Free Presbyterian Church of Scotland took an uncompromisingly negative view on the practice of IVF. The church made the point that the technique should be viewed in the light of its actual practice rather than in the light of some future idealistic practice or of pure theory. They cited many of the objections advanced by the Roman Catholic Church. They also objected to the association of masturbation with IVF and the fact that current IVF techniques were the 'legacy of countless exploited human embryos'.[15] These factors led the church to recommend that IVF should be made a criminal offence.[16] In its response to the Government's consultation paper, the church noted that gamete intrafallopian transfer (GIFT) was a new technique which should be given more financial backing, as it did not carry with it the moral objections associated with IVF and no spare embryos had to be produced.[17]

The Church of Scotland was positive in its attitude to IVF in principle, but had problems over certain aspects of the IVF programme in practice. The church was opposed to the creation of 'spare' embryos, and hence found the practice of super-ovulation unacceptable. As this technique commonly accompanies IVF, the whole concept of IVF had to be questioned. The church also noted that resources spent on developing IVF should not be diverted from other possible infertility treatments which were not morally objectionable. In particular, research into the causes and possible treatment of tubal blockage should not suffer because of the current interest in IVF.[18]

The response by the Church of Scotland illustrates the problem which many Christian groups faced: how to react to a technique which, in theory or in an ideal form, is not necessarily contrary to their moral and theological standards but which, in its application, does frequently contravene acceptable codes of practice. The inevitable consequence of such a dilemma is that some observers who wish to find ecclesiastical support for IVF will simply cite the statement of support in principle while overlooking the causes for concern in practice. Equally, if Christian bodies were not to state that they had examined the issue primarily as a matter of principle, they would be criticized for failing to address central moral propositions – the very criticism that some churches levelled against the Warnock Committee.

The Report *Choices in Childlessness* followed a line of reasoning similar to the Church of Scotland's response to Warnock. The working party responsible for the report declared that its members had no moral objections to IVF in principle within the confines of marriage. The problem of risk to the future life and well-being of embryos conceived through IVF, however, exercised the minds of the working party. The condition laid down for acceptable IVF practice was summarized in a brief but embracing statement: 'The risk ought not to be greater than that involved in normal processes of conception and birth.'[19] This criterion was such as to make it virtually impossible for the working party to accept any IVF programme. It is doubtful if any IVF practitioner would be prepared to give an assurance that IVF poses no greater risk to embryos than does normal conception. Indeed, it may even be argued that since it is difficult to discover the percentage of spontaneous miscarriages within two weeks of conception in normal circumstances, the criterion cannot possibly be met. In practice, the proviso suggested by the report would relegate IVF to the status of a theoretically acceptable treatment which could not be applied in practice.

Guarded acceptance

Other Christian groups were generally positive in their acceptance of IVF, as long as previously stated views on DI and egg or embryo donation were not compromised. The Methodist Church in Great Britain saw IVF within marriage as equivalent to AIH, and saw no legal or moral objections to its practice, though the church did believe that IVF programmes should be controlled by a licensing authority which should dictate a strict code of practice.[20] The Methodist Church in Ireland was equally sympathetic to the application of IVF in appropriate circumstances, though their approval extended also to a combination of IVF with DI or egg donation, in keeping with their previously stated policy.[21]

The Free Church of Scotland initially stated in a response to the Warnock Report that it strongly supported the development of IVF provided that it was conducted within the framework of marriage and that DI or egg donation were not involved.[22] After further deliberation, however, the church modified its support to state, in response to the Government's consultation paper, that other safeguards should also be put in place before IVF could be considered to be morally acceptable. The church was particularly concerned about the treatment of all embryos resulting from an IVF programme. It stated that there should be no experimentation or destruction of 'spare' embryos, and that, in principle, a decision should be taken that all embryos should be transferred to the mother's womb.[23]

The Presbyterian Church in Ireland also found it necessary to outline its position more fully as the debate continued. In the submission of its *ad hoc* committee, a general welcome was given to IVF 'within the moral law of personal relationships'.[24] In 1985, the General Assembly of the church passed a resolution which detailed more fully what the 'moral law of personal relationships' actually entailed. It stated that IVF was acceptable only within marriage, and that no donated gametes or embryos could be used without intruding in an unacceptable way into the marriage relationship of the couple seeking treatment for their infertility problem.[25]

Anglican opinion in the United Kingdom was generally favourable to IVF. The Church of England did acknowledge that if IVF became too common a practice, possible dangers might arise for the status of normal sexual relationships and procreation within marriage. Since fewer than 0.5% of all couples are likely to seek IVF, however, the element of risk is slight. The church stated that

> The ethical question therefore which has to be decided is to what extent the legislation of exceptions (with a good aim and with good results) will depreciate the norm. Judgements here

> will differ; but if the intention behind the practice is good, and
> if the effect on resultant children is not deleterious, it would
> seem to the majority of us that the number of couples who
> would deviate from the norm through the use of this technique
> is too small a proportion of all couples with children to
> endanger the nature of marriage or respect for any embryo.[26]

This viewpoint was shared by the Scottish Episcopal Church, which did not outline any moral objection to IVF in principle, and which recommended that IVF should be controlled, along with other infertility treatments, by a statutory licensing authority.[27] The Church of Ireland was unhappy that IVF and other infertility treatments might divert funds from research into infant mortality and child handicap. Nevertheless, it stated that IVF was acceptable as long as it was conducted within marriage and that couples so treated were under forty years of age.[28] The Mothers' Union accepted IVF within marriage without any further conditions.[29]

A pattern emerged from the Anglican responses in the debate. They demonstrated a desire to deal with the broad principles involved in IVF without dealing with all the possible practical effects of the technique. This approach was also evident in many other Christian responses. It is indicative of the complexity of the issue of IVF, especially combined with DI and other infertility techniques, that most churches did not attempt to cover every aspect of the subject. As we have already seen, this may have given rise to a degree of uncertainty regarding the churches' position on the subject. It is unclear whether silence on a particular aspect of IVF denoted agreement with it or merely an oversight on behalf of the body submitting evidence. We must, therefore, keep in mind that statements regarding IVF have to be read in the light of other statements on other aspects of the Warnock debate.

The Salvation Army accepted IVF within marriage, in principle, but it was not confident about its application. A worry similar to that which exercised the minds of the members of the Church of England's Board for Social Responsibility surfaced in the evidence submitted to the Warnock Committee. The Salvation Army was concerned that IVF or other infertility treatments might supplant other, more natural, means of dealing with the problem of infertility. While not rejecting IVF, the Salvation Army recommended that couples should consider the technique only after counselling, which should include the possibility of accepting childlessness as well as considering either adoption or fostering.[30]

CARE also shared the worry that an excessive use of IVF would lead to a situation where normal sexual intercourse would be bypassed as a means of achieving conception. The result of this would be to impoverish both marriage and society. The group argued, therefore, that IVF should be used only as an emergency measure and never outside marriage.[31] In CARE's response to the Warnock Report, the added safeguard was introduced that all embryos should be transferred to the womb of the mother.[32]

In their response to the Government's consultation document, the Christian Medical Fellowship stated that IVF was an acceptable method of treating infertility in certain cases, though it should be available only to married couples. The Fellowship stated that only a minority of its members could accept DI, egg donation or embryo donation, but that if such practices were to be allowed under eventual Government legislation, then a licensing authority should regulate both them and IVF. The possibility of IVF being combined with other infertility treatments, such as DI, was recognized but not accepted on moral grounds.[33]

Analysis

The practice of IVF was already established when the Warnock Committee issued its report. The committee's acceptance of the practice and the subsequent inclusion of it as an acceptable practice, under licence, in the 1990 Act was to be expected since there was, and is, widespread public support for this technique. This does not mask the fact, however, that there are still a number of ethical issues that need to be resolved.

IVF and the nature of sex

Some have argued that the practice of IVF represents a separation between the unitive and procreative aspects of sex. As with AIH, DI, and egg or embryo transfer, conception does not take place as a direct result of sexual intercourse. While this is so, it does not follow that IVF is an unacceptable method of infertility treatment for Christians. The argument we advanced in our discussion of AIH is still valid.

If a married couple use IVF as part of their whole experience of life together, in which they wish to enjoy both aspects of the gift of sex, then IVF is an acceptable practice. In the overall context of their marriage the couple aims to enjoy both the unitive and procreative goods of marriage. IVF assists them in achieving that goal.

The real problems with IVF lie in its application in practice. This is partly because it is often combined with DI or egg or embryo donation. We have already argued that DI, egg donation and embryo donation are not acceptable forms of infertility treatment, so it follows that when IVF is used in conjunction with any of these techniques, this represents an unacceptable use of the technique. In this context IVF compounds the misuse of the gift of sex.

Superovulation and spare embryos

It is normal for superovulation to be part of the process of IVF and for a number of embryos to be created *in vitro*. Of these, it is usual for three to be implanted, with the understanding that, in most cases, at least two will fail to implant. The success rate for IVF when fewer embryos are transferred is very low.

This leaves a couple considering IVF with three ethical problems to contend with. First, do they accept a practice which will probably result in the loss of at least two embryos? Secondly, how do they determine what is to be done with the remaining untransferred embryos? Thirdly, what ought to be done with those embryos which are known to be malformed? Since it is extremely difficult, if not impossible, for most couples to receive treatment where only one embryo is created and transferred, those considering IVF must face up to all of these problems.

Loss of embryos

While we must not minimize the low success rate of IVF, the fact that most transferred embryos will fail to implant is not an insurmountable obstacle to accepting IVF. Unassisted conception is also a high-risk affair, with many, if not most, embryos failing to implant. As long as the intention in both cases is the same (to achieve an established pregnancy), then there is no moral objection to IVF on these grounds. The idea of accepting a treatment which may result in the loss of such a percentage of transferred embryos may seem rather clinical and calculating, but this hardly represents a moral objection. It does, however, underline the need for good counselling.

Spare embryos

The problem of remaining embryos is a real one, for few centres would be prepared to transfer all suitable embryos on one occasion. If a couple were committed to using the remaining embryos in a future attempt to become pregnant, then the problem is minimized. The difficulty still remains, of course, that a couple cannot be sure that they will attempt a second pregnancy or that it would be medically advisable for them to do so. Nevertheless, if, after counselling, a couple did determine to try IVF, and if they decided to use all suitable embryos within the time limits imposed by the regulations regarding storage, then no moral objection exists.

Even if a couple did have to decline a second attempt at pregnancy because of medical or other serious problems, their original decision was made in good faith. The dilemma is similar to that facing a couple who are told that a pregnancy will create a serious risk to the life of the woman. If they choose to continue to engage in sexual intercourse using contraceptives, they know that a small risk exists that the woman will become pregnant and a termination of the pregnancy will then have to be considered. In taking this risk, it is not the couple's intention to cause a future abortion, since they do not intend a pregnancy ever to occur. They are not acting immorally in electing to continue engaging in sexual intercourse. Similarly, the couple who opt for IVF with the intention of attempting the implantation of all the embryos created will do so knowing that there is a small risk that a second pregnancy will be ruled out on medical grounds. This does not mean that because of this small risk they should not have used IVF in the first place. It does, however, underline once again the risks involved in IVF.

We are still left with the question of what should happen to embryos that are left after a couple are unable to use them because of medical problems. The 1990 Act allows for three possible uses of embryos: transfer to their genetic mother, transfer to another woman, and research. The remaining option is to allow the embryos to die after the stated period of storage has been completed. Where transfer to the genetic mother is not possible, there are no easy choices available.

Assuming that a couple did not deliberately wish to create spare embryos but that they found themselves in the position of being unable to accept them, what advice could be given? We have already argued that embryo transfer represents a separation in the unitive and procreative aspects of sex and a separation of legal and genetic parenthood. In the unusual case of a couple who use their own gametes in IVF with a view to accepting all embryos thus created, but who then find that they are unable to do so, the unitive and procreative aspects of sex were not essentially separated. If these embryos were to be offered to another woman, then, while the problem of separating legal and genetic parenthood would remain, the technique may be seen as an attempt to continue the life of the embryo rather than a deliberate attempt to create an embryo for transfer to another woman.

This situation would, of course, be highly unsatisfactory, but we are placed in this position because we have to try to balance the importance of the life of the embryo with the importance of maintaining the link between genetic and legal parenthood. This is a difficult decision to make, but the most loving and just solution must be to attempt to safeguard the life of the embryo. The options also exist of such a couple using a surrogate mother or of allowing the embryos to be used for research, but we will discuss the ethics of these options later. We must not lose sight of the fact that the scenario we have outlined above would very rarely happen in practice if a couple were determined from the start to attempt implantation with all the embryos created.

Malformed embryos

The issue of malformed embryos is one which couples using IVF must address before they begin any programme of treatment. It is most likely that in the course of IVF treatment some malformed embryos will be created. In some circumstances the defect in these embryos may be so great as to be incompatible with the embryo's ever becoming viable outside the uterus if it were successfully transferred. In other cases the likelihood of implantation may be extremely remote, due to very severe genetic defects. In these cases allowing the embryos to die is not likely to alter their fate, while in some cases the fertilized ovum may be so malformed as not to be a human embryo at all.

At the same time, now that genetic screening has advanced to the stage where certain conditions can be diagnosed in a very early embryo, we are left with the dilemma of choosing what to do with an embryo which, if successfully implanted, will develop into a child with a serious genetic illness such as cystic fibrosis or Huntington's chorea. It is extremely unlikely that any centre offering IVF would be prepared to try to implant such an embryo, even if a couple so desired. Therefore part of the counselling a couple must receive regarding IVF must include this fact. It is even possible that if a child were born with a genetic illness which had been identified at the embryonic stage, a case could be brought against the centre under the Congenital Disabilities (Civil Liability) Act 1976, though this may not be successful if it could be shown that the parents knew of the embryo's genetic defect.

Is this approach to genetically defective embryos correct, or does it undermine the status of disabled people and show a grievous disrespect for human life? Here, we need to make a distinction between creating an embryo with the intention of accepting it for implantation, and creating an embryo with no such intention if it is surplus to requirements. If an embryo is found to be seriously genetically defective, it is then a matter of deciding to take no therapeutic action with regard to it. In this context this means not attempting implantation and so allowing the embryo to die.

This is not the same as aborting a fetus which has been found to be suffering from a serious genetic illness. In the case of abortion, an invasive technique is used to stop development. In the case of the defective IVF embryo, active techniques which may cause implantation are withheld. It must be stressed that this argument is valid only if the embryo has been created with the intention of completing the therapeutic process which, if possible, would lead to implantation. It is now a case of withholding the completion of that treatment because of the nature of the genetic illness, in much the same way as doctors withhold life-support systems from unconscious patients in the final stages of terminal cancer. It would be irresponsible and wrong to create life in order to allow it to die without an overriding moral reason. This could be supplied only by the certainty that a child would be born whose life would be characterized by significant and largely unmitigated suffering.

It may appear that in this discussion we have moved away from our fundamental principle that the human embryo should be treated as a human being even if its full humanity cannot be demonstrated by recourse to arguments based on functional abilities. This is not so, however, since we have already stated that a right to life is not absolute. In the case of a malformed IVF embryo, the right to life must be weighed against the quality of life of the subsequent child and, in particular, the need for invasive treatment to continue that embryo's life. We must also bear in mind the degree of culpability attached to any adults who realize that they will be responsible for bringing a child into the world who will be condemned to a life of significant suffering. In allowing this argument, we are not treating the embryo differently from an adult who may be dying but whose life may be artificially sustained at the cost of significant and unrelieved suffering. The mixture of circumstances does not change the moral principles, but it does indicate how they are to be applied.

A major problem still remains: who decides the degree of severity of a genetic illness necessary for implantation techniques to be withheld from the embryo? Furthermore, on what basis is this decision to be made? The answer to the first question is relatively simple: it should be the parents in association with those who may perform any implantation process.

The second question is much more difficult, and the only answer we can supply is to suggest that the criteria must primarily concern the well-being of the child. Any argument which rests on the parents' unwillingness to have a handicapped child is understandable, but the issue must be settled not on their desires but on any resulting child's welfare. Where, in all conscience, those involved in making the decision believe that the degree of suffering is likely to be a greater ill than that caused by the embryo's not developing further, then withholding implantation techniques would be justified. We cannot completely ignore the needs and desires of the parents in this decision, but the primary concern must be that of the well-being of any resulting child. In this way it would be hoped that the unacceptable possibility of embryos being discarded for minor genetic defects would be avoided, while real suffering would be minimized in genuinely serious cases.

IVF *and embryo research*

Two fundamental issues are involved here. First, is it moral to use a technique which has been developed through programmes of research which have included embryo research? Secondly, is it acceptable that the present success ratio in IVF programmes is likely to be improved only if continued embryo research is allowed?

The status of the human embryo which we have advocated indicates that any technique which is not intended to assist the development and implantation of an embryo is unacceptable. It is not morally acceptable that one embryo should be deliberately sacrificed to gain knowledge which would help others.

In the light of this, it is clear that no further research should be allowed which would cause embryos to be harmed or destroyed, even if IVF programmes might be improved as a result. To argue otherwise would be the equivalent of allowing dangerous or even fatal experiments on children in the hope that other children might benefit from the research. We must also recognize, however, that just as parents may allow their children to undergo treatment with a high degree of risk in the belief that such treatment may directly help them as well as being of potential help to others, so it is acceptable for embryos to be treated using techniques which carry a similar type of risk.

An element of research may, therefore, be involved in some therapeutic treatments, and this research may assist a better under-standing and application of IVF. This being said, any treatment which is not designed primarily to help the development or implantation of an embryo, and which is of greater risk to the embryo than the withholding of such treatment, should not be allowed.

The question of using existing IVF techniques, in the knowledge that many embryos have been destroyed in making the technique possible, is a complex one. We must assume that, in developing the technique, some embryos were deliberately destroyed, and that the conditions outlined above were not met in many cases. Is it right to make use of knowledge gained in this way?

We deplore the fact that unacceptable features of research have taken place, but this is not an adequate reason for abandoning the use of IVF techniques. If we were to abandon IVF because of the use of ethically unacceptable techniques in the past, we would also have to abandon many other medical practices. Knowledge has been gained from unethical treatments which were used on the mentally ill in previous generations. Many treatments derived from research on animals have involved inflicting unacceptable suffering on them. Experiments on soldiers and civilians conducted by governments during the course of this century, particularly in the field of research into the effects of radiation on the human body, have also yielded beneficial information even though the experiments were unethical. None of these things were right and ought not to happen again, but we cannot simply turn our backs on the knowledge gained from them.

All of these moral problems have led many to argue that IVF ought to be rejected because it creates more problems than it solves.[34] Certainly, the sorts of issues outlined above do suggest that, where possible, other infertility treatments should be tried, but we cannot disallow IVF simply because it presents us with new and difficult moral dilemmas.

We may summarize our discussion by stating that IVF is an acceptable technique when used by married couples on its own, but not in conjunction with DI, egg donation or embryo donation. Furthermore, in order to protect the status of the embryo, a couple ought to give an undertaking that they will attempt to implant all embryos created unless medical circumstances dictate otherwise or unless some of the embryos are so seriously genetically malformed as to make the further process of implantation morally unacceptable.

Because IVF affects directly the well-being of embryos and their status, this stipulation regarding the use of embryos in IVF should be a matter for legislation, while IVF ought to be lawful only in attempting to alleviate infertility within marriage. To allow unmarried women to take part in an IVF programme is to undermine the status of the family and is a threat to the stability of society.

10

Surrogacy

Survey

The Warnock Committee and subsequent Government papers

The Warnock Committee defined surrogacy as 'the practice whereby one woman carries a child for another with the intention that the child should be handed over after birth'.[1]

With the available techniques of DI, IVF, and egg and embryo donation, the possible number of permutations in surrogacy arrangements is formidable. There is certainly now no medical reason why the surrogate mother need have sexual intercourse with the man donating the sperm, and she may or may not have a genetic link with the child produced. Equally, it may be the case that the commissioning woman or couple are linked in some way genetically with the child, or no such link may exist. In addition to the moral and social problems which are distinct to surrogacy, therefore, all the objections that we have already noted in connection with other forms of infertility treatment had again to be taken into consideration.

There are few medical conditions which indicate that surrogacy is the only possible form of infertility treatment. A major anatomical problem which cannot be surgically corrected, or a severe chronic illness which pregnancy would exacerbate, are suggested examples. The Warnock Committee was concerned, however, that surrogacy might be used simply as a tool of convenience for those couples or women who did not want the disruption caused by pregnancy to affect their lives adversely.

The committee recognized the many legal problems which surrogacy might encounter. They noted that surrogacy arrangements were unenforceable, that a court was more likely to grant custody of a child to the carrying rather than the commissioning mother, and that the commissioning father, if he were genetically linked to the carrying mother, might find himself facing an affiliation order if the carrying mother decided to keep the child. Added problems could arise if the child were born disabled or if the carrying mother suffered injury or even death as a result of the pregnancy.[2] When the report went to press, surrogacy was not illegal unless the Adoption Act was contravened by the payment of money to effect an adoption.[3]

Following their usual practice, the committee examined arguments for and against surrogacy. They acknowledged that the weight of public opinion was against the practice of surrogacy, mainly because it was seen as an almost complete intrusion into the process of procreation and into a marital or stable relationship. Many also argued that surrogacy was inconsistent with the dignity of women: no woman should have her womb used by others even with her consent, even if she stood to gain financially from the arrangement. The attendant dangers of pregnancy should not be risked in carrying a child destined for another woman. The potential damage done to a child due to the severance of the prenatal bonding at birth was offered as a further criticism of the practice.[4]

The committee also received arguments in favour of the practice. Some argued that if infertility could be remedied in any way at all, then every possible treatment should be permissible. It was also suggested that to prohibit a woman from offering herself as a surrogate mother would be to deny her freedom of choice over the use of her own body. Warnock also accepted that while some may find surrogacy an intrusion into the marital relationship, others may not, and that any argument based on prenatal bonding is likely to be so speculative as to be of little value.[5]

In introducing their recommendations regarding surrogacy, the committee admitted that this topic raised some of the most difficult problems they had to deal with. Although this subject was the cause of the first statement of dissent by two members of the committee,[6] the Warnock Report came down firmly against all surrogacy arrangements. The statement of dissent wished to allow limited surrogacy for medical reasons only, but the majority opinion was opposed to such a procedure.

In addition to recommending that all surrogacy arrangements should be made illegal contracts, and hence unenforceable in the courts,[7] the committee made one of its most wide-ranging recommendations:

> We recommend that legislation be introduced to render criminal the creation or the operation in the United Kingdom of agencies whose purposes include the recruitment of women for surrogate pregnancy or making arrangements for individuals or couples who wish to utilise the services of a carrying mother; such legislation should be wide enough to include both profit and non-profit making organisations. We further recommend that the legislation be sufficiently wide to render criminally liable the actions of professionals and others who knowingly assist in the establishment of a surrogate pregnancy.[8]

Following this strongly worded recommendation, the Government introduced a Bill which was subsequently enacted as the Surrogacy Arrangements Act 1985. The 1985 Act did not attempt to settle all the issues surrounding surrogacy, but it did, in the words of the Government, make it an offence 'to take part in negotiations for a commercial surrogacy agreement, to offer or agree to negotiate such an arrangement or to compile information which is intended to be used in making such arrangements'. This Act fell far short of the Warnock recommendation, but it did prohibit the establishment of commercial surrogacy agencies as well as the advertising of or for surrogacy services.[9] The Act did not affect either the commissioning parents or the carrying mother; only third parties were addressed.

The Government, in its consultation paper, was still undecided on the issue of non-commercial surrogacy agencies, and called for further submissions to be made. In particular, while the Government seemed not to favour making all surrogacy arrangements illegal, it did request views to be expressed on both the principle of non-commercial surrogacy and the extent to which any criminal law, if introduced, should cover the participating parties. For example, should the commissioning parents and the surrogate mother be covered by a new law, or should third parties only be involved? To what extent should a distinction be made between a third party involved in negotiating a surrogacy arrangement and a third party involved in assisting those already in a surrogacy arrangement?[10]

In its White Paper, the Government took the rather surprising decision of ignoring the majority opinion of the Warnock Committee. It argued that while surrogacy would not be encouraged, and while no enforcement of surrogacy arrangements in any of their aspects would be allowed by the courts, private non-commercial surrogacy arrangements as well as non-commercial surrogacy agencies would be lawful. A fear of placing children under the stigma of criminality, and a feeling that non-commercial arrangements could not be properly regulated by law, were important considerations in reaching this conclusion. In effect, the Government proposed that the 1985 Act should be the only relevant law, although its proposed statutory licensing authority was to have the power to recommend to the appropriate ministers suggested changes to the law in this regard.[11]

The Human Fertilization and Embryology Act 1990

The 1990 Act does not alter the provisions of the 1985 Act, but it does state clearly the legal status of a non-commercial surrogacy arrangement. It also establishes a method whereby, in certain circumstances, commissioning parents may be given legal custody of a surrogate child. In these circumstances the surrogate child will be the legal offspring of the commissioning parents.

The fundamental law underpinning all other regulations stated in the Act is that surrogacy arrangements are not enforceable in law either by or against any of the persons making such arrangements.[12] This, as we shall see, does not prohibit such arrangements as long as they are not commercial in nature, but it does provide protection to those who may have entered into a surrogacy arrangement and who wish to change their minds once the reality of a pregnancy or the birth of a child has had time to take effect.

The Act does allow for a married couple to be treated in law as the parents of a child borne by a woman other than the wife if certain conditions are met.[13] These conditions are quite strict and do not negate the principle, already noted, that the carrying mother is always to be regarded as the legal mother of a child at the time of its birth and will remain so unless a court allows either an adoption or the arrangement under review.

The conditions under which a court may allow a commissioning couple to become the legal parents of a surrogate child are as follows.

(1) The gametes of either husband or wife or both must have been used to create the embryo, either *in vitro* or by DI. (2) The husband or wife must apply for the order to give them legal parenthood of the child within six months of its birth. (3) At the time the application is made, the child must be living with the applicants and their home must be within the United Kingdom or Channel Islands or the Isle of Man. (4) The commissioning couple must both be over eighteen years of age. (5) The consent of both the carrying mother and the father of the child (as defined above in our discussion of DI) must be given freely and with full understanding, such consent being given after six weeks have elapsed since the birth. (6) The whole arrangement must not have involved the payment of any monies other than the payment of reasonable expenses.

If all these conditions are met, then the court may decide to grant the commissioning parents full legal parenthood of the child.[14] This law is designed to protect the carrying mother of the child and to ensure that commercial surrogate arrangements are not granted any legal status, while accepting that this method of alleviating childlessness is sought, often as a last measure, by some couples who desperately wish to have children.

Christian submissions

No Christian group commended surrogacy as a treatment for infertility, even in circumstances where DI or egg donation were not required. The only disagreement between the churches arose, not over the principles involved in surrogacy, but over the best way to deal with the practice. Some groups viewed the subject from the pragmatic position that it was likely to continue in spite of anything they would say to the contrary. They argued that it was their task to suggest guidelines for the control of the practice. Other groups condemned the practice and refused to allow any further consideration of the subject in the event that their views were ignored or countered.

A pragmatic approach

The Scottish Episcopal Church took the view that surrogacy was not generally acceptable, but that it had to be recognized that in certain circumstances it did have a possible value to some couples. While unhappy with the idea that children could be seen as little more than commodities in surrogate arrangements, the church argued that since surrogacy was likely to continue, it should attempt to offer guidelines for the control of the practice. Thus it was stated that surrogacy arrangements should be unenforceable by law, that no surrogate mother should be forced to give up the child she has borne or to return any monies received from the commissioning parents, and that neither party in the surrogacy arrangement should have any redress in law should a child be born with any form of disability. Surrogacy arrangements, they argued, should be undertaken only by agencies granted a licence by a statutory licensing authority and only after detailed counselling of both the commissioning and commissioned parents. In any event, even if these guidelines were ignored in certain cases, the commissioning parents and the surrogate mother should be free from prosecution.[15]

The church further argued that since the link between mother and child is of fundamental importance, even in the womb, the carrying mother should be regarded as the legal mother of the child even if a donated ovum was used in the conception of the child. 'The welfare of the mother-and-child viewed as a fundamental unit would be the guiding factor in resolving any problem and dilemma that might subsequently present itself in a surrogacy arrangement.'[16]

The Presbyterian Church in Ireland initially took a mixed view on surrogacy and womb-leasing. The church's *ad hoc* committee stated that these practices 'tend to be derogatory of human values and relationships, to dehumanise the foetus and to denature women'.[17] However, the committee was prepared also to state that

> Special circumstances might be envisaged such as one where a woman might have a functioning ovary but no uterus, where there might be grounds for medical intervention; but this should be treated as exceptional and in no way justification for a general practice.[18]

In the General Assembly debate which followed this report, the church debated and passed a resolution which took a much more conservative view on the matter. It was resolved that the church rejected 'under all circumstances' surrogacy and womb-leasing. The church was, however, aware of the pain and distress caused by childlessness, and urged its members to exercise pastoral care and compassion for those so affected.[19] This debate within the Presbyterian Church in Ireland demonstrates clearly the difficulty many Christian groups had in balancing the principles involved in surrogacy with the practical and pastoral concerns of the church's responsibility to those who suffer from infertility.

The Roman Catholic Church was uniformly hostile to surrogacy. We have already examined this church's position on the issues of separating procreation from sexual intercourse and the intrusion of a third party into the marriage relationship. In arguing that surrogacy contracts should be made illegal, and that anyone assisting in establishing a surrogacy arrangement should be liable to prosecution, the church also argued that surrogacy violates human dignity and reduces the carrying mother to merely the means to an end for others.[20]

These arguments, advanced by the Bishops' Joint Committee on Bio-ethical Issues, were supported by both the National Board of Catholic Women and the Catholic Union of Great Britain. The former cited a number of practical objections to surrogacy in addition to their rejection of the practice on grounds of principle. These included the question of the validity of a surrogacy contract, the issue of the rights of the commissioning parents over the surrogate mother during gestation, the refusal of a surrogate mother to give up a child and the possible rejection of the child by the commissioning parents. The possible and unpredictable effects of the whole process on the child also gave great cause for concern.[21] The Catholic Union of Great Britain endorsed the opinion that it should be a criminal offence to assist in a surrogacy arrangement, but pointed out that this should not include medical assistance given to a woman already pregnant.[22]

The Church of England opposed surrogacy on the grounds that it 'violates the dignity of motherhood' and that it fails to take into account the bonding process which takes place in the womb between a child and its mother.[23] The church favoured the opinion that surrogacy should be made illegal and all surrogacy arrangements non-binding in law. The Children's Society, in affirming its acceptance of the arguments noted above against surrogacy, also commented that even in non-commercial surrogacy arrangements, where the reason for a woman becoming a surrogate mother may be altruistic, the moral basis for surrogacy is still inadequate. Even in womb-leasing, it was pointed out, the reason for the arrangement is not the welfare of the child but rather the desire to meet the needs of the commissioning parents.[24] The Mothers' Union[25] and the Church of Ireland[26] condemned the practice without detailed comment.

The Methodist Church in Great Britain rejected surrogacy on the grounds that 'it deliberately disrupts the normal relationship between mother and her embryo/child and therefore acts irresponsibly and inhumanly'.[27] In making this statement, the church acknowledged that it was following the argument presented in the report *Choices in Childlessness*, where it was stated that surrogate motherhood reduced procreation to nothing more than a biological act, and that surrogate motherhood was hardly motherhood at all.[28] The Methodist Church in Ireland agreed with the disruptive effect that surrogacy has on the bonding between mother and child, and added that surrogacy arrangements are open to the further objections that anonymity is virtually impossible to guarantee in such arrangements, and that the possibility of blackmail at a future date could not be discounted.[29]

The Church of Scotland also referred to *Choices in Childlessness* in its response to the Warnock Report, stating that it agreed with the stance taken by the members of the working party. The church did, however, point out that in opposing surrogacy, it did so on the same basis as in its opposition to DI. Surrogacy, it argued, was different from DI only in detail, not in principle.[30] Surrogacy was also condemned by the Free Church of Scotland[31] and the Free Presbyterian Church of Scotland,[32] without detailed argument in addition to those noted on DI and other infertility treatments.

The Salvation Army opposed surrogacy because it saw the practice as contrary to basic Christian views on marriage and the creation of human life.[33] In its submission to the Warnock Committee, the Salvation Army stated that these principles included the belief that

> . . . no attempt to create new human lives ought to take place at the expense of cherished and fundamental insights on which our civilisation has been built and for which we are indebted to Christianity: the sanctity of marriage, the respect due to the dignity of human beings and their bodies, the need for openness and truthfulness about human relationships, the value of technology to assist or enhance (not replace) natural or instinctive physical capacities and, finally the need to protect weak and vulnerable members of society, particularly the children, whether born or as yet unborn.[34]

Surrogacy, they argued, failed to meet these criteria on a number of counts.

CARE and the Christian Medical Fellowship also voiced their opposition to the practice. The CMF did so without any detailed comment,[35] while CARE opposed surrogacy on the grounds that it violated standards of human affection, identity and responsible parenthood, in addition to the many practical problems which it could cause to those involved in such arrangements.[36]

Analysis

Does surrogacy, then, represent an acceptable form of infertility treatment for the small number of women who may be able to conceive but who are unable to carry a child to full term? We can readily agree that commercial arrangements are unethical because of the possibility of exploitation and the unacceptability of making human life a matter of commercial transaction. It is also clearly unethical for a woman to use another woman's body purely for convenience. We are left, however, with the few purely medical cases where surrogacy may be the only method whereby a couple may have a child which is genetically theirs.

Parenthood and the gift of sex

In cases where a husband and wife donate both gametes, and are given legal custody of a surrogate child, there is no separation of legal and genetic parenthood. Strangely, surrogacy actually meets the criterion of keeping legal and genetic parenthood together more fully than the principal provision of the 1990 Act, which makes the carrying woman the 'natural' mother. Nevertheless, many are still uneasy, feeling that surrogacy represents an unacceptable intrusion into a marriage or that it requires a separation of the unitive and procreative aspects of sex.

In fact, surrogacy does not contravene the principle of keeping together the unitive and procreative aspects of sex, since, within the context of their whole marriage, the commissioning parents are the ones who have created the life of the embryo, not the carrying mother. We can fairly argue that the embryo, probably though not necessarily created *in vitro*, is the result of the union between the commissioning husband and wife; the carrying mother is providing a necessary environment for the nurture of the embryo but is not contributing to its creation.

The intrusive nature of surrogacy

What objections are left then, to the practice? Some argue that surrogacy is an unacceptable intrusion into a marriage. Further, it is often seen as an unacceptable intrusion into the normal processes of pregnancy and motherhood. There is also the danger that it demeans the status of the embryo and consequently of children.

In spite of much popular feeling, mirrored in church submissions to Warnock, that surrogacy negates almost every principle regarding motherhood and the family, it is not possible to sustain this objection on the basis of the principles we have been using to guide us through this debate. Since surrogacy does not compromise the nature of the gift of sex, or cause legal and genetic parenthood to be confused, it is difficult to see how it necessarily represents an unacceptable intrusion into a marriage. It will be the case that for some couples such an arrangement would be emotionally unacceptable, but this will not be so for all couples. Since there is no sexual contact involved, no principles are being sacrificed even though the danger exists of a relationship developing between the commissioning husband and the carrying mother.

This danger, or the danger of feelings of inadequacy or rejection on behalf of the commissioning woman, may cause most couples to choose to live with the pain of infertility rather than opt for surrogacy, but this does not have to be so for all couples. Unlike DI or egg or embryo donation, what is at the heart of such a decision is the strength of the relationship of the commissioning parents. Genetically the child will be theirs, and will have been created from their union; the surrogate mother assists in bringing their child to birth, but not in creating it.

What then of the issue of the possible intrusive nature of surrogacy into pregnancy and motherhood? Is it ever right to have a woman carrying and nurturing a child other than her own? This is the real heart of the surrogacy question.

The first reaction of many is to say that it can never be right for a woman to carry a child other than her own. To allow such a thing to take place is an abuse of the human body, since in God's created order women's bodies are designed to nurture the life which they have conceived. Even many who reject a Christian or religious outlook to life argue that a woman's body must never be so used by another, even with her consent and when no financial inducements have been offered. This first reaction is not, however, as justifiable as it may appear.

We have already argued that only a married couple should be the genetic parents of a child. Consequently, if an embryo were to be created *in vitro* we would normally expect the embryo to be transferred to the genetic mother. Equally, in an unassisted conception we would normally expect the woman who has conceived to continue to provide the environment of nurture and protection for the embryo. This connection between conception and nurture is certainly established in nature, but it need not be seen as an essential connection in principle. Unlike the connection between the unitive and procreative aspects of sex, the connection between conception and nurture is a biological necessity. Where this connection is physically unsustainable, no principle is sacrificed if the nurturing element in an embryo's development is transferred to another woman as long as the genetic mother remains the mother of the child. It is certainly true that in normal circumstances it is preferable for the same woman to conceive and nurture the embryo, and no separation of these functions, other than for medical reasons, would be acceptable; but a principle should not be made out of a biological necessity.

The connection between the dual aspects of sex is quite different, since, as can be seen from observing other species, the procreative aspect of sex does not have to have a corresponding unitive function. Until this generation, the connection between conception and nurture in mammals was a biological necessity and an example of excellent design. It is reasonable to see the dual aspects of sex as a matter of principle, but the connection between conception and nurture as a matter of expediency.

Having said this, we must also accept that the nurturing process is a profound one and has a deep emotional and psychological effect on most women. The connection between conception and nurture is a natural and proper one and should be separated only in exceptional circumstances.

The status of embryos and children

Does surrogacy represent an attack on the status of the embryo and children? Again, at first sight it may seem that this is the case. In creating embryos *in vitro*, transferring them to the womb of a woman other than the genetic mother, and then granting legal parenthood to the genetic mother and her husband, are we not treating embryos and hence children as commodities? This is a serious charge and cannot be dismissed lightly.

While surrogacy, even in the limited form which we are suggesting, may lead some to think of embryos as commodities, this does not have to be the case. The creation of an embryo *in vitro* can be as loving and committed an expression of parental concern and responsibility as a natural means of reproduction. The transfer of the embryo to the womb of a woman other than its genetic mother can be seen as an altruistic act on behalf of the woman concerned. The granting of legal parenthood to the genetic parents can be seen as the genetic parents accepting their parental responsibilities. There is nothing intrinsically wrong with any of these procedures and nothing in them which necessarily demeans the embryo.

Unlike embryo donation, in which an embryo is created for the 'use' of another unknown woman, surrogacy maintains the link between the genetic parents even though the antenatal nurture of the child takes place in another woman's womb. Surrogacy is essentially a form of fostering, and as long as it is conducted within carefully thought-out limits, it is acceptable.

Further objections

Why was surrogacy almost uniformly rejected by Christian contributors to the debate? The main reasons appear to be strongly felt opinions that a woman's body should not be used by another woman and her partner in this way, and that the bonding experience during pregnancy is such that this bond should not be broken after birth other than in exceptional circumstances.

Strongly felt as these opinions are, they do not stand up to scrutiny. Who has the right to determine what a woman can do with her body as long as she is not causing harm to others? It is a particularly curious moral viewpoint which indicates that a woman may choose to have an abortion for non-medical reasons, but should not be allowed to use her body to nurture life. If it is argued that surrogacy does in fact harm the participants even though they may be unaware of it, this is to extend paternalism to an unacceptable degree. As we have already noted, surrogacy does not threaten the institution of marriage or the family, it does not demean the embryo, fetus or child, and society is not likely to be undermined by non-commercial surrogacy arrangements.

The argument regarding the possible damage done to either the carrying mother or to the child as a result of interrupting the bonding process begun in pregnancy is equally open to challenge. No hard research has been offered to prove that the bonding process during pregnancy is so fundamental that it should never be interrupted. Indeed, in the case of surrogacy it is impossible to provide any evidence on the matter until significant numbers of surrogate children have been born. We cannot know what bonding takes place between a woman and a child she knows is not hers genetically, other than by asking such a woman to describe her own experience. We cannot base our understanding of bonding in surrogate pregnancies on our understanding of bonding in more usual pregnancies. Equally, evidence would have to be based on a large number of women, in different circumstances, to be definitive.

It is, of course, the case that some women entering the surrogacy arrangement will wish to change their minds, and elect to keep the child or even to have an abortion. Under current law, either option is available to such women. In one way this is no different from many women carrying their own children; abortions take place because women choose to have them and some women, though admittedly a small minority, elect to have their children adopted. While our principles lead us to argue against abortion other than in exceptional medical circumstances, we must accept that in the present circumstances a woman choosing to enter into a surrogacy arrangement cannot be made to continue with the pregnancy if she changes her mind. This would have to be understood by all parties in any arrangement entered into. Nevertheless, since the child is the child of the genetic parents and not that of the carrying mother, the child ought to be given to them as soon as practicable after birth. Understandably, very few women would want to enter into such an arrangement, but those who wish to do so, from altruistic reasons, should not be prohibited in their chosen course of action. Enforcement of such arrangements is the only safe and fair way of regulating them.

To many, this argument will appear clinical and impersonal, and it has to be admitted that in some cases heartache will follow such arrangements. This does not mean, however, that they will all have this result, and there are instances already where great happiness has been brought both to childless couples and to women who have elected to be surrogate mothers. Certainly, as a solution to infertility, surrogacy is fraught with problems, but it should not be disallowed on moral or legal grounds.

The result of this discussion is, then, to voice concern over the practice of surrogacy and to question whether or not it is too high a price for many couples to pay in alleviating infertility. We cannot, however, say that it is morally wrong in certain cases where medical necessity dictates that a woman cannot carry a child and where another woman is willing, out of altruism, to provide the nurture the natural mother is unable to provide. This is so, of course, only within the limits we have proposed for all infertility treatments: the commissioning couple must be married, no financial rewards should be offered to anyone taking part in the arrangement, and DI and egg transfer must not be part of the procedure. It also follows, from our reasoning, that surrogacy arrangements should, in fact, be enforceable, since only in this way can the contracting parties be assured of the outcome of the arrangement and children be protected from being treated as commodities over which adults may wrangle.

11

Embryo research and other scientific techniques

Survey

The Warnock Committee and subsequent Government papers

Medical science advanced so rapidly during the decade following the birth of the first IVF baby that an array of medical possibilities opened up which even a few years previously would have seemed impossible. Some of these techniques were emerging at the time of the Warnock Report, while others were included in the report as theoretical propositions only. Along with the recommendations on surrogacy, the recommendations of the committee in this area of the debate were the source of most discussion and disagreement.

The committee attempted to sidestep the thorny issue of when life or personhood begins. While this is at the very heart of the matter, the committee elected to opt for a different starting-point. The members argued that since the question of the beginning of life and the equally challenging question of the beginning of personhood are not susceptible of scientific proof, a more fruitful approach was to ask: what is appropriate in the field of research for an embryo of the human species? In other words, without defining exactly the status of the human embryo in terms of its possible personhood, the committee sought to agree on the suitability of research on human embryos, treating them as entities distinct from gametes on the one hand and fetuses on the other. The committee also distinguished between pure research, which is aimed at discovering factual information only, and applied research, which has a therapeutic purpose.[1]

In their customary fashion the committee members considered arguments for and against allowing research on human embryos. Arguments against research centred on the belief that the human embryo was either a person or potential person and as such should be protected from all experimentation. In addition, some felt that to allow scientists to research on human embryos would be to open up the door to unscrupulous practices, no matter how carefully these were controlled in theory.[2]

Those who argued in favour of allowing regulated research did so on the grounds that the human embryo was not a person or potential person, but an embryo. As such, it may be the subject of research if such research can be expected to lead to the alleviation of infertility, genetic disease or certain types of miscarriage. Proponents of research also argued that while some research on animal embryos may be of use in human health care, this was not always the case.[3]

In its recommendations, the Warnock Committee did not seek to deal with embryos *in vivo* but only those *in vitro*. The committee recommended, with three members dissenting,[4] that limited, regulated research should be allowed although the human embryo should also be given some degree of protection in law. They set the limit of fourteen days from conception, excluding time 'frozen', as the time during which embryos may be used in research. Similarly, fourteen days was to be the limit for growing embryos *in vitro* before implantation or destruction. They also stipulated that no embryo which had been used for research should be implanted in a woman seeking treatment or offering herself as a volunteer in a research programme. The majority of the committee also accepted that embryos could be created for the purposes of research, although donors of embryos should be allowed disposal rights over their own embryos.[5] Four committee members who were prepared to allow embryo research dissented from this view.[6]

In its consultation document, the Government outlined four possible benefits of embryo research: infertility treatment, better contraception, detecting genetic illness and gaining knowledge about congenital disease. It was the Government's intention, however, to introduce two mutually exclusive clauses in its eventual Bill. One clause would follow the Warnock majority decision, while the other would prohibit all embryo research.[7]

In its White Paper, the Government continued with this approach. One clause prohibited all techniques except those necessary for the transfer of an embryo from *in vitro* to *in vivo* states. A second clause allowed for embryo research, under the scrutiny of the proposed statutory licensing authority.[8]

The Warnock Committee also discussed the possibilities of trans-species fertilization, cloning (replacing the ovum's nucleus with one from a body cell of the same species), ectogenesis (gestation in an artificial environment), trans-species gestation, parthenogenesis (developing an organism from an unfertilized ovum), nucleus substitution, embryonic biopsy and the prevention of genetic defects. While most of these techniques were only theoretical possibilities, the committee did recommend that it be made a criminal offence to implant a human embryo in the uterus of another species, and that trans-species fertilization be allowed only as part of infertility treatment, with any resultant hybrid not being allowed to proceed beyond the two-cell stage. The committee was happy to leave other techniques to the scrutiny of a licensing authority.[9]

The consultation document published by the Government asked for further views to be made known in regard to trans-species fertilization.[10] In its White Paper the Government upheld the original Warnock proposals and added that it intended to introduce legislation prohibiting cloning, the creation of hybrids and genetic manipulation of the human embryo.[11]

The Human Fertilization and Embryology Act 1990

While, as we have seen, the Government had given Parliament the option of banning embryo research, the 1990 Act does make provision for some research, under licence, subject to certain conditions.

The Act first of all stipulates that the creation and use of embryos for any reason can be practised legally only under licence,[12] and that only live human gametes or embryos may be implanted in a woman.[13] Similarly, a human embryo must not be placed in any animal.[14] Cloning is also prohibited,[15] as is keeping or using an embryo after the appearance of the primitive streak.[16] For the purposes of the Act the primitive streak is said to appear not later than fourteen days after the gametes are mixed, excluding any period of time during which the embryo is frozen.[17] The Act further states that embryos used for research may not subsequently be used for any other purpose;[18] equally, licences issued for research must be kept separate from licences issued for treatment.[19] This makes a clear distinction, in law, between research and treatment.

The Act also makes provision for cross-species fertilization under limited conditions. This term is somewhat misleading; it suggests the creation of a hybrid, with scientists attempting to bring such a creature to birth. In fact, the Act allows only for the mixing of sperm with the egg of an animal for the purposes of testing the fertility or the normality of the sperm. Anything which is formed must be destroyed at the end of the test, and in all cases must not be allowed to proceed beyond the two-cell stage.[20] It is unclear whether or not such fertility tests do in fact ever result in true fertilization, but the Act does allow for this possibility in placing the limit of development at the two-cell stage.

The Act states clearly the limited number of purposes for which a research licence may be granted. They are[21] promoting advances in the treatment of infertility, increasing knowledge about the causes of congenital disease, increasing knowledge about the causes of miscarriages, developing more effective techniques of contraception, and developing methods for detecting the presence of gene or chromosome abnormalities in embryos before implantation. It is not lawful to alter the genetic structure of any cell while it forms part of an embryo, although the Act does leave open the possibility that future regulations may allow for this to happen in specific circumstances.[22]

Christian submissions

In general, Christian opinion was hostile to research or experimentation on human embryos where a risk of the embryos' destruction was greater than that necessary to achieve implantation. This response was, however, not universal, and even within churches a difference of opinion sometimes arose. For some, certain techniques or experiments were unacceptable, while other experiments were permissible. A survey of Christian opinion, therefore, necessitates a comprehensive examination of individual churches' statements on quite a wide range of subjects. Once again, we must be thorough in our investigation, even though we have to accept a good deal of repetition as we examine what the churches said.

Roman Catholic opinion

With the exception of the theoretical possibility of therapeutic research on an embryo which will be implanted, Roman Catholic opinion was entirely and uniformly hostile to embryo research. The Bishops' Joint Committee on Bio-ethical Issues stated unequivocally in its response to the Warnock Report that research on embryos is 'research on Man'.[23] As such, any research other than that intended to benefit the individual embryo is contrary to the Helsinki Declaration and the Hippocratic Oath. In regard to the Warnock Report's recommendation that after fourteen days from fertilization embryos *in vitro* should be destroyed, if they were not transferred to a woman's womb, the bishops' committee continued: 'For the first time in the history of our civilisation, deliberate killing of the harmless is to be made not merely permissible but actually obligatory.'[24] This strong condemnation of embryo research and experimentation ruled out all techniques which did not lead to the transfer of all embryos to the wombs of the mothers who donated the ova. The bishops' committee specifically voiced its opposition to trans-species fertilization,[25] cloning,[26] deliberate twinning by division of the zygote,[27] and gestation in animals.[28] All other forms of embryo research not specifically mentioned were disallowed under the essential principle denoted above.

The National Board of Catholic Women began its submission to the Warnock Committee by stating that it considered human life to begin at conception. In support of this view the Board cited the Declaration of Geneva 1948, revised 1968 (World Medical Association) and the Declaration of Oslo 1970 (World Medical Assembly). Reference was also made to the Declaration of Helsinki 1964, revised Tokyo 1975 (World Medical Assembly), which stated that the needs of the subject must always prevail over the interests of science and society. Consequently, the Board rejected all types of embryo research, including the storage of embryos, apart from brief storage pending the early transfer to the mother's womb. They specifically condemned splitting of embryos, cultivation of genetic material for 'spare parts', selection of the fittest embryo for implantation, sex selection and development of hybrids.[29] In the Board's response to the Warnock Report, they declared trans-species fertilization to be unacceptable, even for the testing of male infertility, and a recommendation was made that it should become a criminal offence.[30]

In a joint response to the Government's consultation paper, the Catholic Union of Great Britain and the Guild of Catholic Doctors drew attention to the distinction between therapeutic and non-therapeutic forms of research. The former was acceptable but the latter unacceptable.[31] All forms of research and experimentation which did not lead to the early implantation of every embryo were discounted. Trans-species fertilization was also considered to be unacceptable.[32]

Anglican opinion

Anglican responses to embryo research and experimentation were less uniform than the Roman Catholic responses noted above. The Scottish Episcopal Church was most forthcoming in its support of the Warnock Committee's recommendations regarding embryo research. The church accepted that research or experimentation should be allowed within the period from fertilization to the development of the primitive streak, noting that some evidence had suggested that 78% of normally conceived embryos are lost through menstruation at the fourteen-day stage.[33] They suggested one proviso, that all research should potentially assist the alleviation of infertility or enable better antenatal diagnosis of genetic illness. In regard to trans-species fertilization, the church went further than the Warnock Committee: it recommended that development of the 'hamster test' be allowed to continue to the sixteen-cell stage rather than the two-cell stage suggested. This condition should apply only to the 'hamster test' and not to any other trans-species fertilization, which would have to be authorized separately by a licensing authority.[34] The church felt that there may be valuable information to be discovered by allowing this later development, and felt assured that there could be no question of a hybrid creature ever being born.

In contrast to the Scottish Episcopal Church, the Church of Ireland was completely opposed to embryo research and trans-species fertilization. In its response to the Government's consultation paper, the church stated that it was opposed in principle to embryo research and urged that greater resources should be expended in conducting research into cot deaths, still births and other causes of infant mortality.[35] Trans-species fertilization was rejected 'even if potentially beneficial medical data may be obtained'.[36]

The Church of England's Board for Social Responsibility acknowledged that a division of opinion existed within the church on the subject of embryo research. Nevertheless, the majority view was stated, namely that since the fertilized ovum cannot be attributed full personhood, at least until after the fourteen-day stage, research should be allowed until that stage had been reached.[37] The church disagreed, however, with the practice of creating embryos specifically for research purposes.[38] 'Spare' embryos created as part of an IVF programme should be used. In the Board's response to the Government's consultation paper, trans-species fertilization was accepted as outlined in the Warnock Report: the resulting hybrid should be terminated at the two-cell stage, and only programmes which have been granted a licence should be allowed by law.[39]

The joint Church of England and Church in Wales body, the Children's Society, was generally favourable to embryo research within certain limits. The Society agreed with the Warnock Committee that experimentation should be allowed only within the first fourteen days from fertilization,[40] and that trans-species fertilization should be allowed in the form of the 'hamster test' as long as the Warnock recommendations were adhered to.[41] The Society did not, however, accept the argument that embryos should be created specifically for research projects or that, in an IVF programme, deliberate over-production of embryos would be acceptable.[42] They rejected cloning[43] and ectogenesis[44] as well as any genetic manipulation of the embryo, except in those circumstances where such intervention was used to remove a genetic abnormality which would give rise to severe disability.[45] The Society was unclear regarding what was intended by use of embryonic material for transplantation. It declared that it was unacceptable to make use of an embryo developed beyond the fourteen-day deadline, but that it was acceptable to use cells grown in culture extracted from an embryo before the fourteen-day limit was reached.[46]

The Mothers' Union reacted cautiously to the issue of embryo research. While it accepted that some research was potentially beneficial to society as a whole, it was unhappy with the fourteen-day limit for research. The Mothers' Union suggested that the limit should be defined by whether or not the embryo was 'capable of sustaining life'. The meaning of this term was explained as the time when implantation became possible.[47] They found the creation of embryos for research unacceptable.[48] Similarly, they rejected gestation of the human embryo in an animal's womb.[49] The majority of the Mothers' Union members also rejected trans-species fertilization.[50]

Presbyterian opinion

The Church of Scotland was opposed to all forms of embryo research and experimentation apart from the therapeutic techniques acceptable to most Christian groups. Even when embryos came into existence as a result of other experiments, such embryos should not be used in research programmes.[51]

The Free Church of Scotland was equally critical of all embryo research and experimentation of a non-therapeutic nature. In its response to the Government's consultation paper, the church examined various arguments which set out to determine when life or personhood should be attributed to the embryo or fetus. The church believed human life to begin at conception, and made the point that the onus is on others to prove that this is not the case. If there is any doubt over the matter, they argued, then the safest option should be adopted. Thus, until it could be proved conclusively that human life could not begin at conception, the human embryo should be offered full protection under the law.[52] Consequently, all forms of research and experimentation were wrong.

The Free Presbyterian Church of Scotland was wholly opposed to experimentation on the human embryo. It recommended that the production of 'spare' embryos, embryo freezing, experimentation on embryos, cloning, attempted parthenogenesis, trans-species fertilization, the placing of a human embryo in the uterus of another animal and ectogenesis should all be criminal offences.[53] In the church's opinion, human life begins at conception, so all experimentation on the human embryo is experimentation on human beings and consequently unacceptable.[54]

The Presbyterian Church in Ireland resolved at its General Assembly of 1985 that human life should be considered as beginning at conception. In the light of this decision, all non-therapeutic techniques of research or experimentation were deemed to be unacceptable.[55] This was the position already taken by the church's ad hoc committee, which had submitted evidence to the Warnock Committee, although it had not stated its belief on the nature of concentration and the beginnings of human life in quite such direct terms. The ad hoc committee had voiced its opposition to cloning,[56] ectogenesis[57] and trans-species fertilization[58] although it did allow that there was some merit in being able to identify the sex of an embryo at an early stage,[59] and in remedial genetic manipulation.[60] In all cases, however, the committee did not wish a licence for uncontrolled experimentation to be granted, so even potentially therapeutic techniques might have to be abandoned in order not to allow the increase of other, non-therapeutic, practices.[61]

Methodist opinion

The Methodist Church in Great Britain followed the reasoning found in the report *Choices in Childlessness*, drawing the attention of the Warnock Committee to the recommendations found there.[62] Both the report and the Methodist Church were uncertain regarding the subject of embryo research within the limits of fourteen days from conception. *Choices in Childlessness* merely stated that some experimentation may be morally acceptable,[63] while the Methodist Church acknowledged that it was split on the issue, with a majority prepared to accept some research within the limits recommended by Warnock.[64]

The Methodist Church in Ireland took as its basic proposition the belief that experimentation on human embryos was unacceptable.[65] Within this general commitment, however, the church did allow a number of exceptions. The choosing of the sex of offspring was acceptable when there was 'good medical reason',[66] as was trans-species fertilization when used as a test for fertility.[67] Therapeutic genetic manipulation[68] was also acceptable, as was cloning under certain circumstances where it was felt to offer a possibility of the elimination of medical defects.[69] Ectogenesis was unacceptable.[70] This approach to the issue of embryo research illustrates the point we observed previously: it is not always clear what is meant by research and experimentation, and different groups inevitably interpreted the concepts in varying ways. At times it is difficult to be sure that two or more churches were in fact saying the same thing even when they used similar language.

Other Christian opinions

The Salvation Army was hostile to the concept of embryo research and experimentation except for therapeutic reasons. It aligned itself with the Statement of Dissent (B) appended to the Warnock Report, which recommended that embryo experimentation be made illegal.[71] Specifically, trans-species fertilization was rejected,[72] as was sex selection.[73]

The Christian Medical Fellowship accepted trans-species fertilization in the form of the 'hamster test'. They felt, however, that such tests must be carefully controlled, and that under no circumstances should the resulting fertilized egg be allowed to proceed beyond the two-cell stage.[74]

CARE was of the opinion that since it is medically impossible to determine precisely when human life begins, the only humane approach to the embryo is to treat it with the respect due to all human beings for all stages of its existence.[75] Thus experimentation on the human embryo is unacceptable, though techniques which seek to further the embryo's life or well-being are acceptable.[76] Consequently, genetic manipulation is acceptable when used under strict controls and only for the alleviation of disability,[77] though sex-selection is undesirable,[78] and trans-species fertilization unacceptable.[79]

Analysis

Our discussion on the status of the human embryo indicates that the standards which are applied in embryo research must be the same as those set in other forms of human research. These include the principle that where consent cannot be given, any technique applied must not be deliberately detrimental to the well-being of the recipient. Since consent cannot be given by the recipient in embryo research, only treatment which is likely to be beneficial to the embryo should be allowed.

A distinction must therefore be made here between research and treatment. This is not an arbitrary distinction, but one which is made in the 1990 Act, where treatment includes any practice designed to assist development of an embryo with a view to implantation, or screening of embryos to ensure that embryos are in a suitable condition for implantation. Research, under the 1990 Act, is by definition an activity which precludes any attempt at implantation, since no licence can be issued allowing both treatment and research in the same project.[80]

This means that we must scrutinize not only embryo research as defined in the 1990 Act, but also some forms of treatment which involve the manipulation of the embryo. It is clear that, under the 1990 Act's definition of research, all research is unacceptable, since all research must result in the destruction of the embryo used. Some forms of treatment would also be problematic if they are shown to result in increased risk to embryos.

Screening

Certain types of screening pose fundamental ethical problems. In most IVF programmes, screening does not involve manipulation of embryos, but rather observation of those embryos which develop normally, and identification of those which are abnormal. We have already dealt with the question of the implantation of abnormal embryos in our discussion of IVF. Difficult ethical issues are involved in this area, but the actual method of screening is not objectionable.

The difficulty arises with embryo biopsy (sometimes termed BABI, blastomere analysis before implantation), where a cell is taken from an embryo at the eight-cell stage in the embryo's development. In such an instance the cell so removed will contain all the embryo's genetic information, and the remaining seven cells may be implanted without any detrimental effect on the embryo. If the removed cell is found to be genetically defective, the parents of the embryo must decide whether or not to continue with implantation. We have already discussed the moral issues involved in making this decision.

The problems associated with BABI are twofold. In the first instance, the removal of a cell is not without some risk to the embryo, since this is a delicate operation. The degree of added risk is, however, small and no intentional harm is done to the embryo in the process. While any form of conception and implantation is a risky affair for the embryo, the small added risk does not seem enough to call the procedure into question.

A greater objection is that the procedure may lead to unacceptable practices following the removal of the single cell for analysis. One fear is that this procedure will lead to a form of twinning (sometimes popularly called cloning, though this term is better used to describe a different technique). This fear exists because it is known that at an early stage in the embryo's development each cell has the potential to develop into a separate embryo. This occurs naturally in identical twins. In spite of media reports to the contrary, however, no such experiment is known to have taken place and the practice is expressly forbidden in the United Kingdom under the 1990 Act. There is, therefore, no question of the removed cell being developed into a twin of the original embryo.[81]

An allied fear is that because each cell has the potential to develop into an embryo, a potential embryo is being destroyed when a cell is removed and experimented upon. This, in fact, is not the case. For a cell to develop into an embryo it must be surrounded by its natural shell, the zona pellucida. In the method of screening described above, the cell is removed from the embryo within this shell. This cell cannot develop into an embryo unless an artificial zona is provided, which very technique is forbidden under the 1990 Act. Thus not only is artificial twinning not an issue, but the destruction of a newly formed embryo is not at stake either.

This means that there is no overriding moral objection to any form of screening currently being practised. In the comparatively small number of cases where an intrusive technique is employed, the additional risk to the embryo is not great enough to discredit the practice.

Use of embryos

One of the most disconcerting factors to emerge in the Warnock debate is the widespread acceptance of the belief that embryos are the possessions of their parents and can be used or disposed of at will. While it is correct to say that parents should exercise guardianship over their embryos, as over their children, it is wrong to view embryos as commodities which can be destroyed, experimented upon or nurtured, depending solely upon the will of the genetic parents.

The 1990 Act states that it ought to be shown, in every instance, that embryo research is necessary or desirable before a licence may be given for a programme of research. The Human Fertilization and Embryology Authority has further strengthened this statement by saying that the Authority must be satisfied that the use of human embryos is essential for the research project being requested. There are those who argue that the use of human embryos is never essential, only desirable in speeding up the research programme. In all cases licences and projects should be monitored to see whether or not, under the HFEA's own regulations, embryo research is being properly limited.

Finally, in the interests of clarity, we need to note that trans-species fertilization for testing sperm quality is not embryo research as such, since no human embryo is formed. The 1990 Act forbids the creation of human-animal hybrids, but the HFEA must ensure that even in fertility tests for human sperm no embryonic entity at all is allowed to develop.

As almost all contributors to the Warnock debate argued, the way in which we treat human embryos is a subject for legislation. Our concern is that the status of the human embryo should be upheld in law and not left as a matter for personal moral judgment.

12

Gamete and embryo storage

Survey

The Warnock Report and subsequent Government papers

The Warnock Committee made a number of recommendations regarding storage and disposal of frozen gametes and embryos. These recommendations included a ten-year limit for the storage of embryos,[1] a five-yearly review for the storage of gametes,[2] the right of use or disposal of an embryo to fall to a surviving partner on the death of a donor,[3] and the right of use or disposal of an embryo to fall to a storage authority if both donors die or cannot be traced after ten years.[4] The Government White Paper subsequently suggested that embryos should be stored for a maximum of five years and gametes for a maximum of ten.

Warnock also recommended that if AIH takes place following the death of the husband, the resulting child should be disregarded for inheritance purposes,[5] and that similar conditions should apply in the case of IVF when an embryo is implanted following the husband's death.[6] In the event of a couple failing to agree on the use or disposal of an embryo, Warnock recommended that a storage authority should determine the matter as though the ten-year period of storage had elapsed.[7] The Warnock Committee was of the opinion that posthumous use of sperm or embryos should be actively discouraged, but not disallowed, in accordance with the recommendations made above.[8]

The Human Fertilization and Embryology Act 1990

The 1990 Act first of all establishes that any storage of gametes or embryos can be legally practised only under licence.[9] This means that, while it is not necessary for a clinic to have a licence to practise AIH if the sperm used are not subject to storage (being frozen and kept for a period before being used in an unfrozen state), it is necessary for a clinic to have a licence if storage is required. The Act also stipulates that the maximum period for the storage of gametes is ten years[10] and embryos five years.[11] The Act does allow, however, that in certain specific cases this time restriction may be extended.[12] In fact, in interpreting this regulation the HFEA has chosen to extend the five-year period for embryo storage where implantation is sought by the donors.

The question of consent receives close attention in the Act. The Act makes every effort to ensure that embryos and gametes are used in a manner acceptable to donors, and that donors are aware of the full implications of donation before they choose to act in that capacity. The relevant schedule states that only written consent is valid,[13] and that such consent remains valid only if it is not withdrawn by the donor.[14] Those whose gametes have been used to create an embryo must specify in their consent the use to which that embryo may be put: either research, or fertility treatment for one of the donors or for a third party.[15] Consent must also be given for the maximum period of storage up to the statutory maximum,[16] and must state what is to be done with the gametes or embryos if a donor dies or is unable to vary or revoke the terms of consent due to incapacity.[17] Other conditions of storage may be specified,[18] with all of the above relating not only to embryo or gamete donation separately, but also to any embryo which may be created from the gametes of a donor.[19]

Those who decide to donate gametes or embryos must first of all receive counselling regarding the full implications of such an act.[20] This counselling must include an explanation that consent may be varied or withdrawn, but that this is not possible once an embryo has been used in treatment services or research.[21] Clearly, counselling which requires that donors are fully aware of the implications of their actions must give detailed information regarding the various types of infertility treatments that are available, and also the types of research which may be pursued.

Consent must be given for the storage of gametes or embryos under any circumstances,[22] and this includes the storage of embryos obtained by lavage or some such technique.[23] In this case the embryo must not be removed from the woman unless consent regarding its use has been obtained. In cases of IVF, both donors must give their consent regarding the use to which the resulting embryo may be put.[24]

Christian submissions
Positive reactions

A number of Christian responses simply stated their basic agreement with the Warnock position. This was the approach taken by the Scottish Episcopal Church,[25] the Salvation Army,[26] the Methodist Church in Ireland,[27] the Christian Medical Fellowship[28] and the working party which produced *Choices in Childlessness*, in a follow-up document.[29] The Church of Scotland was in general agreement with the Warnock recommendations, but felt that once a married couple stated they did not wish to have any more children, the marriage came to an end for whatever reason, or agreement between the marriage partners could not be reached, then the stored embryos should be destroyed. The church also recommended that instead of speaking of 'rights of disposal', the term 'destruction' should be used, thus prohibiting the sale or use of existing embryos.[30]

Mixed reactions

The Mothers' Union and the Children's Society were unhappy about the Warnock recommendations but were not prepared to reject them completely. The Mothers' Union stated that they could neither accept nor totally reject the recommendations, but that members felt that the time limits suggested for storage and review procedures were too long.[31] In response to the Government's consultation paper, the Mothers' Union suggested that while it was unhappy with the whole concept, if storage was to be allowed, then the maximum time limit should be five years and no posthumous use of gametes should be allowed.[32]

The Children's Society found difficulty in believing that embryo storage should ever be necessary except in the short term, and that it seemed something of a luxury for embryos to be frozen in case a couple who were sterilised should later desire a child. While not condemning storage of embryos, the Society was clearly uncertain of the value of the practice as well as of its moral implications.[33] The use of frozen sperm in posthumous AIH was rejected, because it was claimed that such a practice would be likely to take place while a woman was still mourning the loss of her husband and that the resulting child would be more a memorial to the dead than a human being desired in his or her own right.[34]

The Presbyterian Church in Ireland was also unsure of the value of freezing and storing gametes and embryos. Without opposing the practice completely, the *ad hoc* committee which gave evidence to the Warnock Committee did show concern that a system of mass production could be based on such storage, and that adequate safeguards against improper use of stored gametes and embryos would be difficult to enforce.[35]

Negative reactions

With the single exception of short-term storage (a few days) with a view to early implantation of all embryos stored, the remainder of Christian submissions to the Warnock debate were hostile to the freezing and storage of embryos. This was the position of the Church of Ireland in its response to the Government's consultation paper. Implantation of each embryo created was seen as being the only correct way in which to treat fertilized ova, and any storage facility should exist purely to accommodate that desire.[36] Consequently, the issue of freezing and storing embryos for a period of years should not be allowed to arise, for in those circumstances it would be impossible to have a couple's clear commitment from the outset that implantation would in fact be sought.

The Free Presbyterian Church of Scotland voiced its disagreement with the Warnock recommendations in the strongest possible terms. The church recommended that embryo freezing and the use of frozen sperm in AIH after the husband's death should be made criminal offences.[37]

CARE also opposed the freezing and storage of embryos, stating that the possible risks to the embryo, to the child if born, to the family pattern of those concerned and to society's attitude to marriage and the family were such that the practice should be discontinued and made unlawful. It was admitted that the nature of this risk was an unknown factor, but that the potential for damage to the embryo and the family was such that only if no risk was involved should freezing and storage be allowed.[38] Cautious approval of gamete storage was given on the condition that such gametes would be used in fertilization only within marriage and that no payment should be given or received for gamete donation. Even with these safeguards, CARE was not completely satisfied that gamete storage was in the best interests of individuals and society, but was prepared to grant that the issue was not easily resolved: 'To give gametes for storage and examination may not be morally intolerable.'[39] Such a statement can hardly be presented as supportive of gamete storage, but it does grant cautious and guarded approval.

Roman Catholic opinion was united in its opposition to embryo storage. The Catholic Bishops' Joint Committee on Bio-ethical Issues stated in its submission to Warnock that storage could be accepted only if there was a guarantee of subsequent transfer, unimpaired, to the mother's uterus.[40] It is doubtful if any practitioner would be able to give an assurance that a stored embryo could be given a definite prospect of such unimpaired transfer. Similarly, unless the timescale for such storage was only a matter of days, it would not be possible to guarantee that the mother in question would wish, or perhaps even be able, to undergo such a process of transfer and implantation.

This point was recognized by the Bishops' Committee in its response to the Government's consultation document. In that response, the committee suggested that even stricter safeguards should be introduced. Only that number of embryos which can be transferred immediately to the mother's womb with the best possible chance of survival should be created *in vitro*. If that number was one, so be it. In the unlikely event of such a mother having to postpone implantation, it would be acceptable for the embryo to be stored pending implantation at the earliest possible opportunity. In the even more unlikely event of the woman's death before implantation, the life of the embryo may be saved if another woman were prepared to accept it for implantation into her womb. If no such recipient was forthcoming, then the storage authority should retain and care for the embryo as long as it could be said to be alive.[41] None of these measures, however, should mask the fact that the essential Roman Catholic position was to oppose the freezing and storage of embryos, and indeed to suggest that the creation of embryos *in vitro* should be abandoned.

On the question of AIH following the death of the husband, the bishops were strongly opposed to the practice. They recommended that all stored gametes should be destroyed following the death of their donor, so that such a practice could not take place. The question of the legal status of any children born through IVF following the death of their father, the bishops observed, merely underlined the undesirability of the whole issue of creating embryos *in vitro*.[42]

The Catholic Union of Great Britain stated its opposition to embryo freezing and storage for the same reasons as outlined above. Should such techniques be allowed, however, the Union suggested that as long as the interests of the embryos were given precedence over all other considerations, the Warnock recommendations could be accepted.[43] The National Board of Catholic Women consistently opposed embryo freezing and storage except in those cases where the embryos would be transferred at the earliest possible opportunity to their mother's womb.[44] In particular, the Board stated that it was 'appalled at the proposed treatment of human beings as goods to be stored away for up to ten years and then brought out and disposed of at will by a storage authority'.[45] Such long-term storage, it was argued, should be forbidden by law.

Analysis

In not accepting DI, egg donation or embryo donation, and in setting tight restrictions on surrogacy and IVF, the circumstances in which storage of gametes or embryos would be morally acceptable are limited. In cases of AIH, IVF where a husband and wife supply the gametes for their own use, and surrogacy under the conditions described earlier, storage of gametes or embryos is necessary. In principle, there is no moral obstacle to gamete storage for research, or to gamete or embryo storage for the limited techniques listed above.

Two specific areas deserve our attention: the question of donation of sperm from minors, and the fate of stored gametes or embryos when the donor dies.

Minors

The HFEA's statement that, in certain circumstances, sperm from a minor may be stored is acceptable where there is the possibility that the minor may become infertile because of illness, surgery or medical treatment such as radiotherapy. In order to protect minors from exploitation or from acting in a manner which they may later regret, storage and subsequent use of sperm should not be allowed in any other circumstance. In any case, the range of consent for the use of stored gametes should be restricted to use by the donor when he becomes an adult. In such circumstances it may also be necessary to extend the period of storage to more than ten years.

While we object morally to the use of gametes in DI or other similar techniques, even for adults, it should certainly be the case that a minor should be restricted legally from consenting to any such use of his gametes, or the use of them in research, or in creating embryos for research. While we disagree with the 1990 Act on the range of consent possible for adults, we must also recognize that when a minor becomes eighteen he may then consent to any of the practices allowed by the Act. Should the circumstance arise in which a minor donates sperm because of possible sterility, and subsequently dies before reaching adulthood, or fails, as an adult, to give directions regarding the use of his sperm, such sperm should be destroyed.

Donor death

The death of a donor may affect the use or disposal of gametes or embryos in a number of ways.

Where gametes have been stored for AIH, they should be destroyed on the death of the donor. This is, of course, not required by the 1990 Act, but it is the only course of action compatible with the principles suggested in our discussion on AIH.

The disposal or use of embryos is much more complicated, for we are dealing with a qualitatively different entity from gametes. Unlike posthumous AIH, the creation of an embryo *in vitro* with a prospective view to implantation is not affected by the death of the genetic father. The creation of the embryo has already taken place and, should the woman wish to continue with the implantation, she is acting on the basis of an already existing commitment to the embryo, not on the basis of a former relationship with her husband, even though in practice that may be very much in her mind. In such cases counselling is, of course, necessary, but the practice is not unacceptable.

If the woman does not wish to become pregnant after her husband's death, we are faced with another dilemma. It is out of the question to insist that she should do so, but we are also constrained to honour the embryos created with a view to implantation. If the embryos are allowed to die, then this decision should be made in the knowledge that the death of the husband has affected the existence of the embryos previously created. The embryos should not simply be allowed to perish without some conscious decision being taken regarding their fate. In these extreme and rare cases it should also be possible to accept embryo donation, even though, as we have already seen, this is very much a matter of choosing the lesser of two very unsatisfactory courses of action. When a couple are considering opting for IVF, this scenario should be put to them, and the advisability of pursuing other forms of infertility treatment, if appropriate, should be stressed.

In the case of a couple separating or divorcing, it is unlikely that the woman would wish to attempt implantation with any stored embryos, previously created. In this case, the consequences of the divorce must also be shown to include the fate of the embryos. Again, while it is unthinkable that a woman should be pressured into accepting implantation, the future of the embryos must be decided. Embryo donation may be the best, though in itself unsatisfactory, solution to the problem. Should a couple choose to allow the embryos to die, then the gravity of their action should be recognized. As we have already argued, the only acceptable form of IVF is for the technique to be used by a married couple, and any such couple should give an undertaking that they will make use of all embryos created where this is medically possible. The consequences of a divorce for this undertaking should be made clear. It is essential in all of this that consent regarding the use of gametes or embryos in such circumstances is gained at the time of donation; the difficulties in trying to achieve joint consent following a divorce may prove insurmountable.

Where a couple have embarked upon treatment using IVF, embryos have been frozen, and the woman dies, the only solution, other than allowing the embryos to die, would be embryo donation. Where the woman becomes unable to carry a child through illness, then surrogacy may present a way forward, or embryo donation may be necessary.

It must be stressed that these situations are likely to be very rare, and it would not be the intention of any couple to divorce, much less die, when they begin an IVF programme! Thus the possibility of these unusual circumstances causes us to propose prospective means of dealing with them, but they do not alter our essential principles outlined earlier. Because of the necessity of protecting minors, legislation is appropriate in cases of gamete donation by a minor, particularly to stop a minor being exploited by allowing gametes to be used by others. Legislation regarding consent by adults would be appropriate only in order to limit the use of any donated gamete or any stored embryo in line with our discussions on AIH, DI, IVF and embryo research.

13

Abortion

The Warnock Report did not discuss abortion, since this was not within the guidelines laid down by the Government when the committee was established. Consequently, of course, Christian submissions did not deal with the subject either. As the debate continued, it became apparent that, as many of the ethical issues covered in the Warnock Report were also relevant to the ongoing debate on abortion, the 1990 Act would provide a useful opportunity for amending the 1967 Abortion Act. There had been considerable pressure on the Government for some time to allow a free vote in Parliament on the subject. In the end, the 1967 Act was amended as a result of the 1990 Act, but in a manner which surprised many observers.

Legal changes

Two main amendments have been made to the provisions set by the 1967 Act. The first of these lowers the time limit for abortions from 28 to 24 weeks in those cases where the continuance of the pregnancy would involve risk to the mental or physical health of the pregnant woman, or to any existing children of her family, greater than if the pregnancy were terminated.[1] When abortion is carried out in order to prevent grave permanent injury to the physical health of the woman, or to prevent a risk to the pregnant woman's life greater than if the pregnancy were terminated, or where there is a substantial risk that the child will be seriously handicapped either physically or mentally, no time limit is imposed.[2] The Infant Life (Preservation) Act 1929 has been suitably amended.[3]

A paragraph dealing with conscientious objections on the part of anyone asked to participate in any of the activities governed by the Act allows for such objections to be upheld.[4] In those cases where any legal proceedings may result because of a refusal to participate in providing any type of treatment, the burden of proof is on the objector to demonstrate that genuine conscientious objections do exist.[5]

Analysis

The principles regarding the status of the human embryo must guide us in our evaluations of the abortion law, and clearly indicate that abortion is an acceptable option only in extreme cases.

The general clause allowing abortion up to 24 weeks is unacceptably lax in that it allows for a very wide range of conditions and situations in the category of 'risk . . . of injury to the physical or mental health of the pregnant woman or any existing children of her family'. The reduction from 28 to 24 weeks is to be welcomed, but the clause itself is so general as to amount to virtual abortion on demand, as can be evidenced from many actual case histories.

The new regulations allowing abortion right up to full term in the cases cited above raise a new possibility: that of abortion leading to the expulsion from the womb of children who will survive the process. Abortion is the termination of pregnancy, not the wilful destruction of the fetus. While the method of abortion is not specified in late cases, it is most likely that labour would be induced or Caesarean section performed. In these cases, it is likely that a number of babies will survive, and may even become accepted members of their families. It is unclear what requirements, if any, would be made on medical or nursing staff to assist the survival of such babies, given the circumstances of their birth.

The principles we have outlined regarding the status of the human embryo indicate that the general clause allowing abortions up to 24 weeks should be removed completely as being wholly unacceptable. Any cases which would lead us to balance the right to life of the fetus with the right to life of the mother, or with an acceptable quality of life for her, may be dealt with under the remaining clauses.

The clause allowing for abortion where there is a substantial risk of serious handicap to any child who may be born is also too general. The substantial risk would have to be as near to certainty as is possible; where it is not possible to come close to certainty on the issue, the child should be given the benefit of the doubt. The degree of handicap also has to be extreme: either incompatible with life outside the womb, or likely to cause an extreme degree of permanent suffering. Conditions such as Down's syndrome or profound deafness do not fall under the latter category, yet these are conditions which do give rise to abortions at present.

In allowing genetically defective embryos to die, while restricting abortions to extreme cases only, are we being inconsistent? No, for abortion is an invasive technique which stops the life or development of the fetus, while failing to attempt implantation is a withholding of an invasive therapeutic technique which is necessary for the continued development of the embryo. As long as IVF is begun in good faith and defective embryos are withheld from implantation solely on the grounds of serious genetic defects, the principles guiding our enquiry are still adhered to.

In the above discussion, it is apparent that the right to life of the embryo or fetus is not absolute, even though it is a right of prime importance. This is even more important in discussion of the remaining two clauses inserted into the Abortion Act. Abortion is allowed in cases of risk to the life of the mother, and in cases where severe and permanent mental or physical injury will result from the continuance of the pregnancy. When balancing one life with another, it is fair to take into account the quality of life, the personal commitments, and the degree of development of the parties involved. When all of this is taken into account, abortion, in circumstances where the life of the mother is at risk, must be permissible, though not, of course, mandatory.

Where the issue is one of permanent, severe, mental or physical injury to the mother, the decisions involved are more complex. Certainly many pregnancies will result in a degree of injury to women; sadly, this is still part of the process of childbirth. Such injuries, including back damage and post-natal depression, must not be minimized, but they do not constitute grounds for abortion. In other cases, though, it may be argued that the life of the mother would be shortened by a continuation of the pregnancy or that her life would be made psychologically unendurable if the pregnancy were to continue. An example of the latter argument may be a case of rape which results in a pregnancy. In balancing life against quality of life, the tendency should always be to favour life, but we must admit that in certain cases where a woman's life would effectively be destroyed through physical suffering or psychological trauma, the issue really concerns one type of destruction of life balanced against another. In a very limited number of circumstances (rape, incest, severe physical injury likely to shorten life or cause permanent severe disability), abortion may be permissible, though it should be neither mandatory nor automatically assumed.

14

Conclusions

What, then, have we learned from our examination and evaluation of what has become known as the Warnock debate? We can make a number of brief observations by way of conclusion.

First, the Warnock Committee, and subsequently the Government and Parliament, had an unclear basis for morality and an equally unclear theory of the connection between morality and law.

Such basis for morality as may be discerned is inadequate when viewed from a Christian perspective. Principles such as love and justice, understood in the light of the person of Jesus and the Scriptures, and further illuminated by specific scriptural injunctions, are the primary considerations in developing a moral code. The church has much to offer the rest of society in promoting this positive morality. Many will disagree with it and with the basis on which it is founded, but a clear prophetic voice needs to be heard.

In failing to make clear that morality may be given expression in legislation only when harm may be caused to others or to those deemed unable to give informed consent, or when society may be threatened or the natural order seriously compromised, the Warnock Committee failed to provide a consistent approach to legislation. Warnock allowed public sentiment to be the final arbiter. The church is able to provide an alternative approach. While promoting a strong and positive morality, it can also defend society from a legal imposition of morality, good or bad. No law ought to be immoral, but law does not have to reflect morality in all cases. In arguing that morality ought to be enshrined in legislation only under the circumstances outlined above, the church can defend society against despotism while ensuring that laws are not immoral. All the while, a distinctively Christian morality may be promoted as a voluntarily chosen way of life.

Secondly, we have to recognize that Christian contributions to the debate were often inadequate. They failed to attempt to move the debate into the area of morality and law. In one way this is understandable, since everyone took their cue from the Warnock Committee, but it is none the less disappointing. Many Christian submissions were much too short, dealing with specific techniques without presenting cogent arguments for conclusions offered. In particular, a failure to argue towards a view of the status of the human embryo characterized many submissions, even though this issue was agreed by many, including Mary Warnock, to be central to the whole debate.

The fact that the churches made no concerted attempt to present an agreed argument to Warnock must inevitably have lessened the impact of their contributions. In responding to the later HFEA Code of Practice, the Council of Churches in Britain and Ireland showed that a common response, which does not preclude the right of individual churches to make their own submissions, is possible. Even though the CCBI did not exist during the period of the Warnock Committee's existence, it is remarkable that an ecumenical approach was not attempted.

Furthermore, the obvious disparity between various church submissions cannot but have minimized the overall impact made by Christians in the debate. While individual churches or Christian bodies did not always take a consistent approach throughout the debate, nevertheless certain trends were observable. Roman Catholic, Presbyterian and Evangelical churches tended to be conservative in their approach, sometimes arguing from natural morality and sometimes from the Scriptures. Anglican submissions were more varied, being sometimes quite conservative and sometimes much more liberal; the only unifying factor was a willingness to argue not only from Scripture or traditional Christian morality, but also from sociological concerns and an attempt to engage society in dialogue. Methodist contributions tended to be the most liberal of all, with a concern for the individuals or couples facing infertility as the primary consideration.

This disparity masks the fact that churches and other bodies representing a majority of Christians in the United Kingdom were conservative in their approach to most of the subjects under review. In failing to act together on at least some of the issues dealt with in the Warnock debate, the Christian church has allowed a confused and confusing message to be given to society and Government. While no individual or church ought to have been prohibited from making a contribution to the debate, it is regrettable that a united submission was not made at any stage prior to the HFEA's Code of Practice.

As we have seen, the basis of many arguments advanced by Christians in discussion of the issues dealt with in the Warnock debate was often inadequate. This is particularly so in the case of the status of the embryo. Our examination of the issue has shown that a simple appeal to Scripture is inadequate, that an appeal to tradition is unable to present us with a unified Christian approach, and that metaphysics and science alike fail to address the issue properly. Only a dynamic understanding of personhood and the embryo (which not only Christians may adopt), and a theological interpretation of the image of God, can enable us to arrive at an understanding of the embryo which does it justice and which builds on the available biblical evidence. Christians have a responsibility to promote the welfare of the human embryo, to defend their position with vigour and to seek to amend the law where it allows for the misuse of the embryo or fetus.

Thirdly, issues of sexual ethics are extremely complicated in practice, but revolve around a few essential principles: the status of the embryo and children, responsible parenthood, the nature of the link between the unitive and procreative aspects of sex, and the importance of making genetic parenthood the basis of legal parenthood.

These principles are able to steer us through the muddied waters of increasingly complex permutations in infertility treatments. It is often difficult and painstaking to carry an argument or enquiry through to its conclusion, but the principles we have developed are able to bring us through this process successfully.

Not everyone will agree with the conclusions reached in this book. Some Christians, as well as others, will object to some of our findings. Nevertheless, we have conducted a careful examination of the issues, we have promoted certain salient principles and we have suggested practical ways in which Christians ought to act, both in their own lives and in interaction with the rest of society. If this helps to create greater understanding of the subject among Christians, and also helps Christians to engage in meaningful debate with others, the effort will have been well worth while.

Notes

1. The agenda set by Warnock

1. *Report of the Committee of Inquiry into Human Fertilization and Embryology* (London: HMSO, 1984).
2. *Ibid.*, para. 1.2.
3. Department of Health and Social Security, *Legislation on Human Infertility Services and Embryo Research: A Consultation Paper* (London: HMSO, 1986).
4. *Human Fertilization and Embryology: A Framework for Legislation* (London: HMSO, 1987).
5. Offences Against the Person Act 1861 (London: HMSO, 1861), sections 58, 59.
6. (1928) 71 Parliamentary Debate HL 617–618. (Debate on infanticide in the House of Lords 1928, quoting J. Talbot's statement of June 1928 to the Grand Jury at Liverpool Assizes.)
7. Infant Life (Preservation) Act 1929 (London: HMSO, 1929), section 1 (1).
8. *Ibid.*, section 1 (2).
9. *Ibid.*, section 1 (1).
10. (1938) 3 All England Reports 615.
11. *Ibid.*, 618 B, C.
12. Abortion Act 1967 (London: HMSO, 1967), section 1 (1).
13. J. K. Mason and R. A. McCall Smith, *Law and Medical Ethics* (London: Butterworth, 1987), p. 76.
14. P. D. G. Skegg, *Law, Ethics and Medicine* (Oxford: Clarendon, 1988), p. 26.
15. S. Thomas, *Genetic Risk* (Harmondsworth: Penguin, 1986), p. 96.

16. Barton, Walker and Weisner, 'Artificial Insemination', *British Medical Journal*, 13 January 1945.
17. *Artificial Human Insemination: The Report of a Commission Appointed by His Grace the Archbishop of Canterbury* (London: SPCK, 1948).
18. *The Report of the Departmental Committee on Human Artificial Insemination* (London: HMSO, 1960).
19. *Ibid.*, para. 1.
20. *Ibid.*, paras. 74, 100–103, 115.
21. *Ibid.*, paras. 239, 262.
22. *Ibid.*, para. 108.
23. *Ibid.*, para. 117.
24. *Ibid.*, para. 139.
25. *Ibid.*, para. 156.
26. *Ibid.*, paras. 159, 177.
27. *Ibid.*, paras. 171, 187.
28. *Ibid.*, para. 195.
29. *Ibid.*, paras. 112, 113.
30. Memorandum of dissent by Mrs Jay and Mr Ross.
31. *Report of the Committee on the Use of Fetuses and Fetal Material for Research* (London: HMSO, 1972).
32. Footnote to chapter 11, para. 18, of the Warnock Report.
33. *Op. cit.*, para. 42.
34. *Ibid.*, para. 31.
35. *Ibid.*, para. 28.
36. *Ibid.*, para. 35.

2. Warnock, morality and legislation

1. Plato, *Euthyphro*, 10A.
2. E. Brunner, *The Divine Imperative* (Philadelphia: Westminster, 1947), p. 114.
3. *Ibid.*, p. 117.
4. K. Barth, *Church Dogmatics* II/2 (Edinburgh: T. and T. Clark, 1957), p. 522.
5. *Ibid.*, p. 552.
6. D. Bonhoeffer, *Ethics* (London: Fontana, 1964), p. 271.
7. *Ibid.*, p. 277.
8. A. P. Griffiths, 'Religion and Ethics II', in M. Warner (ed.), *Religion and Philosophy*, Royal Institute of Philosophy Supplement 31 (Cambridge: Cambridge University Press, 1992), p. 142.
9. S. Sutherland, 'Religion and Ethics I', in *ibid.*, p. 132.
10. R. G. Swinburne, 'Duty and the Will of God', in P. Helm (ed.), *Divine*

Commands and Morality (Oxford: Oxford University Press, 1981), p. 129.

11. *Ibid.*

12. S. Clark, 'God's Law and Morality', *Philosophical Quarterly* 32 (1982), pp. 339–347.

13. R. M. Adams, 'A Modified Divine Command Theory of Ethical Wrongness', in P. Helm (ed.), *Divine Commands and Morality*, pp. 83ff.

14. R. M. Green, *Religion and Moral Reason* (Oxford: Oxford University Press, 1988), pp. 78–80.

15. *Cf.* D. Z. Phillips, 'God and Ought', in P. Helm (ed.), *Divine Commands and Morality*, pp. 175ff., and P. L. Quinn, *Divine Commands and Moral Requirements* (Oxford: Oxford University Press, 1978), pp. 4ff.

16. *Cf.* J. Rachels, *The Elements of Moral Philosophy* (New York: McGraw-Hill, 1993), pp. 106ff.

17. P. Singer, *Practical Ethics* (Cambridge: Cambridge University Press, 1993), p. 331.

18. J. M. Gustafson, *Protestant and Roman Catholic Ethics* (London: SCM, 1979), p. 62.

19. K. Barth, *op. cit.*, pp. 521–522.

20. *Ibid.*, pp. 525–526.

21. E. Brunner, *op. cit.*, p. 114.

22. *Cf.* J. M. Gustafson, *op. cit.*

23. *Ibid.*, pp. 101ff.

24. *Cf.* R. M. Green, *op. cit.*, p. 119.

25. *Ibid.*, pp. 114–115.

26. P. Singer, *op. cit.*, pp. 319–320. An example given is: 'Everyone must act in my interests.'

27. R. M. Green, *op. cit.*, p. 102.

28. *Ibid.*, p. 106.

29. *Ibid.*, pp. 110–111.

30. *Ibid.*, pp. 114–115.

31. O. O'Donovan, *Resurrection and Moral Order* (1986; 2nd edn, Leicester: Apollos, 1994), p. 19.

32. N. H. G. Robinson, *The Groundwork of Christian Ethics* (London: Collins, 1971), p. 122.

33. *Ibid.*, p. 169.

34. J. M. Gustafson, *op. cit.*, p. 29.

35. R. G. Jones, *Groundwork of Christian Ethics* (London: Epworth, 1984), pp. 45–56.

36. A. Verhey, 'The Bible in Christian Ethics', in J. Macquarrie and J. Childress (eds.), *A New Dictionary of Christian Ethics* (London: SCM, 1992), p. 58.

37. E. Brunner, *op. cit.*, p. 132.

38. K. Barth, *op. cit.*, p. 704.

39. *Ibid.*, p. 707.

40. *Cf.* discussion on this point in W. Ogletree, *The Use of the Bible in Christian Ethics* (Oxford: Blackwell, 1984), pp. 6ff.

41. D. Bonhoeffer, *op. cit.*, p. 295.

42. *Ibid.*, p. 291.

43. *Cf.* W. Ogletree, *op. cit.*, p. 47.

44. O. O'Donovan, *op. cit.*, p. 143.

45. *Ibid.*, p. 146.

46. K. Barth, *op. cit.*, p. 513.

47. *Ibid.*, p. 517.

48. *Cf.* R. Sokolowski, *The God of Faith and Reason* (Notre Dame: University of Notre Dame Press, 1982), chapters 6, 7.

49. W. Ogletree, *op. cit.*, p. 205.

50. The Devlin–Hart debate began with Devlin's reaction to the Wolfenden *Report on Homosexual Offences and Prostitution*, 1957, in *The Enforcement of Morals* (Oxford: Oxford University Press, 1959, updated 1965). Hart responded in an essay, 'Immorality and Treason', in *The Listener* (30 July 1959), and later incorporated in his book *Law, Liberty and Morality* (Oxford: Oxford University Press, 1963). Some of his views had also been earlier presented in 'Positivism and the Separation of Law and Morals', *Harvard Law Review* 593 (1958). These essays have been reproduced in R. M. Dworkin (ed.), *The Philosophy of Law* (Oxford: Oxford University Press, 1977). The page numbers cited in the following account of the Devlin–Hart debate refer to *The Philosophy of Law*. Regarding the inadmissability of religion as the ground for legislation in the United Kingdom, Devlin wrote, 'A state which refuses to enforce Christian beliefs has lost the right to enforce Christian morals': *The Philosophy of Law*, p. 69.

51. *Ibid.*, p. 67.

52. *Ibid.*, p. 18. Hart defined this as the second 'doctrine' of utilitarianism regarding its understanding of law.

53. *Ibid.*, p. 72.

54. *Ibid.*, pp. 73–75.

55. *Ibid.*, p. 77.

56. *Ibid.*, p. 81.

57. *Cf.* B. Mitchell, *Law, Morality and Religion in a Secular Society* (Oxford: Oxford University Press, 1967), pp. 20–21.

58. *Op. cit.*, p. 79.

59. *Ibid.*

60. *Ibid.*, p. 78.

61. *Ibid.*, p. 80.

62. H. L. A. Hart, 'Positivism and the Separation of Law and Morals', in *The Philosophy of Law*, p. 29.

63. *Ibid.*, p. 34. 'We say that laws may be law but too evil to be obeyed.'

64. *Ibid.*, p. 36.

65. *Ibid.*, p. 37.

66. H. L. A. Hart, 'Immorality and Treason', in *The Philosophy of Law*, p. 86.

67. *Cf.* B. Mitchell, *op. cit.*, p. 54.

68. In this vein, Hart writes: 'We have ample evidence for believing that people will not abandon morality, will not think any better of murder, cruelty, and dishonesty, merely because some private sexual practice which they abominate is not punished by the law': 'Immorality and Treason', in *The Philosophy of Law*, p. 86.

69. *Ibid.*, p. 87.

70. *Ibid.*, pp. 87–88.

71. *Cf.* P. Baelz, *Ethics and Belief* (London: Sheldon, 1977), p. 83.

72. *Cf.* B. Mitchell, *op. cit.*, p. 135.

73. S. Lee, *Law and Morals – Warnock, Gillick and Beyond* (Oxford: Oxford University Press, 1986), p. 36.

74. *Ibid.*

75. *Ibid.*, p. 38.

76. J. Harris, 'Embryos and Hedgehogs: On the Moral Status of the Embryo', in A. Dyson and J. Harris (eds.), *Experiments on Embryos* (London: Routledge, 1990), p. 74.

77. M. Lockwood, *Moral Dilemmas in Modern Medicine* (Oxford: Oxford University Press, 1985), p. 177.

78. R. M. Hare, '*In Vitro* Fertilization and the Warnock Report', in R. Chadwick (ed.), *Ethics, Reproduction and Genetic Control* (London: Routledge, 1987), p. 78.

79. *Ibid.*, pp. 82–83.

80. *Ibid.*, p. 84.

81. *Ibid.*, p. 88.

82. M. Warnock, *A Question of Life* (Oxford: Blackwell, 1985).

83. *Cf.* M. Lockwood, *op. cit.*, p. 156.

84. *Report of the Committee of Inquiry into Human Fertilization and Embryology* (London: HMSO, 1984), foreword, para. 1.

85. *Ibid.*, para. 2.

86. *Ibid.*, para. 3.

87. *Ibid.*, para. 4.

88. *Ibid.*

89. *Ibid.*, para. 5.

90. M. Warnock, *A Question of Life*, pp. viii–ix.

91. *Ibid.*, pp. ix–x.

92. *Ibid.*, p. x.
93. M. Warnock, '*In Vitro* Fertilization: The Ethical Issues II', *Philosophical Quarterly* 33 (1983), pp. 241–242.
94. M. Warnock, 'Do Human Cells Have Rights?', *Bioethics* 1.1 (1987), p. 8.
95. M. Warnock, *A Question of Life*, p. xvi.
96. *Ibid.*, p. xiv.
97. *Ibid.*, p. xv.
98. *Ibid.*
99. *Report of the Committee of Inquiry into Human Fertilization and Embryology*, para. 11.22.
100. *Ibid.*, para. 8.17.
101. *Ibid.*, para. 8.10.
102. *Ibid.*, foreword, para. 6.
103. M. Warnock, *A Question of Life*, p. xii.
104. *Cf.* comments made by Hugh Whittall of the HFEA on that body's refusal to grant licences for deliberate twinning of a human embryo. Such decisions were based in part on 'instinctive revulsion'. *Newsweek* (8 November 1993), p. 49.
105. M. Warnock, *A Question of Life*, p. xiv.

3. *The status of the human embryo: a biblical approach*

1. H. H. Rowley, *Job*, New Century Bible (London: Nelson, 1970), p. 42.
2. M. H. Pope, *Job*, Anchor Bible (New York: Doubleday, 1965), p. 28.
3. N. C. Habel, *The Book of Job*, Cambridge Bible Commentary (Cambridge: Cambridge University Press, 1975), p. 22.
4. A. A. Anderson, *Psalms*, 1, New Century Bible (London: Oliphants, 1972), p. 188.
5. M. Dahood, *Psalms*, 1, Anchor Bible (New York: Doubleday, 1965), p. 139.
6. *Op. cit.*, p. 188.
7. P. C. Craigie, *Psalms 1 – 50*, Word Biblical Commentary (Dallas: Word, 1983), p. 199.
8. M. Dahood, *Psalms*, 2, Anchor Bible (New York: Doubleday, 1968), p. 4.
9. J. H. Eaton, *Psalms* (London: SCM, 1967), p. 140.
10. *Op. cit.*, p. 395.
11. *Ibid.*, p. 431.
12. *Op. cit.*, p. 151.
13. *Op. cit.*, p. 58.
14. A. A. Anderson, *Psalms*, 2, New Century Bible (London: Oliphants, 1972), p. 910.
15. *Op. cit.*

16. *Op. cit.*, p. 302.

17. L. C. Allen, *Psalms 101 – 150*, Word Biblical Commentary (Dallas: Word, 1983), p. 252.

18. E. W. Nicholson, *Jeremiah 1 – 25*, Cambridge Bible Commentary (Cambridge: Cambridge University Press, 1973), p. 24.

19. R. R. Carroll, *Jeremiah*, Old Testament Library (London: SCM, 1986), p. 97.

20. J. A. Thompson, *The Book of Jeremiah*, New International Commentary on the Old Testament (Grand Rapids: Eerdmans, 1980), p. 145.

21. R. K. Harrison, *Jeremiah and Lamentations*, Tyndale Old Testament Commentaries (London: IVP, 1973), p. 49.

22. A. Cole, *Galatians*, Tyndale New Testament Commentaries (London: Tyndale, 1965), p. 15.

23. C. Westermann, *Isaiah 40 – 66*, Old Testament Library (London: SCM, 1969), p. 207.

24. C. Westermann, *Genesis 12 – 36, A Commentary* (London: SPCK, 1985), p. 413.

25. R. Davidson, *Genesis 12 – 50*, Cambridge Bible Commentary (Cambridge: Cambridge University Press, 1979), p. 122.

26. E. A. Speiser, *Genesis*, Anchor Bible (New York: Doubleday, 1964), p. 194.

27. G. Von Rad, *Genesis*, Old Testament Library (London: SCM, 1961), p. 260.

28. F. F. Bruce, *Romans*, Tyndale New Testament Commentaries (London: IVP, 1974), p. 193.

29. J. D. G. Dunn, *Romans 9 – 16*, Word Biblical Commentary (Dallas: Word, 1988), p. 549.

30. M. Black, *Romans*, New Century Bible (London: Marshall, Morgan and Scott, 1973), p. 132.

31. R. G. Boling, *Judges*, Anchor Bible (New York: Doubleday, 1975), p. 219.

32. J. Gray, *Joshua, Judges, Ruth*, New Century Bible (London: Marshall, Morgan and Scott, 1986), p. 324.

33. J. A. Fitzmyer, *The Gospel According to Luke, i–ix*, Anchor Bible (New York: Doubleday, 1981), p. 326.

34. L. Morris, *Luke*, Tyndale New Testament Commentaries (London: IVP, 1974), p. 74.

35. E. E. Ellis, *The Gospel of Luke*, New Century Bible (London: Marshall, Morgan and Scott, 1974), p. 76.

36. *Op. cit.*, p. 363.

37. W. Hendrikson, *Matthew* (Edinburgh: Banner of Truth, 1973), p. 132.

38. D. Hill, *The Gospel of Matthew*, New Century Bible (London: Oliphants, 1972), p. 78.

39. *Op. cit.*, p. 74.

40. L. Morris, *The Gospel According to John*, New London Commentary (Grand

Rapids: Eerdmans, 1971), p. 102.

41. R. E. Clements, *Exodus*, Cambridge Bible Commentary (Cambridge: Cambridge University Press, 1971), p. 138.

42. J. P. Hyatt, *Exodus*, New Century Bible (London: Oliphants, 1971), p. 233.

43. *Ibid.*, p. 234.

44. J. I. Durham, *Exodus*, Word Bible Commentary (Dallas: Word, 1987), p. 323.

45. *Ibid.*, p. 324.

46. Free Church of Scotland, *The Sanctity of Human Life: The Report of the Study Panel of the Free Church of Scotland* (unpublished, 1988), p. 9.

47. I. Jakobovits, *Human Fertilisation and Embryology: A Jewish View* (London: Office of the Chief Rabbi, 1984), p. 4.

4. The status of the human embryo: a theological approach

1. *Didache* 2:2.

2. *Epistle of Barnabas* 20:2.

3. Athenagoras, *Supplication for the Christians* 20:2.

4. Tertullian, *Apology* 9:6–8.

5. Clement of Alexandria, *Protrepticus* ii.x.96.1.

6. Minucius Felix, *Octavius* 30:2, 3.

7. *Apocalypse of Peter* 8.

8. *Christian Sibyllines* ii, lines 281–288.

9. Josephus, *Contra Apionem* ii.202.

10. Cf. B. Soane, 'Roman Catholic Casuistry and the Moral Standing of the Human Embryo', in G. R. Dunston and M. J. Seller (eds.), *The Status of the Human Embryo* (London: Kings Fund, 1988), p. 76.

11. Basil of Caesarea, *Ep.* 188, Canon 2.

12. Gregory of Nyssa, *Adversus Macedonianos*.

13. Council of Ancyra, Canon 21.

14. G. R. Dunston, 'The Human Embryo in the Western Moral Tradition', in G. R. Dunston and M. J. Seller (eds.), *The Status of the Human Embryo*, p. 42.

15. Jerome, *Ep.* 22.13.

16. *Didascala et Constitutiones Apostolorum* vii.iii.2.

17. Augustine, *Quaestionum in Heptateuchum* I.II, n. 80.

18. Augustine, *De Civitate Dei* xxii.xi, n.

19. Gratian, *Decretum II* 32.2.7.

20. Innocent III, Canon 5.20.

21. Gregory IX, *Decretales* v.12.5.

22. Raymond de Penafort, *Summa de Casibus Poenitentiae* II.I, *De Homicidio*.

23. Thomas of Chobham, *Summa Confessarum* (1216).

24. Thomas Aquinas, *Summa Theologiae* 2a 2ae 64.8.

25. *Ibid.*, 1a 76.3.

26. Sixtus V, *Effraenatum* (29 October 1588).

27. Gregory XIV, *Sedes Apostolica* (31 May 1591).

28. Pius IX, *Apostolicae Sedis* (12 October 1869).

29. *Cf. Sacred Congregation for the Doctrine of the Faith* AA/LXVI (1973), *Codex Iuris Canonici, Lib.* vi, *Tit.* vi, *Can.* 1398 (1983).

30. *Cf.* W. J. Cameron, 'Soul', in J. D. Douglas *et al.* (eds.), *The Illustrated Bible Dictionary* 3 (Leicester: Inter-Varsity Press, 1980), p. 1476.

31. P. Geach, *God and the Soul* (London: Routledge and Kegan Paul, 1969), p. 18.

32. P. Tournier, *The Meaning of Persons* (London: SCM, 1957), p. 100.

33. *Ibid.*, p. 104.

34. *Ibid.*, p. 106.

35. H. D. Lewis, *The Self and Immortality* (London: Macmillan, 1973), p. 52.

36. *Ibid.*, p. 119.

37. M. Lockwood, *Moral Dilemmas in Modern Medicine* (Oxford: Oxford University Press, 1985), p. 23.

38. F. H. Cleobury, *Biology and Personality*, ed. I. Ramsey (Oxford: Blackwell, 1965), p. 165.

39. *Op. cit.*, p. 38.

40. I. G. Barbour, *Issues in Science and Religion* (London: SCM, 1966), p. 353.

41. *Ibid.*

42. *Ibid.*, p. 354.

43. T. Nagel, *Mortal Questions* (Cambridge: Cambridge University Press, 1979), p. 182.

44. K. Ward, *The Battle for the Soul* (London: Hodder and Stoughton, 1985), p. 139.

45. *Ibid.*, p. 144.

46. D. MacKay, *Behavioural Sciences*, ed. M. A. Jeeves (Leicester: Inter-Varsity Press, 1984), p. 47.

47. D. Scott, *The Common Sense of Michael Polanyi* (London: The Book Guild, 1985), p. 133.

48. E. L. Mascall, *The Importance of Being Human* (Oxford: Oxford University Press, 1959), p. 28.

49. *Ibid.*, p. 35.

50. J. Montgomery, in S. Spitzer (ed.), *Birth Control and the Christian: A Protestant Symposium on the Control of Human Reproduction* (Wheaton: Tyndale House, 1969).

51. *Ibid.*, p. 73.

52. Dt. 4:29; 26:16; 1 Ki. 8:48; 2 Ki. 23:25; Mi. 7:1; Mt. 16:26; 10:28; 22:37; Acts 4:32; 2 Cor. 5:1–10; Heb. 4:12; Rev. 6:9–11.

53. R. Swinburne, *The Evolution of the Soul* (Oxford: Clarendon, 1986).

54. P. Singer, *Practical Ethics* (Cambridge: Cambridge University Press, 1993), pp. 169–174.

55. P. Bristow, *The Moral Dignity of Man: Catholic Moral Teaching on Family and Medical Ethics* (Dublin: Four Courts Press, 1993), p. 24.

56. *Ibid.*, pp. 24–25.

57. P. Helm, 'Soul', in J. D. Douglas (ed.), *The New International Dictionary of the Christian Church* (Exeter: Paternoster, 1978), p. 916.

58. *Op. cit.*, p. 151.

59. *Op. cit.*, p. 164.

60. R. G. Edwards, 'The Current Clinical and Ethical Situation of Human Conception *In Vitro*', *Proceedings of the Annual Symposium of the Eugenics Society* 19 (1983), p. 103.

61. K. T. Kelly, *Life and Love* (London: Collins, 1987), p. 81.

62. J. Foster, 'Personhood and the Ethics of Abortion', in J. H. Charner (ed.), *Abortion and the Sanctity of Human Life* (Exeter: Paternoster, 1985), p. 36.

63. P. Byrne, 'The Animation Tradition in the Light of Contemporary Philosophy', in G. R. Dunston and M. J. Seller (eds.), *The Status of the Human Embryo*, p. 99.

64. G. B. Bentley, 'A Moral and Theological Approach', in J. H. Charner (ed.), *Abortion and the Sanctity of Human Life*, p. 59.

65. R. Higginson, *Reply to Warnock*, Grove Booklets on Ethics 63 (Nottingham: Grove Books, 1986), p. 19.

66. D. G. Jones, *Manufacturing Humans* (Leicester: Inter-Varsity Press, 1982), p. 153.

67. *Ibid.*, p. 156.

68. O. O'Donovan, *The Christian and the Unborn Child*, Grove Booklets on Ethics 1 (Nottingham: Grove Books, 1973), p. 12.

69. O. O'Donovan, *Begotten or Made?* (Oxford: Clarendon, 1984), p. 51.

70. *Ibid.*, p. 54.

71. *Ibid.*, p. 66.

72. O. O'Donovan, 'Again, Who is a Person?', in J. H. Charner (ed.), *Abortion and the Sanctity of Human Life*, p. 127.

73. *Ibid.*, p. 128.

74. *Ibid.*, p. 136.

75. New International Version.

76. *Cf.* C. Ryder Smith, *The Bible Doctrine of Man* (London: Epworth, 1951), p. 94.

77. *Cf.* D. Cairns, *The Image of God in Man* (London: SCM, 1953), p. 19.

78. *Ibid.*, p. 23.

79. New International Version.

80. R. S. Anderson, *On Being Human* (Grand Rapids: Eerdmans, 1982), p. 74.

81. *Ibid.*, p. 75.
82. D. Cairns, *op. cit.*, p. 32.
83. *Ibid.*, pp. 74–75.
84. Irenaeus, *Adv. Haer.* IV.4.3; V.16.2.
85. D. Cairns, *op. cit.*, pp. 84–85.
86. *Ibid.*, p. 90.
87. Augustine, *De Trinitate* XIV.8.
88. *Ibid.*, XIV.5.
89. Aquinas, *Summa Theologiae* 1 93.2.
90. Luther, *Weimarer Ausgabe*, 42.51.
91. *Ibid.*, 42.50.
92. Calvin, *Commentary on Genesis* 1:25.
93. Calvin, *Commentary on Job* 2:1.
94. Calvin, *Commentary on Acts* 15:9.
95. Calvin, *Institutes* III.7.6.
96. E. Brunner, *Natural Theology* (London: Geoffrey Bles, 1946), p. 22.
97. E. Brunner, *Man in Revolt* (Philadelphia: Westminster, 1947), p. 52.
98. *Ibid.*, p. 96.
99. E. Brunner, *Natural Theology*, p. 24.
100. *Ibid.*, p. 18.
101. K. Barth, *Church Dogmatics* III/1 (Edinburgh: T. and T. Clark, 1958), p. 207.
102. *Ibid.*, p. 206.
103. K. Barth, *Church Dogmatics* III/2 (Edinburgh: T. and T. Clark, 1960), pp. 85–86.
104. *Cf.* D. Cairns, *op. cit.*, p. 172.
105. *Ibid.*
106. K. Barth, *op. cit.*, III/2, pp. 296–329.
107. W. Pannenberg, *Anthropology in Theological Perspective* (Edinburgh: T. and T. Clark, 1985), p. 235.
108. *Ibid.*, p. 242.

5. *Sexual ethics*

1. Gn. 1:28.
2. I. Jakobovits, *Human Fertilisation and Embryology: A Jewish View* (London: Office of the Chief Rabbi, 1984), p. 4.
3. Ps. 127:3.
4. Gn. 16:20; 30:1ff.; 1 Sa. 1.
5. Lk. 1.
6. Mt. 19:12.
7. 1 Cor. 7:25–38.

8. 1 Tim. 2:15.

9. *Humanae Vitae: Encyclical Letter of His Holiness Paul VI, Acta Apostolicae Sedis* LX (1968), no. 9 (London: The Incorporated Catholic Truth Society, 1970), para. 14.

10. *Ibid.*, paras. 22–30.

11. *Ibid.*, para. 9.

12. *Ibid.*, para. 11.

13. *Ibid.*, para. 10.

14. *Ibid.*, para. 11.

15. *Ibid.*, para. 24.

16. Eph. 3:15.

17. *Op. cit.*, para. 8.

18. *Ibid.*, para. 12.

19. *Ibid.*, para. 3.

20. *Ibid.*, para. 14.

21. *Ibid.*, para. 11.

22. *Ibid.*, para. 13.

23. *Ibid.*, para. 10.

24. *Ibid.*

25. *Ibid.*

26. *Ibid.*, para. 23.

27. Free Church Federal Council and the British Council of Churches, *Choices in Childlessness* (London: FCFC/BCC, 1982), p. v.

28. *Ibid.*, p. 11.

29. *Ibid.*, p. 7.

30. *Ibid.*, p. 19.

31. *Ibid.*, p. 20.

32. *Ibid.*, p. 22.

33. *Ibid.*, p. 24.

34. *Ibid.*

35. *Ibid.*, pp. 27–28.

36. *Ibid.*, p. 29.

37. *Ibid.*, p. 31.

38. Church of England, *Personal Origins: The Report of a Working Party on Human Fertilization and Embryology of the Board for Social Responsibility of the General Synod of the Church of England* (London: Church Information Office, 1985), p. iii.

39. *Ibid.*, para. 99.

40. *Ibid.*, para. 114.

41. *Ibid.*, para. 101.

42. *Ibid.*, para. 102.

43. *Ibid.*, para. 103.

44. *Ibid.*, para. 104.
45. *Ibid.*, para. 108.
46. *Ibid.*, para. 109.
47. *Ibid.*, p. 42, n. 4.
48. Eph. 5:21 – 6:4.
49. Eph. 3:15.

6. *Artificial insemination by husband (AIH)*

1. *The Report of the Committee of Inquiry into Human Fertilization and Embryology* (London: HMSO, 1984), para. 4.3–4.
2. *Ibid.*, para. 10.8–9.
3. *Human Fertilization and Embryology: A Framework for Legislation* (London: HMSO, 1987), paras. 54, 60.
4. Human Fertilization and Embryology Act 1990 (London: HMSO, 1990), para. 4.1 (b).
5. *Ibid.*, para. 28.6 (b).
6. *Ibid.*, schedule 3, para. 2.2 (b).
7. *Ibid.*, para. 13.6.
8. Catholic Bishops' Joint Committee on Bio-ethical Issues, In Vitro *Fertilization: Morality and Public Policy* (Oxford: Catholic Media Office, 1983).
9. *Ibid.*, p. 18, para. 29.
10. National Board of Catholic Women, *Warnock Committee: Inquiry into Human Fertilization and Embryology* (unpublished, 1983), para. 5.
11. Free Presbyterian Church of Scotland, *Representations by the Free Presbyterian Church of Scotland in Connection with the Report of the Committee of Inquiry into Human Fertilization and Embryology* (unpublished, 1983), p. 4, para. 3 (iii).
12. Church of England Board for Social Responsibility, *Human Fertilization and Embryology: The Response of the Board for Social Responsibility of the General Synod of the Church of England to the DHSS Report of the Committee of Inquiry* (London: Social Policy Committee, Church House, 1984), para. 4.1.
13. Mothers' Union, *Statement by the Committee for Social Concern to the Department of Health and Social Security on the Report of the Committee of Inquiry into Human Fertilization and Embryology under the Chairmanship of Dame Mary Warnock DBE* (unpublished, 1984), p. 3, para. v.
14. Children's Society, *Government Inquiry into Human Fertilization and Embryology: Evidence* (unpublished, 1983), para. 19.
15. Methodist Church, Division of Social Responsibility, *Government Inquiry into Human Fertilization and Embryology* (unpublished, 1983), p. 2, para. 1.
16. Methodist Church in Ireland, *A Response by a Committee of the Methodist Church in Ireland to the Invitation to Comment upon the Government Inquiry into*

Human Fertilization and Embryology (unpublished, 1983), para. 7.

17. Church of Scotland, *Response to the Report of the Committee of Inquiry into Human Fertilization and Embryology* (unpublished, 1984), section 3, para. 3.
18. Free Church of Scotland, *Legislation on Human Infertility Services and Embryo Research: Free Church of Scotland Responses to Consultation Paper* (unpublished, 1987), para. 6.1.
19. Presbyterian Church in Ireland, *Government Inquiry into Human Fertilization and Embryology: Submission by an Ad Hoc Group of the Presbyterian Church in Ireland* (unpublished, 1983), para. 6.1.
20. General Assembly of the Presbyterian Church in Ireland, 1985, resolution 3.
21. Free Church Federal Council and the British Council of Churches, *Choices in Childlessness* (London: FCFC/BCC, 1982), p. 54, para. B. 1 (a).
22. Nationwide Festival of Light, *Human Fertilization and Embryology: Submission to the Committee of Inquiry under the Chairmanship of Mrs Mary Warnock* (unpublished, 1983), para. 4.7.

7. *Donor insemination (DI)*

1. (1958) MacLennon *v.* MacLennon SC105.
2. *Report of the Committee of Inquiry into Human Fertilization and Embryology* (London: HMSO, 1984), para. 4.10.
3. *Ibid.*, paras. 4.11, 14.
4. *Ibid.*, para. 4.16.
5. *Ibid.*, para. 4.17.
6. *Ibid.*, paras. 4.22–24.
7. *Ibid.*, para. 4.24.
8. *Ibid.*, paras. 4.21, 25.
9. Department of Health and Social Security, *Legislation on Human Infertility Services and Embryo Research: A Consultation Paper* (London: HMSO, 1986), paras. 27–32.
10. *Human Fertilization and Embryology: A Framework for Legislation* (London: HMSO, 1987), paras. 71–90.
11. Human Fertilization and Embryology Act 1990 (London: HMSO, 1990), para. 4.3.
12. *Ibid.*, para. 41.2 (c).
13. *Ibid.*, para. 13.5.
14. *Ibid.*, para. 13.6.
15. *Ibid.*, para. 13.7 (a).
16. *Ibid.*, para. 28.2, with 28.5.
17. *Ibid.*, para. 28.3.
18. *Ibid.*, para. 28.2.

19. *Ibid.*, para. 28.7 (a).
20. *Ibid.*, para. 28.7 (b).
21. *Ibid.*, para. 29.1.
22. *Ibid.*, para. 28.6 (a).
23. *Ibid.*, para. 28.6 (b).
24. *Ibid.*, para. 29.4.
25. *Ibid.*, para. 13.2.
26. *Ibid.*, para. 31.3.
27. *Ibid.*, para. 31.4 (b).
28. *Ibid.*, para. 31.4 (a).
29. *Ibid.*, paras. 32, 34.
30. *Ibid.*, paras. 35.1, 2.
31. *Ibid.*, para. 35.4.
32. *Ibid.*, para. 31.6.
33. *Ibid.*, para. 31.7.
34. *Op. cit.*, para. 4.16.
35. Children's Society, *Government Inquiry into Human Fertilization and Embryology: Evidence* (unpublished, 1983), para. 2.C.
36. *Ibid.*, para. 20.
37. *Ibid.*, para. 20 (i).
38. *Ibid.*, para. 20 (ii).
39. Scottish Episcopal Church, *Working Party on Human Infertility and Embryo Research* (unpublished, 1987), paras. 3.93, 94.
40. *Ibid.*, para. 3.95.
41. Methodist Church in Ireland, *A Response by a Committee of the Methodist Church in Ireland to the Invitation to Comment upon the Government Inquiry into Human Fertilization and Embryology* (unpublished, 1983), para. 8.
42. Methodist Church, Division of Social Responsibility, *Government Inquiry into Human Fertilization and Embryology* (unpublished, 1983), p. 2, para. 2.
43. Free Church Federal Council and the British Council of Churches, *Choices in Childlessness* (London: FCFC/BCC, 1982), p. 54, para. B. 1 (b).
44. *Ibid.*, p. 54, para. B.1b (i)–(iv).
45. *Ibid.*, p. 54, para. B.1b (v), (vi).
46. Church of England Board for Social Responsibility, *Evidence to the DHSS Inquiry into Human Fertilization and Embryology* (unpublished, 1983), section 3, para. 1.
47. Lambeth Conference Statement 1958.
48. *Op. cit.*, section 3, para. 2.
49. Church of England Board for Social Responsibility, *Human Fertilization and Embryology: The Response of the Board for Social Responsibility of the General Synod of the Church of England to the DHSS Report of the Committee of Inquiry* (London: Social Policy Committee, Church House, 1984), paras. 5.2 – 5.4.

50. Mothers' Union, *Statement to the Government Inquiry into Human Fertilization and Embryology from the Social Concern Committee of the Mothers' Union* (unpublished, 1983), para. 4.v (a).

51. *Ibid.*, para. 4.iii (a).

52. Mothers' Union, *Statement by the Committee for Social Concern to the Department of Health and Social Security on the Report of the Committee of Inquiry into Human Fertilization and Embryology under the Chairmanship of Dame Mary Warnock DBE* (unpublished, 1984), p. 3, para. 2.

53. *Ibid.*, p. 2, para. 1.

54. Mothers' Union, *Statement by the Committee for Social Concern to the Department of Health and Social Security on the Consultation Paper: Legislation on Human Infertility Services and Embryo Research* (unpublished, 1987), para. 3.

55. *Ibid.*, para. 4.

56. Presbyterian Church in Ireland, *Government Inquiry into Human Fertilization and Embryology: Submission by an Ad Hoc Group of the Presbyterian Church in Ireland* (unpublished, 1983), para. 6.2, 3.

57. General Assembly of the Presbyterian Church in Ireland 1985, resolution 3.

58. Salvation Army, *Written Submission to the Warnock Committee of Inquiry into Human Fertilization and Embryology* (unpublished, 1983), para. iv (6).

59. *Ibid.*, para. iv. (6, 7).

60. Church of Scotland, *Response to the Report of the Committee of Inquiry into Human Fertilization and Embryology* (unpublished, 1984), section 3, para. 3.

61. *Ibid.*, section 3, para. 4.

62. Church of Scotland, *Letter to All Scottish Members of Parliament* (unpublished, 1985), para. 3.

63. Free Church of Scotland, *Letter to Scottish Home and Health Department Regarding Inquiry into Human Fertilization and Embryology* (unpublished, 1984), para. 4.

64. Free Church of Scotland, *Response to Consultation Paper on Legislation on Human Infertility Services and Embryo Research* (unpublished, 1987), para. 6.1.

65. Free Presbyterian Church of Scotland, *Representations by the Free Presbyterian Church of Scotland in Connection with the Report of the Committee of Inquiry into Human Fertilization and Embryology* (unpublished, 1984), p. 2, para 2.

66. *Ibid.*, p. 6, recommendation 3.

67. Baptist Union of Great Britain and Ireland, *Submission to the Warnock Committee Prepared by a Working Party under the Auspices of the Baptist Union Department of Mission, and Approved by the Baptist Union Council* (unpublished, 1983), para. 13.

68. Church in Wales, *Human Fertilization and Embryology: The Response of the Bench of Bishops of the Church in Wales to the Warnock Report*

(unpublished, 1985), p. 4.

69. *Ibid.*

70. Church of Ireland, *Legislation on Human Infertility Services and Embryo Research: A Consultative Document. A Response by the Armagh Diocesan Board of Social Responsibility endorsed by the Northern Ireland Board of Social Responsibility of the Church of Ireland* (unpublished, 1987), para. 6.

71. Catholic Bishops' Joint Committee on Bio-ethical Issues, In Vitro *Fertilization: Morality and Public Policy* (Oxford: Catholic Media Office, 1983), para. 18.

72. Catholic Bishops' Joint Committee on Bio-Ethical Issues, *Response to the Warnock Report on Human Fertilization and Embryology* (London: Catholic Media Office, 1984), para. 22.

73. Catholic Union of Great Britain, *Reply by the Joint Ethico-Medical Committee to 'Legislation on Human Infertility Services and Embryo Research'* (unpublished, 1987), p. 2, paras. 4–6.

74. National Board of Catholic Women, *Warnock Committee: Inquiry into Human Fertilization and Embryology* (unpublished, 1983), para. 4.

75. National Board of Catholic Women, *Warnock Report on Human Fertilization and Embryology: Comments submitted to the Secretary of State for Social Services by the National Board of Catholic Women* (unpublished, 1984), recommendation 4.

76. Nationwide Festival of Light, *Human Fertilization and Embryology: Submission to the Committee of Inquiry under the Chairmanship of Mrs Mary Warnock* (unpublished, 1983), para. 4.8.

77. Christian Medical Fellowship, *Legislation on Human Infertility Services and Embryo Research: The Christian Medical Fellowship's Response to DHSS Invitation to Comment on Consultation Document Cm 46* (unpublished, 1987), p. 1, para. 2.

78. *Ibid.*, p. 2, paras. 4–8.

79. *E.g.* Free Presbyterian Church of Scotland, *Representations by the Free Presbyterian Church of Scotland in Connection with the Report of the Committee of Inquiry into Human Fertilization and Embryology*, p. 2, para. 2; Nationwide Festival of Light, *Human Fertilization and Embryology: Submission to the Committee of Inquiry under the Chairmanship of Mrs Mary Warnock*, para. 4.8.

80. Dt. 25:5–10.

8. *Egg and embryo donation*

1. *Report of the Committee of Inquiry into Human Fertilization and Embryology* (London: HMSO, 1984), para. 6.4.

2. *Ibid.*, para. 6.5.

3. *Ibid.*, para. 6.6.

4. *Ibid.*, para. 6.8.

5. Department of Health and Social Security, *Legislation on Human Infertility Services and Embryo Research: A Consultation Paper* (London: HMSO, 1986), para. 38.

6. *Human Fertilization and Embryology: A Framework for Legislation* (London: HMSO, 1987), paras. 15, 54.

7. *Report of the Committee of Inquiry into Human Fertilization and Embryology*, para. 7.2.

8. *Ibid.*

9. *Ibid.*, paras. 7.4–6.

10. Department of Health and Social Security, *Legislation on Human Infertility Services and Embryo Research: A Consultation Paper*, para. 38.

11. *Human Fertilization and Embryology: A Framework for Legislation*, paras. 15, 54; *Report of the Committee of Inquiry into Human Fertilization and Embryology*, para. 10.10.

12. Human Fertilization and Embryology Act 1990 (London: HMSO, 1990), para. 27.1.

13. *Ibid.*, para. 27.2.

14. Methodist Church in Ireland, *A Response by a Committee of the Methodist Church in Ireland to the Invitation to Comment upon the Government Inquiry into Human Fertilization and Embryology* (unpublished, 1983), para. 2.a–c.

15. Church of England Board for Social Responsibility, *Human Fertilization and Embryology: The Response of the Board for Social Responsibility of the General Synod of the Church of England to the DHSS Report of the Committee of Inquiry* (London: Social Policy Committee, Church House, 1984), para. 7.2.

16. Children's Society, *Government Inquiry into Human Fertilization and Embryology: Evidence* (unpublished, 1983), para. 9 (a).

17. Free Church Federal Council and the British Council of Churches, *Choices in Childlessness* (London: FCFC/BCC, 1982), p. 54, para B.2.

18. Nationwide Festival of Light, *Human Fertilization and Embryology: Submission to the Committee of Inquiry under the Chairmanship of Mrs Mary Warnock* (unpublished, 1983), para. 5.5.

19. Church of Scotland, *Response to the Report of the Committee of Inquiry into Human Fertilization and Embryology* (unpublished, 1984), para. 3.

20. *Op. cit.*, para. 1.

21. *Op. cit.*, para. 8.b.

22. Salvation Army, *Response by the Salvation Army to the Consultation Paper: Legislation on Human Infertility Services and Embryo Research* (unpublished, 1987), para. 10.

23. *Op. cit.*, para. 8.4.

24. Catholic Bishops' Joint Committee on Bio-ethical Issues, *Response to the Warnock Report on Human Fertilization and Embryology* (London: Catholic

Media Office, 1984), para. 30.

25. Catholic Union of Great Britain, *Reply by the Joint Ethico-Medical Committee to 'Legislation on Human Infertility Services and Embryo Research'* (unpublished, 1987), p. 3, para. 1.

9. *In vitro* fertilization (IVF)

1. *Report of the Committee of Inquiry into Human Fertilization and Embryology* (London: HMSO, 1984), paras. 5.6–8.

2. *Ibid.*, para. 5.9.

3. *Ibid.*, para. 5.11.

4. *Human Fertilization and Embryology: A Framework for Legislation* (London: HMSO, 1987), para. 15.

5. Human Fertilization and Embryology Act 1990 (London: HMSO, 1990), schedule 2, para. 1.1 (a).

6. *Ibid.*, schedule 3, para. 2.1.

7. *Ibid.*, schedule 3, para. 6.1.

8. Catholic Bishops' Joint Committee on Bio-ethical Issues, In Vitro *Fertilization: Morality and Public Policy* (Oxford: Catholic Media Office, 1983), para. 24.

9. *Ibid.*, para. 25.

10. *Ibid.*, paras. 11, 12.

11. *Ibid.*, paras. 8, 9.

12. Catholic Bishops' Joint Committee on Bio-ethical Issues, *Response to the Warnock Report on Human Fertilization and Embryology* (London: Catholic Media Office, 1984), para. 26.

13. National Board of Catholic Women, *Warnock Committee: Inquiry into Human Fertilization and Embryology* (unpublished, 1983), para. 3.

14. National Board of Catholic Women, *Warnock Report on Human Fertilization and Embryology: Comments submitted to the Secretary of State for Social Services by the National Board of Catholic Women* (unpublished, 1984), recommendation 5.

15. Free Presbyterian Church of Scotland, *Representations by the Free Presbyterian Church of Scotland in Connection with the Report of the Committee of Inquiry into Human Fertilization and Embryology* (unpublished, 1983), p. 3, para. 2. (1).

16. *Ibid.*, p. 6, recommendation 4.10.

17. Free Presbyterian Church of Scotland, *Representation of the Free Presbyterian Church of Scotland Regarding Consultation Paper (Cm 46): Legislation on Human Infertility Services and Embryo Research* (unpublished, 1987), p. 1, para. 5.

18. Church of Scotland, *Response to the Report of the Committee of Inquiry into Human Fertilization and Embryology* (unpublished, 1984), section 3, para. 6.

19. Free Church Federal Council and the British Council of Churches, *Choices in*

Childlessness (London: FCFC/BCC, 1982), p. 54, para. B.2.

20. Methodist Church, Division of Social Responsibility, *Government Inquiry into Human Fertilization and Embryology* (unpublished, 1982), p. 2, para. 3.

21. Methodist Church in Ireland, *A Response by a Committee of the Methodist Church in Ireland to the Invitation to Comment upon the Government Inquiry into Human Fertilization and Embryology* (unpublished, 1983), para. 1.

22. Free Church of Scotland, *Letter to Scottish Home and Health Department Regarding Inquiry into Human Fertilization and Embryology* (unpublished, 1984), para. 4.a.

23. Free Church of Scotland, *Response to Consultation Paper on Legislation on Human Infertility Services and Embryo Research* (unpublished, 1987), para. 6.2.

24. Presbyterian Church in Ireland, *Government Inquiry into Human Fertilization and Embryology: Submission by an Ad Hoc Group of the Presbyterian Church in Ireland* (unpublished, 1983), para. 3. 2.

25. General Assembly of the Presbyterian Church in Ireland 1985, resolution 3.

26. Church of England Board for Social Responsibility, *Human Fertilization and Embryology: The Response of the Board for Social Responsibility of the General Synod of the Church of England to the DHSS Report of the Committee of Inquiry* (London: Social Policy Committee, Church House, 1984), para. 6.4.

27. Scottish Episcopal Church, *Working Party on Human Infertility and Embryo Research* (unpublished, 1987), para. 3.74.

28. Church of Ireland, *Submission to the Warnock Committee by the Armagh Diocesan Board of Social Responsibility* (adopted by the Northern Ireland Board of Social Responsibility of the Church of Ireland) (unpublished, 1983), recommendation 4.

29. Mothers' Union, *Statement to the Government Inquiry into Human Fertilization and Embryology from the Social Concern Committee of the Mothers' Union* (unpublished, 1983), para. 5 (i) a.

30. Salvation Army, *Written Submission to the Warnock Committee of Inquiry into Human Fertilization and Embryology* (unpublished, 1983), para. iv.3.

31. Nationwide Festival of Light, *Human Fertilization and Embryology: Submission to the Committee of Inquiry under the Chairmanship of Mrs Mary Warnock* (unpublished, 1983), para. 4.6.

32. CARE Trust, *Response to Warnock From CARE Trust* (unpublished, 1984), para. 14 (iii).

33. Christian Medical Fellowship, *Legislation on Human Infertility Services and Embryo Research: The Christian Medical Fellowship's Response to DHSS Invitation to Comment on Consultation Document Cm 46* (unpublished, 1987).

34. *E.g.* the Bishops' Commission on Doctrine of the Irish Episcopal Conference, *In Vitro Fertilisation* (Dublin: Veritas, 1986).

10. Surrogacy

1. *Report of the Committee of Inquiry into Human Fertilization and Embryology* (London: HMSO, 1984), para. 8.1.
2. *Ibid.*, paras. 8.5–9.
3. Adoption Act 1958 (London: HMSO, 1958), section 50.
4. *Op. cit.*, paras. 8.10–12.
5. *Ibid.*, paras. 8.13–16.
6. *Ibid.*, Expression of Dissent: A. Surrogacy, Dr W. Greengross, Dr D. Davies.
7. *Ibid.*, para. 8.19.
8. *Ibid.*, para. 8.18.
9. Department of Health and Social Security, *Legislation on Human Infertility Services and Embryo Research: A Consultation Paper* (London: HMSO, 1986), para. 14.
10. *Ibid.*, paras. 41–44.
11. *Human Fertilization and Embryology: A Framework for Legislation* (London: HMSO, 1987), paras. 73, 74.
12. Human Fertilization and Embryology Act 1990 (London: HMSO, 1990), para. 36.1.
13. *Ibid.*, para. 30.1.
14. *Ibid.*, paras. 30.1–7.
15. Scottish Episcopal Church, *Working Party on Human Infertility and Embryo Research* (unpublished, 1987), paras. 4.21–24.
16. *Ibid.*, para. 4.31.
17. Presbyterian Church in Ireland, *Government Inquiry into Human Fertilization and Embryology: Submission by an Ad Hoc Group of the Presbyterian Church in Ireland* (unpublished, 1983), para. 4.1.
18. *Ibid.*, para. 4.3.
19. General Assembly of the Presbyterian Church in Ireland 1985, resolutions 3, 4.
20. Catholic Bishops' Joint Committee on Bio-ethical Issues, *Response to the Warnock Report on Human Fertilization and Embryology*, paras. 51, 52.
21. National Board of Catholic Women, *Warnock Committee: Inquiry into Human Fertilization and Embryology* (unpublished, 1983), para. 6.
22. Catholic Union of Great Britain, *Reply by the Joint Ethico-Medical Committee to 'Legislation on Human Infertility Services and Embryo Research'* (unpublished, 1987), p. 3, para. 9.
23. Church of England Board for Social Responsibility, *Human Fertilization and Embryology: The Response of the Board for Social Responsibility of the General Synod of the Church of England to the DHSS Report of the Committee of Inquiry* (London: Social Policy Committee, Church House, 1984), para. 9.3.

24. Children's Society, *Government Inquiry into Human Fertilization and Embryology: Evidence* (unpublished, 1983), para. 10.

25. Mothers' Union, *Statement to the Government Inquiry into Human Fertilization and Embryology from the Social Concern Committee of the Mothers' Union* (unpublished, 1983), para. 5.i (b).

26. Church of Ireland, *Legislation on Human Infertility Services and Embryo Research: A Consultative Document. A Response by the Armagh Diocesan Board of Social Responsibility endorsed by the Northern Ireland Board of Social Responsibility of the Church of Ireland* (unpublished, 1987), para. 14.

27. Methodist Church, Division of Social Responsibility, *Government Inquiry into Human Fertilization and Embryology* (unpublished, 1983), p. 2, para. 4.

28. Free Church Federal Council and the British Council of Churches, *Choices in Childlessness* (London: FCFC/BCC, 1982), p. 48.

29. Methodist Church in Ireland, *A Response by a Committee of the Methodist Church in Ireland to the Invitation to Comment upon the Government Inquiry into Human Fertilization and Embryology* (unpublished, 1983), para. 3.

30. Church of Scotland, *Response to the Report of the Committee of Inquiry into Human Fertilization and Embryology* (unpublished, 1984), section 3, para. 12.

31. Free Church of Scotland, *Response to the Consultation Paper on Legislation on Human Infertility Services and Embryo Research* (unpublished, 1987), para. 4.d.

32. Free Presbyterian Church of Scotland, *Representations by the Free Presbyterian Church of Scotland in Connection with the Report of the Committee of Inquiry into Human Fertilization and Embryology* (unpublished, 1983), p. 6, recommendation 3.

33. Salvation Army, *Written Submission to the Warnock Committee of Inquiry into Human Fertilization and Embryology* (unpublished, 1983), para. iv.11.

34. *Ibid.*, para. ii.7.

35. Christian Medical Fellowship, *Legislation on Human Infertility Services and Embryo Research: The Christian Medical Fellowship's Response to DHSS Invitation to Comment on Consultation Document Cm 46* (unpublished, 1987), para. 25.

36. Nationwide Festival of Light, *Human Fertilization and Embryology: Submission to the Committee of Inquiry under the Chairmanship of Mrs Mary Warnock* (unpublished, 1983), para. 5.6.

11. Embryo research

1. *Report of the Committee of Inquiry into Human Fertilization and Embryology* (London: HMSO, 1984), paras. 11.9, 10.

2. *Ibid.*, paras. 11.11–13.

3. *Ibid.*, para. 11.14.
4. *Ibid.*, Expression of Dissent: B. Use of Human Embryos in Research, Mrs M. Carriline, Professor J. Marshall, Mrs J. Walker.
5. *Ibid.*, paras. 11.17, 18, 22, 24, 30.
6. *Ibid.*, Expression of Dissent: C. Use of Human Embryos in Research, Mr T. S. Baker, Professor A. Dyson, Mrs N. Edwards, Dr W. Greengross.
7. Department of Health and Social Security, *Legislation on Human Fertility Services and Embryo Research: A Consultation Paper* (London: HMSO, 1986), paras. 48, 59.
8. *Human Fertilization and Embryology: A Framework for Legislation* (London: HMSO, 1987), para. 30.
9. *Op. cit.*, paras. 12.2–16.
10. *Op. cit.*, paras. 39–140.
11. *Op. cit.*, paras. 37–42.
12. Human Fertilization and Embryology Act 1990 (London: HMSO, 1990), para. 3.1.
13. *Ibid.*, para. 3.2.
14. *Ibid.*, para. 3.3 (b).
15. *Ibid.*, para. 3.3 (d).
16. *Ibid.*, para. 3.3 (a).
17. *Ibid.*, para. 3.4.
18. *Ibid.*, para. 15.4.
19. *Ibid.*, schedule 2, para. 4.2 (a).
20. *Ibid.*, schedule 2, paras. 1.1 (f); 3.5.
21. *Ibid.*, schedule 2, para. 3.2.
22. *Ibid.*, schedule 2, para. 3.4.
23. Catholic Bishops' Joint Committee on Bio-ethical Issues, *Response to the Warnock Report on Human Fertilization and Embryology* (London: Catholic Media Office, 1984), para. 33.
24. *Ibid.*, para. 34.
25. *Ibid.*, para. 40.
26. Catholic Bishops' Joint Committee on Bio-ethical Issues, In Vitro *Fertilization: Morality and Policy Policy* (Oxford: Catholic Media Office, 1983), para. 18.
27. *Ibid.*, para. 18, n. 6.
28. *Op. cit.*, para. 49.
29. National Board of Catholic Women, *Warnock Committee: Inquiry into Human Fertilization and Embryology* (unpublished, 1983), para. 3.
30. National Board of Catholic Women, *Warnock Report on Human Fertilization and Embryology: Comments submitted to the Secretary of State for Social Services by the National Board of Catholic Women* (unpublished, 1984), recommendation 15.

31. Catholic Union of Great Britain, *Reply by the Joint Ethico-Medical Committee to 'Legislation on Human Infertility Services and Embryo Research'* (unpublished, 1987), p. 1, para. 7.

32. *Ibid.*, p. 3, para. 7.

33. Scottish Episcopal Church, *Working Party on Human Infertility and Embryo Research* (unpublished, 1987), para. 4.45.

34. *Ibid.*, para. 4.11.

35. Church of Ireland, *Legislation on Human Infertility Services and Embryo Research: A Consultative Document. A Response by the Armagh Diocesan Board of Social Responsibility endorsed by the Northern Ireland Board of Social Responsibility of the Church of Ireland* (unpublished, 1987), para. 15.

36. *Ibid.*, para. 13.

37. Church of England Board for Social Responsibility, *Human Fertilization and Embryology: The Response of the Board for Social Responsibility of the General Synod of the Church of England to the DHSS Report of the Committee of Inquiry* (London: Social Policy Committee, Church House 1984), paras. 2.6, 7.

38. *Ibid.*, para. 10.6.

39. Church of England Board for Social Responsibility, *Legislation on Human Infertility Services and Embryo Research, A Consultation Paper produced by the DHSS: Response by the Board for Social Responsibility of the General Synod of the Church of England* (unpublished, 1987), para. 8.

40. Children's Society, *Government Inquiry into Human Fertilization and Embryology: Evidence* (unpublished, 1983), para. 27.

41. *Ibid.*, para. 26.

42. *Ibid.*, para. 27.

43. *Ibid.*, para. 11.

44. *Ibid.*, para. 28.

45. *Ibid.*, para. 29.

46. *Ibid.*, para. 30.

47. Mothers' Union, *Statement to the Government Inquiry into Human Fertilization and Embryology from the Social Concern Committee of the Mothers' Union* (unpublished, 1983), para. 4.v (c).

48. Mothers' Union, *Statement by the Committee for Social Concern to the Department of Health and Social Security on the Report of the Committee of Inquiry into Human Fertilization and Embryology under the Chairmanship of Dame Mary Warnock DBE* (unpublished, 1984), para. D.

49. *Ibid.*

50. Mothers' Union, *Statement by the Committee for Social Concern to the Department of Health and Social Security on the Consultation Paper: Legislation on Human Infertility Services and Embryo Research* (unpublished, 1987), para. 6.

51. Church of Scotland, *Response to the Report of the Committee of Inquiry into Human Fertilization and Embryology* (unpublished, 1984), section 3, para. 9.

52. Free Church of Scotland, *Legislation on Human Infertility Services and Embryo Research: Free Church of Scotland Response to Consultation Paper* (unpublished, 1987), para. 7.

53. Free Presbyterian Church of Scotland, *Representations of the Free Presbyterian Church of Scotland Regarding Consultation Paper (Cm 46): Legislation on Human Infertility Services and Embryo Research* (unpublished, 1987), p. 6. para. 4.

54. *Ibid.*, p. 2, para. 3.

55. General Assembly of the Presbyterian Church in Ireland 1985, resolution 2.

56. Presbyterian Church in Ireland, *Government Inquiry into Human Fertilization and Embryology: Submission by an Ad Hoc Group of the Presbyterian Church in Ireland* (unpublished, 1983), para. 5.2.

57. *Ibid.*, para. 9.

58. *Ibid.*, para. 8.

59. *Ibid.*, para. 7.

60. *Ibid.*, para. 10.1.

61. *Ibid.*, para. 7.

62. Methodist Church, Division of Social Responsibility, *Government Inquiry into Human Fertilization and Embryology* (unpublished, 1983), p. 2, para. 1.

63. Free Church Federal Council and the British Council of Churches, *Choices in Childlessness* (London: FCFC/BCC, 1982), p. 54, para B.2.

64. Methodist Church, Division of Social Responsibility, *Report on Medical Ethics to Methodist Conference* (unpublished, 1985), para 3.

65. Methodist Church in Ireland, *A Response by a Committee of the Methodist Church in Ireland to the Invitation to Comment upon the Government Inquiry into Human Fertilization and Embryology* (unpublished, 1983), para. 11.

66. *Ibid.*, para. 9.

67. *Ibid.*, para. 10.

68. *Ibid.*, para. 13.

69. *Ibid.*, para. 5.

70. *Ibid.*, para. 12.

71. Salvation Army, *A Response to the Department of Health and Social Security on Reading the Warnock Report* (unpublished, 1984), para. ii. (2).

72. Salvation Army, *Response by the Salvation Army to the Consultation Paper: Legislation on Human Infertility Services and Embryo Research* (unpublished, 1987), para. 11.

73. *Op. cit.*, para. iii. (6).

74. Christian Medical Fellowship, *Legislation on Human Infertility Services and Embryo Research: The Christian Medical Fellowship's Response to DHSS Invitation to Comment on Consultation Document Cm 46* (unpublished, 1987), para. 21.

75. Nationwide Festival of Light, *Human Fertilization and Embryology:*

Submission to the Committee of Inquiry under the Chairmanship of Mrs Mary Warnock (unpublished, 1983), para. 3.5.

76. CARE Trust, *Response to Warnock from CARE Trust* (unpublished, 1984), para. 14.iv.
77. *Op. cit.*, para. 5.9.
78. *Ibid.*, para. 5.10.
79. *Ibid.*, para. para. 5.12.
80. Human Fertilization and Embryology Act 1990, schedule 2.
81. While many embryos have been split at the 4–8 cell stage, the twinning occurs only when both new embryos are allowed to develop. At the time of writing this has been shown to be possible in the US, but has not actually happened yet.

12. Gamete and embryo storage

1. *Report of the Committee of Inquiry into Human Fertilization and Embryology* (London: HMSO, 1984), para. 10.10.
2. *Ibid.*, para. 10.8.
3. *Ibid.*, para. 10.12.
4. *Ibid.*
5. *Ibid.*, para. 10.9.
6. *Ibid.*, para. 10.15.
7. *Ibid.*, para. 10.13.
8. *Ibid.*, paras. 4.4; 10.9, 15.
9. Human Fertilization and Embryology Act 1990 (London: HMSO, 1990), paras. 3.1 (b); 4.1 (a).
10. *Ibid.*, para. 14.3.
11. *Ibid.*, para. 14.4.
12. *Ibid.*, para. 14.5.
13. *Ibid.*, schedule 3, para. 1.
14. *Ibid.*
15. *Ibid.*, schedule 3, para. 2.1.
16. *Ibid.*, schedule 3, para. 2.2 (a).
17. *Ibid.*, schedule 3, para. 2.2 (b).
18. *Ibid.*, schedule 3, para. 2.
19. *Ibid.*, schedule 3, para. 8.2.
20. *Ibid.*, schedule 3, para. 3.1 (a).
21. *Ibid.*, schedule 3, para. 4.
22. *Ibid.*, schedule 3, para. 8.1.
23. *Ibid.*, schedule 3, para. 7.
24. *Ibid.*, schedule 3, para. 6.3.
25. Scottish Episcopal Church, *Working Party on Human Infertility and Embryo*

Research (unpublished, 1987), para. 4.0.

26. Salvation Army, *Response by the Salvation Army to the Consultation Paper: Legislation on Human Infertility Services and Embryo Research* (unpublished, 1987), para. 8.

27. Methodist Church in Ireland, *A Response by a Committee of the Methodist Church in Ireland to the Invitation to Comment upon the Government Inquiry into Human Fertilization and Embryology* (unpublished, 1983), para. 6.

28. Christian Medical Fellowship, *Legislation on Human Infertility Services and Embryo Research: The Christian Medical Fellowship's Response to DHSS Invitation to Comment on Consultation Document Cm 46* (unpublished, 1987), para. 19.

29. Free Church Federal Council and the British Council of Churches, *A Response to the Warnock Report by Members of the Working Party which produced 'Choices in Childlessness'* (unpublished, 1984), para. 11.

30. Church of Scotland, *Response to the Report of the Committee of Inquiry into Human Fertilization and Embryology* (unpublished, 1984), section 3, paras. 10, 11.

31. Mothers' Union, *Statement by the Committee for Social Concern to the Department of Health and Social Security on the Report of the Committee of Inquiry into Human Fertilization and Embryology under the Chairmanship of Dame Mary Warnock DBE* (unpublished, 1984), para. B.7.

32. Mothers' Union, *Statement by the Committee for Social Concern to the Department of Health and Social Security on the Consultation Paper: Legislation on Human Infertility Services and Embryo Research* (unpublished, 1987), para. 5.

33. Children's Society, *Government Inquiry into Human Fertilization and Embryology: Evidence* (unpublished, 1983), paras. 13, 16a.

34. *Ibid.*, para. 16.a (i), (ii).

35. Presbyterian Church in Ireland, *Government Inquiry into Human Fertilization and Embryology: Submission by an Ad Hoc Group of the Presbyterian Church in Ireland* (unpublished, 1983), para. 5.

36. Church of Ireland, *Legislation on Human Infertility Services and Embryo Research: A Consultative Document. A Response by the Armagh Diocesan Board of Social Responsibility endorsed by the Northern Ireland Board of Social Responsibility of the Church of Ireland* (unpublished, 1987), para. 11.

37. Free Presbyterian Church of Scotland, *Representation of the Free Presbyterian Church of Scotland Regarding Consultation Paper (Cm 46): Legislation on Human Infertility Services and Embryo Research* (unpublished, 1987), recommendations 4.2, 9.

38. CARE Trust, *Response to Warnock from CARE Trust* (unpublished, 1984), para. 14. (v).

39. Nationwide Festival of Light, *Human Fertilization and Embryology: Submission to the Committee of Inquiry under the Chairmanship of Mrs Mary*

Warnock (unpublished, 1983), para. 5.3.

40. Catholic Bishops' Joint Committee on Bio-ethical Issues, In Vitro *Fertilization: Morality and Public Policy* (Oxford: Catholic Media Office, 1983), para. 11.3.

41. Catholic Bishops' Joint Committee on Bio-Ethical Issues, *On Human Infertility Services and Embryo Research* (London: Catholic Media Office, 1987), para. 19.

42. *Ibid.*, para. 20.

43. Catholic Union of Great Britain, *Reply by the Joint Ethico-Medical Committee to 'Legislation on Human Infertility Services and Embryo Research'* (unpublished, 1987), p. 3, para 4.

44. National Board of Catholic Women, *Warnock Report on Human Fertilization and Embryology: Comments submitted to the Secretary of State for Social Services by the National Board of Catholic Women* (unpublished, 1984), recommendations 9, 10.

45. National Board of Catholic Women, *Legislation on Human Infertility Services and Embryo Research Consultation Paper Issued by the Department of Health and Social Security: Views of the National Board of Catholic Women* (unpublished, 1987), para. 6.

13. Abortion

1. Human Fertilization and Embryology Act 1990 (London: HMSO, 1990), para. 37.1(a).

2. *Ibid.*, para. 37.1 (b)–(d).

3. *Ibid.*, para. 37.4.

4. *Ibid.*, para. 38.1.

5. *Ibid.*, para. 38.2.

Sources

Abortion Act 1967 (London: HMSO, 1967).

Adoption Act 1958 (London: HMSO, 1958).

M. Ah-Moye and I. Craft, 'The GIFT Technique – A New Fertility Option?' *The Practitioner* 232 (January 1988).

L. C. Allen, *Psalms 101 – 150*, Word Biblical Commentary (Dallas: Word, 1983).

A. A. Anderson, *Psalms*, New Century Bible, 2 vols. (London: Oliphants, 1972).

M. Anderson, *Infertility* (London: Faber and Faber, 1987).

R. S. Anderson, *On Being Human* (Grand Rapids: Eerdmans, 1982).

Apocalypse of Peter.

Artificial Human Insemination: The Report of a Commission Appointed by His Grace the Archbishop of Canterbury (London: SPCK, 1948).

Athenagoras, *Supplication for the Christians.*

Augustine, *De Civitate Dei.*

Augustine, *De Trinitate.*

Augustine, *Quaestionum in Heptateuchum.*

I. D. Baillie, letter to HFEA, 16 May 1991.

P. Baelz, *Ethics and Belief* (London: Sheldon, 1977).

Baptist Union of Great Britain and Ireland, *Submission to the Warnock Committee Prepared by a Working Party under the Auspices of the Baptist Union Department of Mission, and Approved by the Baptist Union Council* (unpublished, 1983).

I. G. Barbour, *Issues in Science and Religion* (London: SCM, 1966).

K. Barth, *Church Dogmatics* (Edinburgh: T. and T. Clark), II.2 (1957), III.1 (1958), III.2 (1960).

Barton, Walker and Weisner, 'Artificial Insemination', *British Medical Journal* (13 January 1945).

Basil of Caesarea, *Epistle* 188, Canon 2.

Bishops' Commission on Doctrine of the Irish Episcopal Conference, In Vitro *Fertilization* (Dublin: Veritas, 1986).

M. Black, *Romans*, New Century Bible Commentary (London: Marshall, Morgan and Scott, 1973).

R. G. Boling, *Judges*, Anchor Bible (New York: Doubleday, 1975).

D. Bonhoeffer, *Ethics* (London: Fontana, 1964).

P. Bristow, *The Moral Dignity of Man: Catholic Moral Teaching on Family and Medical Ethics* (Dublin: Four Courts Press, 1993).

British Medical Journal 286 (May 1983), 289 (July 1984), 290 (January 1985).

F. F. Bruce, *Romans*, Tyndale New Testament Commentaries (London: IVP, 1974).

E. Brunner, *The Divine Imperative* (Philadelphia: Westminster, 1947).

——— *Man in Revolt* (Philadelphia: Westminster, 1947).

——— *Natural Theology* (London: Geoffrey Bles, 1946).

D. Cairns, *The Image of God in Man* (London: SCM, 1953).

J. Calvin, *Commentary on Acts*.

——— *Commentary on Genesis*.

——— *Commentary on Job*.

——— *Institutes of the Christian Religion*.

N. M. de S. Cameron, *Embryos and Ethics: The Warnock Report in Debate* (Edinburgh: Rutherford House, 1987).

CARE Trust, *Response to Warnock From CARE Trust* (unpublished, 1984).

——— *HFEA Code of Practice Consultation Document: Comments by CARE* (unpublished, 1991).

R. R. Carroll, *Jeremiah*, Old Testament Library (London: SCM, 1986).

Catholic Bishops' Joint Committee on Bio-ethical Issues, In Vitro *Fertilization: Morality and Public Policy* (Oxford: Catholic Media Office, 1983).

——— *Response to the Warnock Report on Human Fertilization and Embryology* (London: Catholic Media Office, 1984).

——— *On Human Infertility Services and Embryo Research* (London, Catholic Media Office, 1987).

Catholic Union of Great Britain, *Reply by the Joint Ethico-Medical Committee to 'Legislation on Human Infertility Services and Embryo Research'* (unpublished, 1987).

R. Chadwick (ed.), *Ethics, Reproduction and Genetic Control* (London: Routledge, 1987).

J. H. Charner (ed.), *Abortion and the Sanctity of Human Life* (Exeter: Paternoster, 1985).

Children's Society, *Government Inquiry into Human Fertilization and Embryology:*

Evidence (unpublished, 1983).

Christian Medical Fellowship, *Legislation on Human Infertility Services and Embryo Research: The Christian Medical Fellowship's Response to DHSS Invitation to Comment on Consultation Document Cm 46* (unpublished, 1987).

——— *Submission to the HFEA on the Consultation Document for their Code of Practice* (unpublished, 1991).

Christian Sibyllines.

Church in Wales, *Human Fertilization and Embryology: The Response of the Bench of Bishops of the Church in Wales to the Warnock Report* (unpublished, 1985).

Church of England, *Personal Origins: The Report of a Working Party on Human Fertilization and Embryology of the Board for Social Responsibility of the General Synod of the Church of England* (London: Church Information Office, 1985).

Church of England Board for Social Responsibility, *Evidence to the DHSS Inquiry into Human Fertilization and Embryology* (unpublished, 1983).

——— *Human Fertilization and Embryology: The Response of the Board for Social Responsibility of the General Synod of the Church of England to the DHSS Report of the Committee of Inquiry* (London: Social Policy Committee, Church House, 1984).

——— *Legislation on Human Infertility Services and Embryo Research, A Consultation Paper produced by the DHSS: Response by the Board for Social Responsibility of the General Synod of the Church of England* (unpublished, 1987).

Church of Ireland, *Submission to the Warnock Committee by the Armagh Diocesan Board of Social Responsibility* (adopted by the Northern Ireland Board of Social Responsibility of the Church of Ireland) (unpublished, 1983).

——— *Legislation on Human Infertility Services and Embryo Research: A Consultative Document. A Response by the Armagh Diocesan Board of Social Responsibility endorsed by the Northern Ireland Board of Social Responsibility of the Church of Ireland* (unpublished, 1987).

Church of Scotland, *Response to the Report of the Committee of Inquiry into Human Fertilization and Embryology* (unpublished, 1984).

——— *Letter to All Scottish Members of Parliament* (unpublished, 1985).

S. Clark, 'God's Law and Morality', *Philosophical Quarterly* 32 (1982).

Clement of Alexandria, *Protrepticus*.

R. E. Clements, *Exodus*, Cambridge Bible Commentary (Cambridge: Cambridge University Press, 1971).

F. H. Cleobury, *Biology and Personality*, ed. I. Ramsey (Oxford: Blackwell, 1965).

Clinical Theology Association, *Response to HFEA Code of Practice Consultation Document* (unpublished, 1991).

Codex Iuris Canonici, Lib. vi, *Tit.* vi, *Can.* 1398 (1983).

A. Cole, *Galatians*, Tyndale New Testament Commentaries (London: Tyndale, 1965).

D. Cook, *The Moral Maze* (London: SPCK, 1983).

Council of Ancyra, Canon 21.

Council of Churches for Britain and Ireland, *Response to the Consultation Document Issued by the HFEA* (unpublished, 1991).

P. Coyle (Honorary Secretary of the Guild of Catholic Doctors), letter to author, 7 July 1991.

P. C. Craigie, *Psalms 1 – 50*, Word Biblical Commentary (Dallas: Word, 1983).

M. Dahood, *Psalms*, Anchor Bible, 2 vols. (New York: Doubleday, 1965, 1968).

R. Davidson, *Genesis 12 – 50*, Cambridge Bible Commentary (Cambridge: Cambridge University Press, 1979).

Department of Health and Social Security, *Legislation on Human Infertility Services and Embryo Research: A Consultation Paper* (London: HMSO, 1986).

Didache.

Didascala et Constitutiones Apostolorum.

J. D. Douglas (ed.), *The New International Dictionary of the Christian Church* (Exeter: Paternoster, 1978).

J. D. G. Dunn, *Romans 9 – 16*, Word Biblical Commentary (Dallas: Word, 1988).

G. R. Dunston and M. J. Seller (eds.), *The Status of the Human Embryo* (London: Kings Fund, 1988).

J. I. Durham, *Exodus*, Word Biblical Commentary (Dallas: Word, 1987).

R. M. Dworkin (ed.), *The Philosophy of Law* (Oxford: Oxford University Press, 1977).

A. Dyson and J. Harris (eds.), *Experiments on Embryos* (London: Routledge, 1990).

J. H. Eaton, *Psalms* (London: SCM, 1967).

R. G. Edward, 'The Current Clinical and Ethical Situation of Human Conception *In Vitro*', *Proceedings of the Annual Symposium of the Eugenics Society* 19 (1983).

E. E. Ellis, *The Gospel of Luke*, New Century Bible (London: Marshall, Morgan and Scott, 1974).

Epistle of Barnabas.

J. A. Fitzmyer, *The Gospel According to Luke i–ix*, Anchor Bible (New York: Doubleday, 1981).

Free Church Federal Council and the British Council of Churches, *Choices in Childlessness* (London: FCFC/BCC, 1982).

———— *A Response to the Warnock Report by Members of the Working Party which produced 'Choices in Childlessness'* (unpublished, 1984).

Free Church of Scotland, *Letter to Scottish Home and Health Department Regarding Inquiry into Human Fertilization and Embryology* (unpublished, 1984).

———— *Response to Consultation Paper on Legislation on Human Infertility Services and Embryo Research* (unpublished, 1987).

———— *The Sanctity of Human Life: The Report of the Study Panel of the Free Church of Scotland* (unpublished, 1988).

Free Presbyterian Church of Scotland, *Representations by the Free Presbyterian Church of Scotland in Connection with the Report of the Committee of Inquiry into Human Fertilization and Embryology* (unpublished, 1983).

———— *Representations of the Free Presbyterian Church of Scotland Regarding Consultation Paper (Cm 46): Legislation on Human Infertility Services and Embryo Research* (unpublished, 1987).

P. Geach, *God and the Soul* (London: Routledge and Kegan Paul, 1969).

General Assembly of the Presbyterian Church in Ireland, 1985 (report).

Gratian, *Decretum II*.

J. Gray, *Joshua, Judges, Ruth*, New Century Bible (London: Marshall, Morgan and Scott, 1986).

R. M. Green, *Religion and Moral Reason* (Oxford: Oxford University Press, 1988).

Gregory IX, *Decretales*.

Gregory XIV, *Sedes Apostolica* (31 May 1591).

Gregory of Nyssa, *Adversus Macedonianos*.

J. M. Gustafson, *Protestant and Roman Catholic Ethics* (London: SCM, 1979).

N. C. Habel, *The Book of Job*, Cambridge Bible Commentary (Cambridge: Cambridge University Press, 1975).

R. K. Harrison, *Jeremiah and Lamentations*, Tyndale Old Testament Commentaries (London: IVP, 1973).

P. Helm (ed.), *Divine Commands and Morality* (Oxford: Oxford University Press, 1981).

W. Hendrikson, *Matthew* (Edinburgh; Banner of Truth, 1973).

R. Higginson, *Dilemmas* (London: Hodder and Stoughton, 1988).

———— *Reply to Warnock*, Grove Booklets on Ethics 63 (Nottingham: Grove Books, 1986).

D. Hill, *The Gospel of Matthew*, New Century Bible (London: Oliphants, 1972).

Human Fertilization and Embryology: A Framework for Legislation (London: HMSO, 1987).

Human Fertilization and Embryology Act 1990 (London: HMSO, 1990).

Human Fertilization and Embryology Authority, *Code of Practice* (London: HFEA, 1991).

———— *Code of Practice: Explanation* (unpublished, 1991).

———— *Letter to All Interested Parties*, 21 March 1991.

Humanae Vitae: Encyclical Letter of His Holiness Paul VI, Acta Apostolicae Sedis LX (1968), no. 9 (London: The Incorporated Catholic Truth Society, 1970).

J. P. Hyatt, *Exodus*, New Century Bible (London: Oliphants, 1971).

Infant Life (Preservation) Act 1929 (London: HMSO, 1929).

Innocent III, Canon 5.20.

Irenaeus, *Adversus Haereses*.

I. Jakobovits, *Human Fertilisation and Embryology: A Jewish View* (London: Office of the Chief Rabbi, 1984).

Jerome, *Epistle* 22.

Joint Ethico-Medical Committee of the Guild of Catholic Doctors and Catholic Union of Great Britain, *Reply to Consultation Document on 'Code of Practice' of HFEA* (unpublished, 1991).

D. G. Jones, *Manufacturing Humans* (Leicester: Inter-Varsity Press, 1982).

R. G. Jones, *Groundwork of Christian Ethics* (London: Epworth, 1984).

Josephus, *Contra Apionem*.

K. T. Kelly, *Life and Love* (London: Collins, 1987).

Lambeth Conference Statement 1958.

S. Lee, *Law and Morals* (Oxford: Oxford University Press, 1986).

J. Lejuene, P. Ramsay and G. Wright, *The Question of In Vitro Fertilization: Studies in Medicine, Law and Ethics* (London: SPUC Educational Trust, 1984).

H. D. Lewis, *The Self and Immortality* (London: Macmillan, 1973).

LIFE, *Warnock Dissected* (Leamington Spa: LIFE, 1984).

————— *Comments from LIFE on the HFEA's Code of Practice: Consultation Document* (unpublished, 1991).

M. Lockwood, *Moral Dilemmas in Modern Medicine* (Oxford: Oxford University Press, 1985).

M. Luther, *Weimarer Ausgabe*.

D. MacKay, *Behavioural Sciences*, ed. M. A. Jeeves (Leicester: Inter-Varsity Press, 1984).

J. McLean, 'Early Embryo Loss', in *Upholding Human Dignity: Ethical Alternatives to Human Embryo Research* (London: The Parliamentary Medical and Scientific Advisory Committee to the All-Party Parliamentary Pro-Life Group, 1987).

J. Macquarrie and J. Childress (eds.), *A New Dictionary of Christian Ethics* (London: SCM, 1992).

E. L. Mascall, *The Importance of Being Human* (Oxford: Oxford University Press, 1959).

J. K. Mason and R. A. McCall Smith, *Law and Medical Ethics* (London: Butterworth, 1987).

Methodist Church, Division of Social Responsibility, *Government Inquiry into Human Fertilization and Embryology* (unpublished, 1983).

————— *Report on Medical Ethics to Methodist Conference* (unpublished, 1985).

Methodist Church in Ireland, *A Response by a Committee of the Methodist Church in Ireland to the Invitation to Comment upon the Government Inquiry into Human Fertilization and Embryology* (unpublished, 1983).

Minucius Felix, *Octavius*.

B. Mitchell, *Law, Morality and Religion in a Secular Society* (Oxford: Oxford University Press, 1967).

L. Morris, *The Gospel According to John*, New London Commentary (Grand Rapids: Eerdmans, 1971).

———— *Luke*, Tyndale New Testament Commentaries (London: IVP, 1974).

Mothers' Union, *Statement to the Government Inquiry into Human Fertilization and Embryology from the Social Concern Committee of the Mothers' Union* (unpublished, 1983).

———— *Statement by the Committee for Social Concern to the Department of Health and Social Security on the Report of the Committee of Inquiry into Human Fertilization and Embryology under the Chairmanship of Dame Mary Warnock DBE* (unpublished, 1984).

———— *Statement by the Committee for Social Concern to the Department of Health and Social Security on the Consultation Paper: Legislation on Human Infertility Services and Embryo Research* (unpublished, 1987).

T. Nagel, *Mortal Questions* (Cambridge: Cambridge University Press, 1979).

National Board of Catholic Women, *Warnock Committee: Inquiry into Human Fertilization and Embryology* (unpublished, 1983).

———— *Warnock Report on Human Fertilization and Embryology: Comments submitted to the Secretary of State for Social Services by the National Board of Catholic Women* (unpublished, 1984).

———— *Legislation on Human Infertility Services and Embryo Research Consultation Paper Issued by the Department of Health and Social Security: Views of the National Board of Catholic Women* (unpublished, 1987).

Nationwide Festival of Light, *Human Fertilization and Embryology: Submission to the Committee of Inquiry under the Chairmanship of Mrs Mary Warnock* (unpublished, 1983).

E. W. Nicholson, *Jeremiah 1 – 25*, Cambridge Bible Commentary (Cambridge: Cambridge University Press, 1973).

O. O'Donovan, *Begotten or Made?* (Oxford: Clarendon, 1984).

———— *The Christian and the Unborn Child*, Grove Booklets on Ethics (Nottingham: Grove Books, 1973).

———— *Resurrection and Moral Order* (1986; 2nd edn, Leicester: Apollos, 1994).

Offences against the Person Act 1861 (London: HMSO, 1861).

W. Ogletree, *The Use of the Bible in Christian Ethics* (Oxford: Blackwell, 1984).

W. Pannenberg, *Anthropology in Theological Perspective* (Edinburgh: T. and T. Clark, 1985).

Pius IX, *Apostolicae Sedis* (12 October 1869).

Plato, *Euthyphro*.

M. H. Pope, *Job*, Anchor Bible (New York: Doubleday, 1965).

Presbyterian Church in Ireland, *Government Inquiry into Human Fertilization and Embryology: Submission by an Ad Hoc Group of the Presbyterian Church in Ireland* (unpublished, 1983).

P. L. Quinn, *Divine Commands and Moral Requirements* (Oxford: Oxford University Press, 1978).

J. Rachels, *The Elements of Moral Philosophy* (New York: McGraw-Hill, 1993).

Raymond de Penafort, *Summa de Casibus Poenitentiae*.

Reformed Presbyterian Church in Ireland and the Evangelical Presbyterian Church, *The Beginnings of Life* (unpublished, 1986).

Report of the Departmental Committee on Human Artificial Insemination (London: HMSO, 1960).

Report of the Committee on the Use of Fetuses and Fetal Material for Research (London: HMSO, 1972).

Report of the Committee of Inquiry into Human Fertilization and Embryology (London: HMSO, 1984).

N. H. G. Robinson, *The Groundwork of Christian Ethics* (London: Collins, 1971).

H. H. Rowley, *Job*, New Century Bible (London: Nelson, 1970).

C. Ryder Smith, *The Bible Doctrine of Man* (London: Epworth, 1951).

Sacred Congregation for the Doctrine of the Faith AA/LXVI (1973).

Salvation Army, *Written Submission to the Warnock Committee of Inquiry into Human Fertilization and Embryology* (unpublished, 1983).

————— *A Response to the Department of Health and Social Security on Reading the Warnock Report* (unpublished, 1984).

————— *Response by the Salvation Army to the Consultation Paper: Legislation on Human Infertility Services and Embryo Research* (unpublished, 1987).

D. Scott, *The Common Sense of Michael Polanyi* (London: The Book Guild, 1985).

Scottish Episcopal Church, *Working Party on Human Infertility and Embryo Research* (unpublished, 1987).

M. E. Setchell and G. I. Scott, 'In Vitro Fertilization', *Update* (1 February 1988).

P. F. Sims, 'Test Tube Babies in Debate', *Ethics and Medicine* 4.3 (1988).

P. Singer, *Practical Ethics* (Cambridge: Cambridge University Press, 1993).

Sixtus V, *Effraenatum* (29 October 1588).

P. D. G. Skegg, *Law, Ethics and Medicine* (Oxford: Clarendon, 1988).

R. Snowden and G. D. Mitchell, *The Artificial Family* (London: Unwin, 1981).

Society for the Protection of the Unborn Child, *Comments of SPUC on the HFEA Code of Practice* (unpublished 1991).

R. Sokolowski, *The God of Faith and Reason* (Notre Dame: University of Notre Dame Press, 1982).

E. A. Speiser, *Genesis*, Anchor Bible (New York: Doubleday, 1964).

S. Spitzer (ed.), *Birth Control and the Christian: A Protestant Symposium on the Control of Human Reproduction* (Wheaton: Tyndale House, 1969).

R. Swinburne, *The Evolution of the Soul* (Oxford: Clarendon, 1986).

Tertullian, *Apology*.

Thomas Aquinas, *Summa Theologiae*.

Thomas of Chobham, *Summa Confessarum*.

S. Thomas, *Genetic Risk* (Harmondsworth, Penguin, 1986).

J. A. Thompson, *The Book of Jeremiah*, New International Commentary on the Old Testament (Grand Rapids: Eerdmans, 1980).

P. Tournier, *The Meaning of Persons* (London: SCM, 1958).

G. Von Rad, *Genesis*, Old Testament Library (London: SCM, 1961).

K. Ward, *The Battle for the Soul* (London: Hodder and Stoughton, 1985).

M. Warner (ed.), *Religion and Philosophy*, *Royal Institute of Philosophy* Supplement 31 (Cambridge: Cambridge University Press, 1992).

M. Warnock, 'Do Human Cells Have Rights?' *Bioethics* 1.1 (1987).

————— '*In Vitro* Fertilization: The Ethical Issues II', *Philosophical Quarterly* 33 (1983).

————— *A Question of Life* (Oxford: Blackwell, 1985).

C. Westermann, *Genesis 12 – 36, A Commentary* (London: SPCK, 1985).

————— *Isaiah 40 – 66*, Old Testament Library (London: SCM, 1969).

R. Winston, *Infertility* (London: Macdonald, 1986).

C. Wood and A. Traunson, 'Current State and Future of IVF', *Periodical of Clinical Obstetrics and Gynaecology* 12 (1985).

(1928) 71 Parliamentary Debate HL 617–618. (Debate on infanticide in the House of Lords 1928, quoting J. Talbot's statement of June 1928 to the Grand Jury at Liverpool Assizes.)

(1938) 3 All England Reports 615.

(1958) MacLennon *v.* MacLennon SC105.